In Defence of Modernity

British Idealist Studies Series 1: Oakeshott

1: Roy Tseng, *The Sceptical Idealist*
2: Luke O'Sullivan, *Oakeshott on History*
3: Ian Tregenza, *Michael Oakeshott on Hobbes*
4: Efraim Podoksik, *In Defence of Modernity*

Series Editor:
Noël O'Sullivan, University of Hull

Editorial Board:
Wendell John Coats Jr. (Connecticut)
Richard Flathman (Johns Hopkins)
Paul Franco (Bowdoin)
Robert Grant (Glasgow)
John Gray (European Institute, LSE)
John Kekes (SUNY, Albany)
Kenneth Minogue (LSE)
Terry Nardin (Wisconsin)
Lord Parekh (Hull)
Patrick Riley (Harvard)

In Defence of Modernity

Vision and Philosophy in Michael Oakeshott

Efraim Podoksik

ia

IMPRINT ACADEMIC

Copyright © Efraim Podoksik, 2003

The moral rights of the authors have been asserted
No part of any contribution may be reproduced in any form
without permission, except for the quotation of brief passages
in criticism and discussion.

Published in the UK by Imprint Academic
PO Box 200, Exeter EX5 5YX, UK

Published in the USA by Imprint Academic
Philosophy Documentation Center
PO Box 7147, Charlottesville, VA 22906-7147, USA

ISBN 0 907845 665

A CIP catalogue record for this book is available from the
British Library and US Library of Congress

www.imprint-academic.com/idealists

Printed and bound in Great Britain by
Biddles Ltd., King's Lynn, Norfolk

Contents

Preface vi

List of Abbreviations of Oakeshott's Works viii

Prologue 1

Chapter 1: Oakeshott and Modernity 9

Chapter 2: Philosophy of Experience 35
    Introduction: Philosophy and Plurality 35
    Science 56
    History 78
    Poetry 103
    Conclusion 120

Chapter 3: Philosophy of Society 127
    Introduction 127
    Practice, Morality, Individuality 131
    Liberalism 158
    The Civil Philosophy 180
    Conclusion 207

Chapter 4: Education 211

Epilogue 231

Bibliography 233

Index 251

Preface

Traditions are born inadvertently, and most fade away before reaching maturity. Their existence is at first precarious, and the measure of significance acquired by each of them is a matter of chance rather than design. In the course of time, however, those which survive the struggle for meaningfulness within our imaginations are bestowed with a life and logic of their own, thus becoming a part of the world we inhabit and, therefore, a part of ourselves.

Such is the case with hallowed cultural traditions belonging to all of humanity or great civilisations. But this is no less true for the personal traditions of each of us, our memories, habits and affections. When I am asked what first led me to read Oakeshott, I answer that there was nothing remarkable about the beginning. Chance first brought me to his works. Yet, at the moment I found myself becoming familiar with his writings, something else emerged which attracted me to his thought, arresting my attention at this point as I tried to understand what I had just read. This something was the feeling of surprise, a feeling which grew more acute the more I studied Oakeshott.

Oakeshott is an elegant and modest author, yet readers should beware of a too-great fascination with his style, because they then risk overlooking the real significance of his thought. For when one reads Oakeshott and learns more of him, one comes to appreciate a subtlety of meaning behind his elocution, a nuanced movement of mind behind his clarity of presentation, and a profound familiarity with our cultural heritage behind his sparing use of quotations from distinguished authors.

This is why I spent several years in a dialogue with his fascinating mind, in an attempt to understand him without distorting his ideas. How far I have succeeded in this enterprise is for the reader to judge. What I can offer here is a certain perspective, and no single perspective can ever be complete. Yet, however imperfect the final product, much of its success here is due to the support of a number of individuals, and I would like to take this opportunity to thank them.

My gratitude first goes to Dan Avnon, Shmuel Eisenstadt and Mario Sznajder from the Hebrew University of Jerusalem for their encouragement when I studied for my Master's degree, and to the academic community of Hughes Hall, Cambridge for providing an excellent scholarly environment during my PhD studies.

Sandy Berkovski, Richard Evans, Raymond Geuss, Steven Grosby, Peter Lipton, Derek Matravers, Kenneth Minogue, Yoel Regev and Kevin Williams read various parts of this work, and without their advice and criticisms it would have been more incomprehensible than it is now, and would have contained more mistakes. I would also like to thank James Alexander, Stefan Collini, John Dunn, John Gray, Simon Oakeshott, Luke O'Sullivan, Quentin Skinner and Andrew Sullivan for interesting conversations about the philosophy of Michael Oakeshott and for their insights.

Finally, I am especially indebted to three individuals without whose support this book would have never been written. David Runciman's advice and care guided me through the years of my PhD research, and to him my work owes much of the clarity it possesses. And Melissa Lane and Noël O'Sullivan encouraged me to revise and improve my thesis in preparation for its publication, and their comments and criticisms were invaluable in the final stage of writing.

This book's section on poetry was published as 'The Voice of Poetry in the Thought of Michael Oakeshott', *Journal of the History of Ideas* 63(4), 2002, pp. 717-733. A revised version of the section on science appears as 'The Scientific Positivism of Michael Oakeshott', *British Journal for the History of Philosophy*, forthcoming. And some of the material of this book is used in 'How Oakeshott Became an Oakeshottean', *European Journal of Political Theory*, forthcoming.

While this work has benefited greatly from the contributions of the individuals named above, all responsibility for its errors or shortcomings is mine alone.

Abbreviations

CBP	'Contemporary British Politics,' *Cambridge Journal*, 1(8), 1948, pp. 474–490.
CPJ	'The Concept of a Philosophical Jurisprudence,' *Politica* 3, 1938, pp. 203–222, 345–360.
CSPS	'The Cambridge School of Political Science,' [April 1924], LSE Archives.
DSM	'A Discussion of Some Matters Preliminary to the Study of Political Philosophy,' LSE Archives.
DU	'The Definition of a University,' *Journal of Educational Thought* 1, 1967, pp. 129–142.
EB	'Edward Bullough,' *Caian* 43(i), 1934, pp. 1–11.
EM	*Experience and Its Modes* (Cambridge: University Press, 1933).
ERPPR	'An Essay on the Relations of Philosophy, Poetry, and Reality,' LSE Archives.
HC	*On Human Conduct* (Oxford: Clarendon Press, 1975).
HCA	*Hobbes on Civil Association* (Indianapolis: Liberty Fund, 2000).
IC	'The Idea of "Character" in the Interpretation of Modern Politics,' [1954], LSE Archives.
JL	'John Locke,' *Cambridge Review* 54, 1932, pp 72–73.
LA	'Lord Acton,' *Caian* 31(i), 1922, pp. 14–23.
MPME	*Morality and Politics in Modern Europe*, S.R. Letwin (ed.) (New Haven: Yale University Press, 1993).
OH	*On History and Other Essays* (Indianapolis: Liberty Fund, 1999).
PFPS	*The Politics of Faith and the Politics of Skepticism* (New Haven: Yale University Press, 1996).
RIP	*Rationalism in Politics and Other Essays* (Indianapolis: Liberty Fund, 1991).
RPML	*Religion, Politics and the Moral Life*, T. Fuller (ed.) (New Haven: Yale University Press, 1993).
SJ	'Shylock the Jew,' *Caian* 30(i), 1921, pp. 61–67.
SPD	*The Social and Political Doctrines of Contemporary Europe* (Cambridge: University Press, 1939).
SPP	'A Study of Political Thought' (A Series of Lectures of Michael Oakeshott), LSE Archives.
SS	'Science and Society,' *Cambridge Journal* 1(11), 1948, pp. 689–697.
VLL	*The Voice of Liberal Learning*, T. Fuller (ed.) (New Haven: Yale University Press, 1989).
WP	'Work and Play,' *First Things* 54, 1995, pp. 29–33.

Prologue

I

This study is an interpretation of Michael Oakeshott's thought as a whole. As every interpretation involves a point of view, it is necessary to begin by outlining the ideas which guide it.

Generally speaking, there are two conflicting views of the character of Oakeshott's philosophy. On the one hand, he is often perceived as mainly a political theorist concerned with specific issues of his time. Although this approach reveals different views about how Oakeshott's ideas should be classified, (for example, whether they should be seen as 'conservative' or 'liberal'), these have in common an attempt to find some political doctrine in his writings.[1]

On the other hand, an opposite view asks us to take seriously Oakeshott's own claims about the irrelevance of philosophy to practical affairs and to see him not as an advocate of some political view but as a detached philosopher interested in exploring the presuppositions of every activity.[2]

Both approaches have richly contributed to our understanding of Oakeshott's ideas. Yet it seems that neither of them is entirely satisfactory, since both miss something important about his thought. It is true that Oakeshott cannot be understood as a political theorist in the narrow sense.[3] Whenever he discusses politics, he does so in the

---

[1] Paul Franco, *The Political Philosophy of Michael Oakeshott* (New Haven: Yale University Press, 1990). See also Benjamin R. Barber, 'Conserving Politics: Michael Oakeshott and Political Theory,' *Government and Opposition* 11, 1979, pp. 446-463; Charles Covell, *The Redefinition of Conservatism: Politics and Doctrine* (London: Macmillan, 1986).

[2] Terry Nardin, *The Philosophy of Michael Oakeshott* (University Park: The Pennsylvania State University Press, 2001). See also Ian Holliday, 'On Michael Oakeshott,' *Government and Opposition* 27(2), 1992, pp. 131-147; Glenn Worthington, 'Oakeshott's Claims of Politics,' *Political Studies* 45, 1997, pp. 727-738.

[3] See ch. 3, introduction.

most general terms, connecting his analysis with a wider social and philosophical outlook. There is nothing politically partisan about his philosophy, and so it cannot be reduced to an advocacy of this or that political platform.

To say this, however, does not mean claiming that Oakeshott's philosophy should be seen as completely detached from the concerns of its time and as possessing no evaluative message. On the contrary, it is possible to understand his philosophy as one that is saying something significant about the condition of modern civilisation and giving us advice. Oakeshott's ideas reflect a certain vision of the character of the modern age. This vision drives his entire thought, lying behind its specific aspects, connecting them and turning them into a coherent statement. To reveal the essence of this vision is the purpose of the current work.

It is true that Oakeshott denied any connection between philosophy and value judgements. Yet this study is dealing not merely with the explicit arguments of Oakeshott's thought but also with the broader context of the vision which underlies these arguments. Certainly, any philosophy deserves to be taken at its face value. Although a philosophical writing is partly an outcome of the contingent historical circumstances in which it was composed, in so far as it is really philosophical it possesses a significance far beyond the particularities of place and time. Whatever the vision contributing to our thought may be, this vision cannot be the criterion of the validity of a philosophical doctrine. Therefore, it is possible and desirable to discuss Oakeshott's philosophy from a purely philosophical standpoint in which everything that he said is looked at from the standpoint of the internal logic of his arguments and of the overall consistency of his ideas.

Nevertheless, the analysis of Oakeshott's thought from the standpoint of what he intended to say to our age — in other words, from the standpoint of a contextualised analysis of his ideas — is not fruitless. Firstly, we still live in the same epoch, and his view of the predicament of man in modern society therefore remains as relevant for us as it was for him.

Secondly, to understand what Oakeshott wanted to say is also to contribute to our understanding of what he did say, and to find the meaning of many aspects of his thought which would otherwise remain obscure. Even though such a study will not aim at demonstrating the validity of his views, it is capable of suggesting a plausible interpretation of their meaning.

II

The vision underlying Oakeshott's philosophy bestows on it a certain character which often remains unnoticed at first reading. The two most important features revealed in it are that his philosophy is self-consciously coherent and that it contains quintessential expressions of the central intellectual concerns of his time.

Such an understanding of Oakeshott's thought challenges a common perception of it as being unsystematic and detached from its age. This perception is partly an outcome of the hostility that his writings faced at the time of their publication, and of the demonstrative unwillingness of some commentators to read Oakeshott seriously and carefully.[4] Yet even those sympathetic to his thought often take at face value his ironical attitude to his own philosophy, thus reinforcing the accusations of his critics. This precludes a more profound appreciation of his philosophy, preventing us from finding answers to its many puzzling elements. Only when Oakeshott's ideas are understood as possessing a coherent and relevant message, can the meaning and significance of his philosophy become clear.

It is true that Oakeshott often denied that his philosophy offered a system, and that he was also reluctant to acknowledge his debt to his contemporaries. Indeed, the idiosyncratic style of many of his writings only strengthened a perception of him as being isolated from his contemporary intellectual context. Yet his style is esoteric precisely because, in some sense, it represents a radical synthesis of ideas already made familiar to us in their more moderate forms by his contemporaries. It is therefore essential to trace parallels and connections between Oakeshott and other thinkers of his time for a proper understanding of his thought. Sometimes, influences on his thought are clear and direct. Other writings, however, absorb multiple influences from the general cultural climate, transforming those influences in a more radical manner. They are more distant from the immediate context and are not easily reducible to the ideas of particular authors and works. Here, grasping the cogency of Oakeshott's argument and its connection with a more general tradition makes better sense than discerning specific influences.

As for the question of coherence, it is true that Oakeshott was opposed to attempts to construct a rigid logical structure or build a holistic concept of the universe. However, he distinguished system

---

[4] See, for example, Bernard Crick, 'The World of Michael Oakeshott: Or the Lonely Nihilist,' *Encounter* 20(6), 1963, pp. 65-74; Sheldon S. Wolin, 'The Politics of Self-Disclosure,' *Political Theory* 4(3), 1976, pp. 321-334.

from the capacity for systematic thinking and praised Locke for '[having] thought systematically and ... escaped making a system'.[5] Systematic thinking appears to be even more important when an overall system is regarded to be neither possible anymore nor desirable. Oakeshott's philosophy is not the rejection of systematic reasoning. It is about how to think systematically in a sceptical age. Although such thinking will not claim to be building a rigid and perfectly consistent system, it will be able to avoid confusion, to make our minds clear and, moreover, to compose a coherent message. Or, as Oakeshott himself said in the introduction to his first book, 'all I have desired is to achieve a general point of view, neither complete nor final, but *systematic* as far as it goes and presented as a reasoned whole.'[6]

Furthermore, this study claims not only that Oakeshott is systematic when he deals with specific issues, but also that all his main writings together comprise a coherent body of thought. Oakeshott hints at this possibility when he argues that the principle of coherence is the criterion by which philosophy must be judged.[7] Moreover, a brief glance at his various writings reveals a remarkable continuity which persists, notwithstanding the many modifications of his thought. This suggests that there is some coherence in his philosophy waiting to be explored.

Thus, this interpretation is based on a view that Oakeshott's philosophy contains a coherent vision of modern civilisation. Such an interpretation is not a piece of intellectual biography because it does not provide a literal account of everything that Oakeshott ever wrote. Instead, it tries to focus on the essential elements of his thought. However, it is not properly described as a piece of philosophy because it is concerned with the intellectual context of his ideas and with a possible relationship between this context and his writings, rather than with discussing the strengths and weaknesses of his assertions.

With these qualifications in mind, Oakeshott's texts will be approached with caution, with the element of interpretation mainly confined to the arrangement of material and the analysis of connections and parallels between various texts or between texts and their context. I have drawn on the whole range of Oakeshott's published and unpublished writings. These include his major philosophical publications, his occasional articles and reviews, his typescripts, manuscripts, notebooks, lecture notes and some letters. A different

[5] JL, p. 72.
[6] EM, p. 8. Italics mine – E.P.
[7] 'Introduction to *Leviathan*,' HCA, p. 12.

significance, however, has been assigned to different texts, with the main emphasis placed on Oakeshott's major published writings. The reason is that even a brief comparison between his published and unpublished works reveals that the former are superior to the latter in the quality of their style and argument. This suggests that Oakeshott published those writings which best reflected the achievements of his philosophy. I have assumed, that is, that if there is any coherent vision in his thought, it must be found in his primary published works. Although other sources are referred to, these are secondary to the main thesis, providing nuances and hinting at possible ways to resolve ambiguities.

III

The contribution of this book to Oakeshott studies lies, therefore, in the attempt to see his philosophy as the expression of a certain vision of modern civilisation, elaborated more or less coherently in his major writings, and offering a particular response to many of the important intellectual issues of his time. To conclude this introduction, it will be useful to present briefly the central thesis advanced about Oakeshott's philosophy, outlining the formal structure of the book.

One of the foremost problems of Oakeshott scholarship has been an artificial and confused separation of his social, or 'political', philosophy from the rest of his thought. The existence of the connection between Oakeshott's general and social philosophy is often recognised,[8] but the character of this connection remains unclear. Oakeshott's idea of the social and political is sometimes regarded as a reflection of a particular concept or an approach belonging to the realm of pure philosophy, be it the notion of the 'concrete universal',[9] or of 'practice',[10] or of some form of 'scepticism' underlying his writings.[11] Politics is also occasionally claimed to play the role of another form of experience alongside history or poetry.[12]

The problem here is that none of these interpretations has provided a clear and coherent picture of the place of the social and polit-

---

[8] W.H. Greenleaf, *Oakeshott's Philosophical Politics* (London: Longman's Green, 1966).
[9] Paul Franco, 'Oakeshott's Critique of Rationalism Revisited,' *Political Science Reviewer* 21, 1992, pp. 15-43.
[10] John Casey, 'Philosopher of Practice,' in J. Norman (ed.), *The Achievement of Michael Oakeshott* (London: Duckworth, 1993), p. 60.
[11] Steven Gerencser, *The Skeptic's Oakeshott* (New York: St. Martin's Press, 2000).
[12] Nevil Johnson, 'Die Politische Philosophie Michael Oakeshotts,' *Zeitschrift für Politik* 32(4), 1985, p. 348.

ical within Oakeshott's thought as a whole. This is not surprising, as Oakeshott does not say much about subjects such as metaphysics or logic and it is thus not clear what his 'general philosophy' is. Besides, he does not consider politics as a distinct mode of experience, and he even denies that politics is a coherent discipline of inquiry.[13] His exposition of modes such as history and science therefore cannot help us to understand his view of politics.

The interpretation that this study offers is different in the sense that it does not consider Oakeshott's social and political ideas to be just one subject among the many different concerns of his philosophy. Rather, his thought is seen here as exploring our world from two standpoints. One deals with the question of the character of our reflective imagining of the world. The other is concerned with the pragmatic perception of our social life.

Oakeshott's later works suggest the possibility of such a distinction. He seems more especially to distinguish between two different levels, namely 'understanding' and 'doing'.[14] The level of understanding can be understood as containing various ways of explaining and imagining the world around us. It includes, among other things, science, history and art. Oakeshott's first philosophical book, *Experience and Its Modes* can be seen as the most articulate exploration of this level, although many of his other writings also deal with it. This aspect of his thought will be called here 'philosophy of experience'.

By contrast, the level of 'doing' can be seen as concerned with the interaction of human beings in the world in order to change it. 'Doing' involves a certain kind of understanding; however, this understanding is not an end in itself, but is instrumental to acting. The most coherent presentation of this aspect of Oakeshott's thought, called here 'philosophy of society', is found in *On Human Conduct*.

Philosophy of experience, then, deals with the level of 'understanding' in Oakeshott's thought, whereas philosophy of society deals with the level of 'doing'. This study will show that, when seen in this light, each of the two aspects is found to possess a significant measure of coherence, and this fact reveals a great deal of systematic reasoning.

These two aspects, moreover, though reflecting different standpoints, are not completely isolated from each other: there is a certain relation between them. Although they are not directly connected, their structures are analogous to each other, both being driven by the

---

[13] 'The Study of "Politics" in a University,' RIP, p. 212.
[14] HC, p. 33. Cf. Nardin, *The Philosophy of Michael Oakeshott*, p. 55.

same concern. In order to understand the vision inspiring Oakeshott's philosophy, it is therefore necessary not only to know the features of both its aspects but also to understand the nature of their relation.

In this sense, what this study shows is that Oakeshott's philosophy conforms to the criterion of coherence which he himself attributed to Hobbes, when he claimed that 'the coherence of [Hobbes'] philosophy, the system of it, lies not in an architectonic structure, but in a single "passionate thought" that pervades its parts.'[15]

More precisely, what is claimed is that Oakeshott's central concern is the idea of modernity understood as inescapable fragmentation and irreducible plurality. His main preoccupation is to understand the 'modern' in two respects. One deals with the question of what it is to be modern in our imagining of the world. The other explores what it is to be modern in the pragmatic view of our social life. The answer to both questions is that to be modern means to recognise radical plurality. And the sentiment underlying this answer is an attempt to reconcile ourselves with modernity by learning to appreciate and enjoy this plurality.

The structure of the book is as follows. Chapter 1 introduces Oakeshott's vision by highlighting the idea of modernity. Chapter 2 analyses his philosophy of experience. It presents the general framework of his idea of radical plurality and exemplifies his approach by discussing his philosophies of science, history and aesthetics in their intellectual context. The subject of chapter 3 is Oakeshott's philosophy of society. It analyses his ideas of practice, ethical life and civil conduct, and argues that his mature achievement is the transformation of the ideas of European liberalism into a coherent philosophy, based on the notion of radical plurality. It also shows how Oakeshott's philosophy of society is analogous to his philosophy of experience. Finally, chapter 4 is an attempt to demonstrate how Oakeshott's idea of education corresponds to his understanding of modernity and how it influenced the philosophy of education of his day. In other words, this chapter deals with the question of what kind of education modern society should encourage, given the kind of world in which we live and in which we want to continue to live.

The final chapter is particularly important for understanding the significance of Oakeshott's vision. It presents his writings on education, which was of great importance to him, in a new light. Before we can approach his view of education, however, it is necessary to understand the main body of his ideas, since his ideas on education

---

[15] 'Introduction to *Leviathan*,' HCA, p. 17.

depended on them. Oakeshott's passionate defence of liberal education was very timely, and it remains so today, especially when what can be called a post-modernist spirit challenges its main foundations. Oakeshott can be seen as one of the most profound and eloquent opponents of this spirit. Long before the term post-modernism itself came into use, he was fully aware of the dangers which the relativism associated with it poses. Confronted by that threat, his thought presents a sincere, elegant and courageous defence of the values of modern liberal Western civilisation.

Chapter 1
Oakeshott and Modernity

> Here there was no promise or salvation for the race or prevision that it would late or soon be gathered into one fold, no anticipation of a near or distant reassemblage of a 'truth' fragmented at the creation of the world...
> *On Human Conduct*, 1975

> No settlement with our enemies will ever be satisfactory unless it arises from a real confidence in our civilization.   [*On Peace with Germany*], 1943

I

This chapter aims to provide a contextual framework for subsequent discussion of the vision behind Oakeshott's ideas, for it is claimed in this study that his vision is best understood when related to the intellectual debates of his time. The specific context which reveals this vision most clearly is one characterized by the perception of modern civilisation as marked above all by the fragmentation of knowledge and the individualisation of society. This perception is important in particular for Oakeshott's idea of radical plurality. In order to show this, attention will initially be focused on the moment when Oakeshott presented in full, for the first time, the idea which would guide him in his later writings — the idea, that is, that radical plurality is inherent in modern civilisation. That moment is the publication of *Experience and Its Modes*.[1] The present chapter seeks to show that that book, besides being a self-contained philosophical treatise, can be seen as inspired by a wider vision. When the nature of that vision

---
[1] On the development of Oakeshott's ideas prior to the publication of *Experience and Its Modes* see ch. 2, introduction, and, in more detail, in Efraim Podoksik, 'How Oakeshott Became an Oakeshottean,' *European Journal of Political Theory*, forthcoming.

is revealed, the ideas underlying the rest of Oakeshott's philosophy will be more easily appreciated.

The significance of *Experience and Its Modes* in the wider context of Oakeshott's thought as a whole is best understood when juxtaposed with the ideas of R.G. Collingwood. The significance of the implicit Oakeshott–Collingwood argument, in turn, only emerges when it is related to philosophical and social questions which were especially prominent in continental European thought at that period. What links the two philosophers is their concern with fragmentation as the distinguishing feature of the modern age: in this fundamental respect, both thinkers share a specific vision of the meaning of modernity. Placing Oakeshott's ideas in this framework is indispensable for understanding what his philosophy is and, no less important, what it is not. More generally, this mode of analysis will reveal that the vision behind Oakeshott's philosophy permits him to defend what is called 'modernity' not only against the attacks of conservative critics but, more recently, against those of so-called post-modern ones.

II

At first glance, *Experience and Its Modes* is a book of pure philosophy, detached from intellectual debates of its time. This impression is, nevertheless, deceptive. The work is very closely connected with another impressive piece of writing, which is an early philosophical work of the British Idealist thinker R.G. Collingwood, *Speculum Mentis, or the Map of Knowledge* (1924).[2] Oakeshott's work should be understood, in part at least, as an argument with the ideas Collingwood presents there.

Various commentators noticed parallels between the two books.[3] Yet what often escapes attention is that Oakeshott, while following Collingwood's path in many respects, consistently opposes him on fundamental points. To understand the nature of Oakeshott's disagreement with Collingwood is to take a step forward in our understanding of Oakeshott's vision.

Speculum Mentis is a philosophical work, yet Collingwood makes it absolutely clear that his concerns are not purely philosophical in

---

[2] R.G. Collingwood, *Speculum Mentis or the Map of Knowledge* (Oxford: Clarendon Press, 1924).
[3] See W.H. Greenleaf, *Oakeshott's Philosophical Politics* (London: Longman's Green, 1966), pp. 10-11, 25, 33, 95; Terry Nardin, *The Philosophy of Michael Oakeshott* (University Park: The Pennsylvania State University Press, 2001), pp. 41, 79n.

their nature. In the prologue he shares with readers his worries about the state of modern civilisation. He reveals that his work is an attempt to diagnose what he calls the *'maladie du siècle'*,[4] and perhaps to see whether it is possible to find some solution to this disease of modernity.

Specifically, Collingwood starts with what he sees as the miserable condition in which philosophers, artists, and religious devotees — all those who form the spiritual elite of society — find themselves in the modern age. They are not listened to, certainly not revered any more, what they produce can hardly interest a wider audience, and their economic condition is completely dependent on market demands. Collingwood compares this situation to the past, which is idealistically described as the time 'when young men of every degree crowded to Oxford to hear Duns Scotus, or when Cimabue's Madonna went through the streets of Florence...'[5] The reason for this current misery is not that the public has lost interest in the product that artists, philosophers or religious leaders can offer. On the contrary, today people need art, religion and philosophy not less, but perhaps even more than they needed them in the past. The problem is that people feel that they are not offered what they want and need. Why is this so?

According to Collingwood, this situation is the symptom of the special feature of modern life. Modern man is characterised by the loss of the unity of mind that medieval man possessed. Once, all the activities of the mind co-existed in some state of harmony, and 'there was a general interpretation of the various activities of the mind, in which each was influenced by all'.[6] This harmony has disappeared in modern life, since the activities of the mind developed in different directions, splitting from each other. Previously, art and religion mutually supported each other, and an artist who worked in a monastery could both fulfil his artistic needs and feel his work to be required and appreciated by his fellows. Today, however, there is a prolonged battle between religion, art, and science, an international war, in which each activity claims priority, but in which there is no judge. In fact, every activity needs all the others for its harmonious fulfilment, but is unable to accommodate them.

Yet Collingwood believes that one may still try to find some resolution even in the condition of separation. Perhaps the very fragmentation of different activities may contain in itself the way to overcome this fragmentation. Collingwood's project is therefore to

[4]   Collingwood, *Speculum Mentis*, p. 22.
[5]   *Ibid.*, p. 19.
[6]   *Ibid.*, p. 27.

scrutinise various activities of the mind and their pretences to autonomy. He distinguishes between art, religion, science, history and philosophy, calling them 'forms of experience'.[7] He attempts to show that their claims for autonomy are false, that, in fact, all forms of experience are incoherent modes of knowledge. He builds a hierarchy of these forms according to the degree of their adequacy in reaching absolute knowledge. When the inadequacy of each form is exposed from within, such a form necessarily transforms itself into a higher form of knowledge. Art for him is the most primitive form of experience in this sense, while philosophy stands closest to the Absolute.

Yet, in the conclusion, Collingwood argues that his analysis has shown that no system of relationship between various activities can be found. According to him, a map of knowledge, in which every activity will be assigned its proper place, is impossible.[8] Each form pretends to comprehend the whole, but this claim is a mere illusion. Every form of experience is merely a modification of the whole, an abstraction which will vanish under philosophical scrutiny. Yet this philosophical journey is not fruitless, because, through the analysis and supersession of those different degrees of knowledge, the mind learns to recognise itself in its own activity. It learns that there is no real autonomy of each activity. 'There are no autonomous and mutually exclusive forms of experience, and, what is more, it is in no one's interest to assume that there are.'[9] Such autonomy is illusory and can lead only to conflict. The philosophical journey through these activities is fruitful only if the mind learns to overcome them, and thereby to become more aware of itself.

Speculum Mentis is perhaps the most Hegelian of the books written by Collingwood. Not accidentally, there are apparent similarities between it and *Phenomenology of Spirit*, and it is supposed to be a guide to the perplexed modern mind, which gradually comes to be conscious of itself in the process of analysing and dissecting various forms of knowledge.

This book was not Collingwood's last word in philosophy. In fact, throughout his intellectual career, Collingwood continuously modified his views on various philosophical subjects, and later his philosophy turned to a rather more historicist direction, emphasising the

---

[7] *Ibid.*, p. 39.
[8] *Ibid.*, p. 306.
[9] *Ibid.*

primacy of history rather than of philosophy and the Absolute.[10] Yet here I am concerned only with Collingwood's views expressed in *Speculum Mentis*, for it is this book which seems to have provoked Oakeshott to write *Experience and Its Modes* in the way he did.

Though Oakeshott never mentions Collingwood's treatise in his book, the parallels between the two works are obvious. Both books focus on the analysis of various forms of experience. Both are written in a neo-Hegelian idiom. Both are preceded by a declaration of the intention behind writing the book. Collingwood's prologue is very long, and it explicitly refers to the contemporary historical situation, whereas Oakeshott's introduction is short and deliberately detached. However, the latter can be seen as a response to the former. Collingwood begins with the assertion that

> all thought exists for the sake of action. We try to understand ourselves and our world only in order that we may learn how to live. The end of our self-knowledge is not the contemplation by enlightened intellects of their own mysterious nature, but the freer and more effectual self-revelation of that nature in a vigorous practical life.[11]

This sort of claim is rejected by Oakeshott at the start of his book:

> An interest in philosophy is often first aroused by an irrelevant impulse to see the world and ourselves better than we find them... Thinking is at first associated with an extraneous desire for action... But we must learn not to follow the philosophers upon these holiday excursions.[12]

Later in the book Oakeshott almost literally quotes the assertion of Collingwood to which he objects: 'All thought exists for the sake of action... and we try to understand the universe only in order to learn how to live.'[13]

There are other similarities. Collingwood praises 'the childishness of medieval man',[14] and Oakeshott speaks of 'the childhood of thought, when knowledge appears undifferentiated'.[15] Collingwood introduces the terms 'modifications' and 'forms of experience';[16] Oakeshott uses the term 'modes of experience'.

Yet the most important point is that Oakeshott's entire work is an argument, which, though being similar in form, is actually the precise opposite of Collingwood's. Whereas Collingwood rejects the

---

[10] Allan Megill, '"Grand Narrative" and the Discipline of History,' in F. Ankersmit & H. Kellner (eds.), *A New Philosophy of History* (London: Reaktion Books, 1995), pp. 151-173.
[11] Collingwood, *Speculum Mentis*, p. 15.
[12] EM, p. 1.
[13] EM, p. 317.
[14] Collingwood, *Speculum Mentis*, p. 29.
[15] EM, pp. 1-2.
[16] Collingwood, *Speculum Mentis*, pp. 39, 48.

idea of the exclusivity of each form of experience, Oakeshott affirms it. As we shall see in more detail in the following chapters, Oakeshott argues that every mode of experience is irrelevant to all others, that each mode forms a homogeneous world of ideas, and that to pass an argument from one mode of experience to another is to commit a grave logical error. In other words, the idea of the complete autonomy and homogeneity of various worlds of experience is at the heart Oakeshott's philosophy. We will also see how Oakeshott parts ways with Collingwood almost at each juncture of his thought. Meanwhile, however, it is enough to notice that Oakeshott adheres to the view which Collingwood rejects.

Moreover, the disagreement between Oakeshott and Collingwood's *Speculum Mentis* does not centre only on the issue of the analysis of the modern mind. Collingwood links this analysis to his view of the state of modern society. And he sees the condition of modern society in no more favourable light. He argues that the fragmentation of mind did not happen by itself but was the outcome of a profound social change which Western civilisation underwent since the Middle Ages. According to Collingwood, medieval life was governed by the idea of institutions:

> The individual counted for nothing except as the member of his guild, his church, his monastic order, his feudal hierarchy. Within these institutions he found a place where he was wanted, work for him to do, a market for his wares. He could devote himself to fulfilling the duties assigned him by his station in that great organism within which he found himself lodged.[17]

The Renaissance broke this culture. It gave birth to modern individualism, expressed in 'the freedom of discovering that one can leave one's ordained place and march out into the world without being struck dead by an offended God'.[18] This quest for freedom also led to the freedom of various activities of mind to become mature and separate from each other. But God was offended, for this freedom was bought at the price of an internal conflict, which is the disease of modernity. The curse of modern individualism is, therefore, the deep cause of the miserable condition of modern consciousness.

Oakeshott had little to say about this idea in *Experience and Its Modes*. But everyone familiar with his later writings will hardly overlook the parallels. Like Collingwood, Oakeshott believes that the modern individual is a child of the Renaissance age, and that this individuality is expressed in his ability to choose his way for him-

---
[17] *Ibid.*, p. 23.
[18] *Ibid.*, pp. 30-31.

self, to embark on the long journey in a search for the place for a person like *him*. This idea can be found in Oakeshott's writings of the middle fifties and in his later book *On Human Conduct* (1975).

Oakeshott is therefore engaged with ideas similar to those of Collingwood. The difference between the two authors, however, is to be found in their attitude. While, for Collingwood, modern individualism is just another symptom of the disease of the modern age, for Oakeshott, the birth of the ideas of freedom and individuality is, perhaps, the most praiseworthy of all historical events. The cherishment of individuality for him is, in fact, the only adequate response to modernity.

Thus, as one can already see, that single book of Collingwood contained the ideas with which Oakeshott was preoccupied during his entire lifetime. This is not to suggest, of course, that Oakeshott's philosophy should be described as a prolonged argument with Collingwood. This would be to underestimate its significance. Rather it can be said that both authors struggle with the same kind of problems but solve them differently. It is, nevertheless, fruitful to begin with this particular connection between Oakeshott and Collingwood for, when Collingwood's ideas are placed together with those of Oakeshott, the specific character of Oakeshott's view becomes clearer.

III

There is, however, another reason why it is important to highlight the relation of *Experience and Its Modes* to *Speculum Mentis*. Collingwood's book was a well-written and quintessential presentation of the set of problems which engaged many other authors. That is, it was directly related to a wider intellectual debate. What was at stake in this debate? Collingwood is known as a follower of the school of British Idealism in the years when Idealism went out of fashion in Britain. Thus, *Speculum Mentis* was written as a neo-Hegelian book, and it attempted to offer a quasi-Hegelian solution to the problems of the modern time. Yet Collingwood cannot be regarded as fully belonging to the neo-Hegelian trend, exemplified by Green, Bosanquet and others. This is to misunderstand the nature of his position.

The subject of *Speculum Mentis*, its philosophical and social problems, and the emotional intensity with which these problems were outlined, were not typical for the British philosophical life of that period. British philosophy of the early twentieth century was dominated by British Idealism and, later, by realism and logical positivism. Of course, British Idealists borrowed many ideas from continental philosophical schools. Yet these ideas were not accompanied by the sense of a sharp crisis so apparent in Collingwood's book. British Idealism was in many respects a native movement.[19] Although many British Idealists claimed to have learnt much from Hegel, this was a rather moderated form of Hegelianism, employed as an alternative to empiricism and utilitarianism. And, certainly, their metaphysical preoccupations with the Absolute were out of touch with the trends in contemporary continental philosophy. Although Collingwood was indebted to his older British Idealist contemporaries, the source of his concerns lay elsewhere. He was perhaps the most continental of all British Idealists, being very familiar with, and deeply influenced by, his contemporaries such as Croce.[20] Moreover, he was influenced not only by a certain set of ideas, but also by an acute sense of the crisis of modernity.

If we are to look for statements similar to those of Collingwood we should travel across the Channel. For example, just a few years earlier, Alfred Weber gave a similar diagnosis to the problem of modernity, accusing German intellectuals of becoming too professional. According to him, intellectuals, concentrating on their narrow fields of study, abandoned the quest for the truth.[21] The intellectual fragmentation was the main disease of modern time, and the intellectuals who succumbed to this fragmentation lost the ability to be spiritual leaders of the nation. Weber was not alone in his concerns about fragmentation. The perception of modernity as fragmentation and of fragmentation as a tragedy was characteristic of Central European thought at the beginning of the twentieth century.

The turning point here was the collapse of Hegelianism in the middle of the nineteenth century and the rise of neo-Kantianism, indicating the end of many attempts to find a unified system of knowledge. Neo-Kantianism can be described as a critique of Absolute Idealism.[22] Neo-Kantians, each in their own way, postulated the impossibility of the unified philosophical system and insisted on the autonomy and irreducibility of different axiological spheres.

This idea was, in some sense, a radicalisation of the notion of the diversity of knowledge characteristic of earlier German philosophy.

[19] On British Idealists see, for example, David Boucher and Andrew Vincent, *British Idealism and Political Theory* (Edinburgh: Edinburgh University Press, 2000), pp. 1-26.
[20] *Ibid.*, p. 185.
[21] Alfred Weber, 'Die Bedeutung der geistigen Führer in Deutschland,' *Die neue Rundschau* 29, 1918, pp. 1249-1268.
[22] Frédéric Vandenberghe, *Comparing Neo-Kantians: Ernst Cassirer and Georg Simmel* (Manchester: University of Manchester, 1996), p. 10.

It was the self-proclaimed task of German philosophy to restore unity in the condition of this diversity. Diversity seen as a problem may already be found in Leibniz's writings. It is certainly one of Kant's main preoccupations. For Schiller, who speaks about the polytheism of the new age, this is the most important characteristic of the modern epoch. And the predominant motive of Hegel and the romantic philosophers of his generation is an attempt to find unity in diversity, which they see as the main task of philosophical inquiry.[23] The revived idea of philosophy as the centre of knowledge and the ultimate arbiter between rival claims of different faculties, advanced by Kant, Fichte, and, in some sense, developed by Hegel, was a desperate attempt to reclaim systematic unity even in the condition of this diversity.[24]

The rise of Neo-Kantianism, therefore, led to the radicalisation of that perception of diversity and to its transformation into the notion of fragmentation. Almost every one of the neo-Kantian thinkers postulated, in a more or less radical form, the autonomy of different spheres of knowledge and value. This perception, however, should not be reduced only to neo-Kantian philosophy, though neo-Kantians were, perhaps, most consistent among the proponents of this view. The idea of fragmentation was a commonplace in the intellectual life of that period, signifying the advent of what was called 'modernity'. This idea of modernity was indeed a popular subject of discussion in Europe, and especially among the intellectuals in the German-speaking countries, from the collapse of the 1848 revolutions onwards, culminating in the *fin-de-siècle* climate at the turn of the nineteenth and twentieth centuries.[25] The idea of modernity as fragmentation can be found in the philosophy of Nietzsche, in the social theory of Max Weber, or in novels such as *The Sleepwalkers* by Hermann Broch.

Thus, Collingwood was engaged with a widespread notion of modernity, yet his specific target seems to have been the

[23] 'The basic theme to emerge from Schiller's *Letters*, then, and from the writings of other early romantic critics of existing society is that the highest human aspiration is the drive for unity. However, this is a unity of a special kind. It is a unity that presupposes and even welcomes diversity and conflict.' Steven B. Smith, *Hegel's Critique of Liberalism: Rights in Context* (Chicago: The University of Chicago Press, 1989), p. 34.

[24] See Terry Pinkar, *Hegel: A Biography* (Cambridge: Cambridge University Press, 2000), pp. 93-95.

[25] See Carl E. Schorske, *Fin-de-Siècle Vienna: Politics and Culture* (New York: Alfred A. Knopf, 1980), pp. xix-xx. On the intellectual situation within German universities see also Fritz K. Ringer, *The Decline of the German Mandarins: The German Academic Community, 1890-1933* (Cambridge, Mass: Harvard University Press, 1969).

neo-Kantian assumption of the autonomy of different spheres of knowledge and value. He presented a neo-Hegelian alternative to this view. The main adversary of Collingwood's Hegelian treatise was, therefore, not English empiricism, but the neo-Kantian frame of mind.

Oakeshott too was well read in German philosophy. Although it is difficult to trace the particular ideas by which he was influenced, there is no doubt that he was very familiar with the Central European intellectual climate. He certainly undertook a very serious study of German philosophy in the middle twenties in the original language. If Collingwood's work is a neo-Hegelian attack on the idea of the autonomy of different spheres of knowledge, Oakeshott's *Experience and Its Modes* is a restatement of the basic neo-Kantian position, although expressed through neo-Hegelian terminology. Oakeshott turns Absolute Idealism upside down in order to offer a response to Collingwood on his own territory. Whether this combination of methodological holism and neo-Kantian influences is successful, and how far, if at all, Oakeshott's book can be seen as lying within the neo-Hegelian tradition, will be discussed later. Meanwhile, it is important to point out that Oakeshott's main idea — the mutual irrelevance of various modes of experience — while original in the British intellectual atmosphere, was not new in itself and was quite familiar to anyone immersed in the Central European debate.

One of the most unequivocal proponents of this idea was Georg Simmel, who was the most widely read social thinker at the time.[26] Twenty years before Oakeshott, Simmel presented a view almost identical to that of Oakeshott, using sometimes the same terms. Simmel, like other neo-Kantians, recognised the plurality of the forms of understanding in modern experience. He regarded the fragmentation of culture as a tragedy but, unlike many of his pessimistic contemporaries, he did not regard plurality itself as a problem. He insisted that, when all forms of experience are taken in their purity, they are absolutely irrelevant to each other. This claim is maintained throughout many of his different writings. Thus, he speaks about countless modifications (*Modifikationen*) of knowledge, such as science, art, or religion, each assuming totality (*Ganzheit*) of the world as its content.[27] Each form of experience can

---

[26] On the personality and philosophy of Simmel see Rudolph H. Weingartner, *Experience and Culture: The Philosophy of Georg Simmel* (Middletown, Co.: Wesleyan University Press, 1962).

[27] Georg Simmel, 'On the Nature of Philosophy,' in K.H. Wolff (ed.), *Georg Simmel, 1858-1918: A Collection of Essays with Translations and a Bibliography* (Columbus:

be recognised as a world (*Welt*) since it pretends to represent totality under a general principle (*Gesamtprinzip*).[28] Yet there can be no overlap or meeting between these forms, and therefore no clash.[29] Thus, Simmel does not see any problem in the principle of the existence of a plurality of categorically distinct forms of experience. The problem for him is practical, and it arises from the imperfection of human understanding. In reality none of these worldviews is able to be perceived in its completeness, since our knowledge is always limited, and this is what drives us to confuse different forms of experience.[30]

Oakeshott uses the same idea of irrelevance in order to reject what is, in fact, Collingwood's thesis. Whilst Collingwood draws the map of knowledge in order to show that the separation between different realms is impossible to maintain, Oakeshott argues that all modes of experience, if taken in their pure form, are homogeneous within themselves and completely irrelevant to each other. Moreover, these modes have an identity of their own which may be worth defending.

Thus, one can argue that Oakeshott started his intellectual career not with an obscure work of philosophy, as is often supposed, but with a treatise which can be properly seen as an elaboration of the idea of the radical plurality existing in the modern mind. This plurality should not be fought against. Instead of exploding each form of knowledge from within, as Collingwood does, it is necessary to maintain strict limits between them. *Experience and Its Modes* is, therefore, a statement defending the radical plurality of different forms of experience, and this statement is affirmed in further writings of Oakeshott, such as 'The Voice of Poetry in the Conversation of Mankind' (1959) and *On History* (1983). At the time it was published, it had little relevance to the mainstream concerns of British philosophy. Yet it was very much in line with contemporary debates in Central Europe.

IV

As we have seen, Collingwood rejected the notion of the autonomy of different spheres of knowledge, attacking it from the position of Absolute neo-Hegelian Idealism. From Collingwood's standpoint, such an attack was probably very timely. Neo-Kantianism looked to

---

The Ohio State University Press, 1959), p. 288. Originally published in *Hauptprobleme der Philosophie* (Leipzig: Sammlung Goschen, 1910), pp. 8-43.

[28] Georg Simmel, *Lebensanschauung: vier metaphysische Kapitel* (München: Duncker & Humboldt, 1918), p. 30.

[29] Georg Simmel, 'Christianity and Art,' in *Essays in Religion*, trans. H.J. Helle (New Haven: Yale University Press, 1997), p. 76; *Lebensanschauung*, p. 30.

[30] Simmel, 'Christianity and Art,' p. 76.

have won this particular battle against methodological holism. Yet this does not mean that the recognition of fragmentation was greeted without concern. Actually, it was perceived as a burden rather than as an achievement, the symptom of a crisis rather than progress. Fragmentation was often perceived as a tragedy inherent in modernity, although it was recognised as a tragedy with no escape.

This pessimistic modernism which admits the loss of unity and predicts an eternal conflict, dominated the intellectual atmosphere in the German socio-philosophical debate of that time. It can be found in some of Nietzsche's writings, where he mourns the absence of unity of style in modern German culture,[31] and it is most sharply exemplified by Max Weber's value pluralism. Even Simmel, perhaps the most optimistic among the theorists of fragmentation, perceived it as a tragedy.

What is interesting about Oakeshott is that he recognises radical fragmentation without expressing any uneasiness about it. For him, fragmentation leads to the radical plurality existing in modern experience, and this plurality should be wholeheartedly cherished and not mourned. It is in this sense that Oakeshott can be called a defender of modernity.

There is, however, an additional reason why it is fruitful to interpret the vision that drives Oakeshott's philosophy in this way: if we situate Oakeshott in this context, we can more easily discern the differences between his position and that of other thinkers with whom he is often associated. Oakeshott is sometimes perceived either as a conservative anti-modernist or as a proto-post-modernist before his time.[32] Yet it seems that both views are somewhat misplaced. The similarities between his views and those of some conservatives and so-called post-modernists can be found, but these similarities are superficial. What is important and significant about Oakeshott are the points where he differs from post- and pre-modernists. To understand this is to understand the essence of the vision of Oakeshott's philosophy.

For this purpose, it will be necessary to establish a coherent idea of what the notion of modernity as fragmentation entails and what is wrong with it from the point of view of its critics. The intention is not

---

[31] Friedrich Nietzsche, *Untimely Meditations*, trans. R.J. Hollingdale (Cambridge: Cambridge University Press, 1983), pp. 5-6.
[32] The terms 'modernity', 'pre-modernity' and 'post-modernity' are used here in their general socio-cultural meaning and not in the sense they are used in the theory of aesthetics. There may be some parallels between the two spheres; however it is important not confuse them.

to suggest here a full scope analysis of these terms. It is true that the concepts of 'modernity' and 'post-modernity' are overused in current debate in Anglo-American social philosophy, and that they may refer to many different, even contradictory phenomena of contemporary life, seen in whatever perspective, and artificially abstracted from any other aspects of reality. It is even possible to speak about different 'modernities'.[33]

However, there are two main reasons which determine the choice of such a line of interpretation in this book. Firstly, the wide-spread debate on modernity and post-modernity, however ambiguous it may appear, is an indication of our intuitive understanding that something essential is at stake in this debate, even though the definite idea of what it is may be unclear. It is not an accident that many interpreters of Oakeshott have placed him somewhere in this debate. Thus, Richard Rorty includes him among 'post-modern bourgeois liberals'.[34] Several other commentators regard him as a conservative critic of modernity.[35] And John Gray, at least at some points, finds in Oakeshott a follower of the philosophers who were 'unequivocal modernists'.[36] All these characterisations are not merely metaphors. They are designed to make important claims about the way one should understand Oakeshott's philosophy. Therefore, to claim that Oakeshott is a defender of modernity is to make a certain assertion about what Oakeshott's thought is, and, no less importantly, what it is not. Saying, that Oakeshott is a critic of both post-modernist and anti- or pre-modernist positions, implies the direction in which this interpretation of Oakeshott's philosophy leads.

Secondly, as is already clear, the term 'modernity' is limited here to a particular set of ideas prominent in continental European thought at the beginning of the twentieth century and, above all, to the idea of fragmentation, which may serve as a relevant background to the development of Oakeshott's philosophy. The present

---

[33] See, for example, Peter J. Taylor, *Modernities: A Geohistorical Interpretation* (Minneapolis: University of Minneapolis Press, 1999).
[34] Richard Rorty, *Objectivity, Relativism, and Truth* (Cambridge: Cambridge University Press, 1997), p. 197.
[35] See, for example, Matthew Johnson, *Michael Oakeshott's Critique of Modernity: Science, Ideology and Reason* (PhD diss., Nebraska University, 1999). On Oakeshott as a conservative see also Perry Anderson, 'The Intransigent Right at the End of the Century,' *London Review of Books* 14, September 24, 1992, pp. 7-11; Robert Devigne, *Recasting Conservatism: Oakeshott, Strauss, and the Response to Postmodernism* (New Haven: Yale University Press, 1994).
[36] John Gray, *Liberalisms: Essays in Political Philosophy* (London: Routledge, 1989), p. 206.

aim, it should be emphasized, is not to offer a comprehensive theory of modernity, which is bound to remain one of those contested and ambiguous concepts which fill today's intellectual climate. It is rather to illuminate some of the problems which shaped Oakeshott's thought and to clarify a few terms so that they can be meaningfully used in reference to his ideas.

Thus, the notion of modernity is understood here to focus on the idea of the fragmentation of worldviews, values and individuals within contemporary Western civilisation.[37] Fragmentation may be understood to exist in two different realms. It may be seen as characterising either the state of modern knowledge and culture, or the condition of modern society. Various thinkers have understood the relationship between the realms of culture and society in different ways. Thus, the fragmentation of culture may be seen as related to the fragmentation of society, so that the two compose one philosophical system (as that of Hegel), or the two phenomena can be grasped as independent developments of the modern age. In any case, both the development of modern culture and of modern society can be understood through the idea of fragmentation.

Collingwood's book, for example, was driven by this vision of modernity. The problem may be generally described as follows. During the preceding period the world had been perceived to be a more or less consistently unified whole, so that it had been possible to build an interdependent system of knowledge. In this system all elements could be unified in an hierarchical order with the religious-ethical realm at the top of the pyramid, and other branches of knowledge derivative from it. This hierarchy was destroyed when other systems of knowledge revolted against the religious worldview and presented themselves as alternative systems independent of it. Science was the primary adversary, but other disciplines also put forward their claims to autonomy. Thus, the eighteenth century witnessed the appearance of aesthetics as an independent discipline and of the concept of genius as the ideal of an

---

[37] Fragmentation is not the only way to define modernity. It can be seen just as a symptom of another phenomenon such as, for example, the experience of 'newness' and 'transitoriness' in modern civilisation. David Frisby, *Fragments of Modernity: Theories of Modernity in the Work of Simmel, Kracauer and Benjamin* (Cambridge: Polity Press, 1985) presents modernity as 'the modes of experiencing that which is "new" in "modern" society.' (p. 1) Yet the fragmentarity of modernity plays a prominent part in this experience. It is the basic element of what is seen here as modernity. Intimations of such understanding can be often found in the literature. See, for example, William Rasch, *Niklas Luhmann's Modernity: Paradoxes of Differentiation* (Stanford: Stanford University Press, 2000).

independent artist.[38] Later, from the end of the eighteenth century onwards, historical inquiry was often seen as the ultimate umpire of knowledge.[39]

The breakdown of the old hierarchical system of values could be perceived as unique because it had not been followed by the formation of an alternative comprehensive worldview. There were, of course, adherents of various worldviews who put them forward as substitutes for religion. Thus, early 'positivists' such as St-Simon and Comte found in science their new religion.[40] Proponents of aestheticism, such as Walter Pater or Stefan George, suggested that art could be such a religion.[41] And post-Hegelian German historicism of the nineteenth century might have wished history to be at the top of the comprehensive system of knowledge.[42]

Nevertheless, it was clear that none of these attempts had been successful, because all of the different worldviews continued to flourish. Within the spheres of science, history and art, moreover, there was a tacit tension between the demand for autonomy and the claim to supremacy.[43] Indeed, many of the proponents of the ideas of art for art's sake, or science for science's sake, or history for history's sake, were prone to adopting the view that their sphere was the one which was supreme and that all other spheres should be subject to it. Had one of these claims been accepted, a new hierarchical structure would have emerged.

However, the different spheres continued to co-exist, each refining its own individuality, and thereby denying the claim to supremacy of the others. Yet each sphere produced by the fragmentation of the old integrated worldview was itself in danger of disintegration since, without being supported by a comprehensive philosophical

---

[38] See, for example, Paul Kaufman, 'Heralds of Original Genius,' in *Essays in Memory of Barrett Wendell* (New York: Russell & Russell, 1967), pp. 189-217; Kineret S. Jaffe, 'The Concept of Genius: Its Changing Role in Eighteenth-Century French Aesthetics,' in P. Kivy (ed.), *Essays on the History of Aesthetics* (Rochester: University of Rochester Press, 1992), pp. 224-244.

[39] Reinhart Koselleck, 'Historia Magistra Vitae: The Dissolution of the Topos into the Perspective of a Modernized Historical Process,' in *Futures Past: On the Semantic of Historical Time*, trans. K. Tribe (Cambridge, Mass: The MIT Press, 1985), pp. 21-38.

[40] Edward Caird, *The Social Philosophy and Religion of Comte* (Bristol: Thoemmes Press, 1999); Frank E. Manuel, *The New World of Henri Saint-Simon* (Cambridge, Mass: Harvard University Press, 1956).

[41] Gene H. Bell-Villada, *Art for Art's Sake and Literary Life* (Lincoln: University of Nebraska Press, 1996), p. 177.

[42] Koselleck, 'Historia Magistra Vitae'.

[43] See, for example, Wolf Lepenies, *Between Literature and Science: The Rise of Sociology*, trans. R.J. Hollingdale (Cambridge: Cambridge University Press, 1988).

system, none could preserve its own unified character and prevent itself from being further divided into different branches. The danger of further fragmentation can already be felt in the concerns intimated, for example, in Nietzsche's essays or Broch's novels. These concerns would be later transformed by French philosophers into the ideas of deconstruction and post-modernism. To use the current jargon, the conclusion might be drawn that after the religious grand narrative had been deconstructed, the time was ripe for the deconstruction of the fragments of this narrative such as scientific or historical positivism, or the autonomy of art.

Thus, one can imagine a scale of different attitudes towards the possible ways of co-existence of the various spheres. There are two extreme poles in this scale. At the one pole, there is a hierarchical system, which is advanced by those who would welcome the return to some form of primordial certainty. Here this position will be called 'pre-modernist'. Included among its proponents are those who are usually regarded as conservative or religious critics of modernity, like Leo Strauss, Eric Voegelin, or Alasdair MacIntyre. At the other pole, there is a situation of permanent instability, in which all value systems are constantly scrutinised and deconstructed. This position will be called 'post-modernist'. For example, Gilles Deleuze, Jean-François Lyotard and Richard Rorty can be included in this category as 'post-modernist' critics of modernity. The distinction between pre- and post-modernists is not perfect, given, especially, that 'pre-modernist' and 'post-modernist' critiques of modernity can often co-exist. Moreover, a critique of modernity can often serve as a meeting point of these two extremes. This is the reason for similarities between some strains of conservative and postmodernist thought.

Nevertheless, a different position is possible, which is not the combination of pre-modern and post-modern critiques of modernity, but a point in the middle of the scale. This position will be called 'modernist'. Included among the proponents of this view are the aforementioned theorists of fragmentation at the end of the nineteenth and the beginning of the twentieth centuries, and it is with this view that we began our discussion. These theorists deny hierarchy but at the same time do not anticipate the relativism and deconstruction associated with post-modernist theories. They, therefore, subscribe neither to the 'pre-modern' nor to the 'post-modern' view.

The 'modernist' position is in some respects similar to pre- and post-modernist positions, for it is situated somewhere in the middle between these extremes. But at the same time it is the rejection of both. To adhere to a pre- or post-modernist critique of modernity, or to both, is to commit oneself to the denial of the autonomy of various spheres such as science, history or art. The only difference between the two is that pre-modernists deny this autonomy because they want to impose their comprehensive worldview, whilst post-modernists want to explode any coherent view, including that of these spheres. By contrast, 'modernists' postulate the autonomy of several well-established spheres.

Now, apart from the idea of the fragmentation of modern culture, a parallel development may also be found in the fragmentation of modern society. Not only may our worldview be seen as fragmented, but the structure of our society may be presented as undergoing an analogous process. Reflection on this social aspect of 'modernity' originates, perhaps, in the political economy of the Scottish Enlightenment with its emphasis on the importance of the division of labour. The Scottish school's analysis was borrowed by German philosophers, and especially by Hegel, who transformed division of labour into one of the main elements of his philosophy of mind.[44] The idea of the centrality of the functional differentiation of modern society lies at the heart of the modern sociological theories of Tönnies and Simmel.[45] This coincides with the idea of the appearance of individuality as a modern phenomenon salient in Hegel, and later developed by Burckhardt and Nietzsche.

The specific understanding of 'modernity' to which this study refers when claiming that Oakeshott's thought implies a defence of modernity should now be clear. This understanding is not idiosyncratic. Besides being quite common in the historical period in which Oakeshott's philosophy originates, this view incorporates many familiar ideas about modernity and even helps to resolve the paradoxes which result when 'modernity' is associated with developments and ideas such as objectivity, secularisation, science, aesthetic enjoyment, individualism, liberalism and many others. To put them together in a coherent fashion is not a simple matter. Thus, individualism, pushed to its extreme, revolts against the standards of objectivity. But if we use the idea of plurality as a heuristic term for the various aspects of modernity, many contradictions disappear. For

[44] On the influence of the Scottish political economists on Hegel's thought see, for example, Laurence Dickey, *Hegel: Religion, Economics and the Politics of Spirit 1770-1807* (Cambridge: Cambridge University Press, 1987).

[45] Ferdinand Tönnies, *Community and Civil Society*, trans. J. Harris & M. Hollis (Cambridge: Cambridge University Press, 2001); Georg Simmel, *The Sociology of Georg Simmel*, trans. K.H. Wolff (Glencoe, Ill: The Free Press, 1950). See also, Roy Pascal, *Culture and the Division of Labour: Three Essays on Literary Culture in Germany* (Coventry: University of Warwick, 1974).

example, modernity is, of course, characterised by the development of the modern scientific mind as creating the most rigorous rules of scientific research, yet scientific activity is limited and it relates only to a particular sphere of modern consciousness. This is why Oakeshott is able to combine his adherence to the strictest scientific positivism with an appreciation of the limitations of science.[46] He is a philosopher not of some specific part of the fragmented reality of the modern age, but of modernity in its entirety.

The understanding of modernity as fragmentation, therefore, can provide an explanation of many aspects of modern civilisation. Yet, theoretically speaking, 'modernity' is a problematic and elusive concept. It promotes a view which is internally unstable and even contradictory. On the one hand, it rejects an overall system of values; on the other hand, it retains several different spheres of values. It rejects the unified system, but maintains that every system of values is sovereign in its autonomous sphere. In other words, it is both the rejection and affirmation of value. Modernity is the attempt to preserve value in a devalued world.

It also becomes clear why 'modernity' is referred to in so many different and contradictory ways. It itself is situated between two contradictory drives, and therefore it can be seen as merely an imperfect type of either of them. Thus, for 'post-modern' critics, modernity is just a continuation of pre-modernity, with its affirmation of value, by other means. This is why Adorno and Horkheimer, or Lyotard, identify modernity with the Enlightenment and despotism of Reason.[47] On the other hand, 'pre-modern' critics such as Leo Strauss or Roger Scruton associate modernity with an almost post-modern nihilism, or at least see it as leading to such nihilism.[48]

The figure of Max Weber is particularly relevant here, because Weber as a theorist of modernity takes to the extreme the combination of fragmentation with an insistence on the objectivity of value-spheres. Therefore, one can find Weber being attacked not

---

[46] See ch. 2, science.
[47] Theodor W. Adorno and Max Horkheimer, *Dialectic of Enlightenment*, trans. J. Cumming (London: Verso, 1979); Jean-François Lyotard, *The Postmodern Condition: A Report on Knowledge*, trans. G. Bennington & B. Massumi (Manchester: Manchester University Press, 1984).
[48] 'The ruin of meaning would never be sanctioned by a philosopher who is merely modern; but it lies in the agenda of those modernists and post-modernists from Sartre to Rorty whose world is bereft of all authority.' Roger Scruton, *Modern Philosophy* (London: Sinclair-Stevenson, 1994), p. 477. See also his definition of 'modern', 'modernist', 'post-modernist' in *ibid.*, pp. 1-2; also Leo Strauss, *Natural Right and History* (Chicago: The University of Chicago Press, 1953).

only by conservative authors such as Voegelin and Alan Bloom, for whom he is the prophet of a dangerous nihilism of values,[49] but also by radical authors, for whom he is the advocate of old-fashioned notions of objectivity and value-neutrality.[50] In fact, both kinds of critic are right, since modernity itself is Janus-faced: it involves, that is, both the preservation and rejection of value.

However, even the 'modernist' recognition of the existence of several established independent spheres may provoke different responses. The danger of 'modernity' can be seen, for example, as lying in the clash between different systems of value, though not in the disintegration of the spheres themselves. One extreme response will be to retreat to some form of the pre-modern position disguised as modernism. Thus, a scientific positivist who advocates the independence of science is a 'modernist'. But if he is tempted to claim that science is the only true form of knowledge he simply falls back into hierarchy. This is why, for example, Communism with its emphasis on technology and science can be seen as an anti-modern phenomenon.

Another response would be to retain some kind of a compromised 'modernist' position, which would shore up diversity with at least some loose kind of unity. Certain aspects of Hegelian philosophy may be interpreted in this way, and this is the direction to which Collingwood seems to be heading in his rejection of the neo-Kantian idea of the autonomy of various spheres of knowledge.

Finally, there can be a recognition that this plurality is irreducible to any kind of unity. Pluralism of different worldviews is recognised, and at the same time relativism is not yet respectable. However, as it has already been indicated, this basic irreducibility of the established value spheres often provokes a deep pessimism with regard to the condition of modern culture, mostly because of the fear of a war between different value spheres, for example between science and art.[51]

The idea of the fragmentation of society and the development of individualism is no less problematic. That view also provokes attacks from two opposite directions. Conservative (pre-modern) criticism sees in the modern individual a dangerous abstraction, a phantom of the 'atomist' approach, which fails to recognise that

---

[49] Eric Voegelin, *The New Science of Politics: An Introduction* (Chicago: The University of Chicago Press, 1987), pp 1-26; Allan Bloom, *The Closing of American Mind* (London: Penguin Books, 1988), pp. 150-151.
[50] See, for example, John Horton, 'The Fetishism of Sociology,' in J.D. Colfax & K.L. Roach (eds.), *Radical Sociology* (New York: Basic Books, 1971), pp. 171-193.
[51] See Lepenies, *Between Literature and Science*, pp. 199-219.

individuals can exist only as members of social institutions within the succession of many generations. 'Post-modernists' like Deleuze may attempt to attack the notion of individuality from the opposite side, denying the existence of unified personality and promoting what is now known as the 'multiple self'.[52]

Yet the idea of differentiation and individualisation may be seen as the predicament of modern social life and supported by the political doctrine of modern liberalism. Like the idea of the plurality of independent values, liberalism (as an idea of the plurality of independent individuals) is an essentially unstable doctrine based on two opposing drives — the one affirming the independence of the individual, and the other emphasising the moral responsibility of such an individual and the social harmony achieved through the free development of independent members of society. Again, this view can be attacked from two sides. Pre-modernists may see in liberalism a disguised nihilism, leading towards anarchy and disorder.[53] Post-modernists may see in liberalism just a disguised doctrine of oppression and domination designed to preserve the old system of privileges.[54]

Thus, modernity understood as fragmentation, either in the cultural or the social dimension, appears to be an inherently unstable and contradictory concept. Any defence of modernity will necessarily involve a battle on two fronts — against the traditional hierarchical systems on the one hand and against nihilism and relativism on the other. Those who undertake this task will also need to respond to the scepticism of pessimistic modernists about whether and where such defence is possible.

V

It has been a rather long excursion, but it has helped us to construct a theoretical framework based on which we can discern what is essential in Oakeshott's thought. First of all, he is not a pre-modernist. He accepts the modernist notion of radical plurality. Partly to emphasise this point, I took the liberty of substituting an apparently more straightforward expression — 'Western civilisation' — for the

---

[52] Gilles Deleuze and Félix Guattari, *Anti-Oedipus: Capitalism and Schizophrenia*, trans. R. Hurley, M. Seem & H.R. Lane (New York: The Viking Press, 1977). See also Jon Elster (ed.) *The Multiple Self* (Cambridge: Cambridge University Press, 1986).
[53] See Carl Schmitt, *The Crisis of Parliamentary Democracy*, trans. E. Kennedy (Cambridge, Mass: The MIT Press, 1985).
[54] Ernesto Laclau and Chantal Mouffe, *Hegemony and Socialist Strategy: Towards a Radical Democratic Politics* (London: Verso, 1985).

notion of modernity. Oakeshott himself would perhaps choose the former to describe his own views and call himself a defender of Western civilisation. Yet I would like to insist on this notion in order to make clear the gap between him and those conservative thinkers who, like Leo Strauss, tend to assign what is valuable in Western civilisation to its pre-modern heritage. True, Oakeshott also venerates the ancient heritage of our civilisation. However, in his philosophy, he puts an emphasis on the value of what is specifically modern in the Western world. The central element of this modernity is an appearance of the plurality of different spheres.

The idea that the modern age is qualitatively different from all other ages, and that modern Western civilisation is perhaps exceptional compared to all other civilisations, is present, even when it is not explicitly stated, in Oakeshott's major works. For example, as we shall see later, Oakeshott regards poetry, science and history as activities characteristic of the specifically modern consciousness. Some may argue that this presentation of his position is puzzling, given the salient historicism of many of his writings. It is true, that in his historical or quasi-historical mood Oakeshott is always averse to the idea of historical discontinuity. He prefers to present the historical process in terms of gradual change. Thus, he qualifies Strauss' view of Thomas Hobbes's philosophy as representing a complete break with previous thought because he believes that its seeds can be found in the Stoic-Christian tradition.[55] Oakeshott also attributes some of the ideas developed by himself to ancient thinkers such as Aristotle.[56] And on other occasions, Oakeshott argues that the modern morality of individuality did not appear suddenly, but resulted from the gradual development of moral attitudes during several centuries.[57] Similarly, the two different understandings of the character of the modern European state, though fully developed in the modern period, had been intimated in the character of the institutions and legal thought of the medieval epoch.[58] Indeed, the idea of social development as the process of gradual change in which a society can use only those resources which are already intimated in its tradition is the subject of one of the most famous of Oakeshott's essays.[59]

However, the idea that a certain phenomenon is the outcome of gradual development is perfectly compatible with the attempt to

---
[55] 'Dr. Leo Strauss on Hobbes,' HCA, pp. 153-154.
[56] HC, pp. 109-111, WP.
[57] MPME.
[58] HC, ch. III.
[59] 'Political education,' RIP, pp. 43-69.

present it as qualitatively new. For, whatever his admiration for historical study might be, Oakeshott himself was not an historian, certainly not according to his own rigid criteria of what historical writings should look like.[60] His method of presentation is not an account of change for its own sake, but the formulation of ideal types through which a certain condition can be understood. And here Oakeshott maintains a clear dichotomy between the modern and pre-modern age. Though he recognises that historically the development of our civilisation into what we recognise as modernity was gradual, complex and ambiguous, he thinks that it is important to maintain a clear distinction between the modern Western and other civilisations. Thus, while in *Experience and Its Modes* he mentions the modes of history, science and practice as historical phenomena, he nevertheless analyses them from a purely theoretical standpoint. In *On Human Conduct* he speaks about two modes of understanding of the modern state, and his analysis is, again, theoretical, and not historical. He also speaks about new types of morality which are clearly distinguished from the medieval morality of communal ties. And in this sense, the philosophy of Hobbes is seen as an analysis which is suitable to a specifically modern moral sensibility.[61]

Furthermore, Oakeshott often refers to the modern age as the situation of maturity of the human race, and this maturity indicates the break between the previous, childish and primordial condition, when 'death was close, leisure was scarce',[62] and sophisticated modern culture. This consciousness of the exceptional character of modern civilisation is supported by the significance that Oakeshott attributes to seeing the world in the category of presentness, to the feeling of the importance of what is truly present. He praises all of those whose life in the present is not dominated by the considerations of the past and the future.[63] Oakeshott is deeply aware of the gap between the modern and the ancient age. The exceptional character of modernity is understood by him to pose new and serious questions with regard to the human condition, and these questions require serious reflection.

Secondly, the choice of the term 'modernity' implies that Oakeshott is *not* a post-modernist philosopher, and this is an especially important point in the face of a growing tendency to study

---

[60] 'The Activity of Being a Historian,' RIP, pp. 151-183.
[61] HC, chs. II and III; 'The Masses in Representative Democracy,' RIP, pp. 363-383; 'The Moral Life in the Writings of Thomas Hobbes,' RIP, pp. 295-350.
[62] 'The Voice of Poetry in the Conversation of Mankind,' RIP, p. 488; see also EM, pp. 1-2.
[63] 'Religion and the World,' RPML, p. 33.

Oakeshott's thought in the context of various post-modernist philosophies.[64] Such study may, perhaps, render his thought more popular but only at the price of losing what is distinctive and valuable in it and of ignoring his deeply felt beliefs.

Bruce Pilbeam, in a recently published article, argues that there are interesting similarities between conservative and postmodernist thought yet these similarities remain largely unnoticed, as most conservatives regard postmodernism as an enemy, and thereby become defenders of rationalism and universality contrary to what one might expect from a traditional conservative.[65] Unlike them, Oakeshott is more radical in his critique of rationalism and this is why he is one of a few conservatives 'to be given by postmodernists either attention or respect'. At the same time, Pilbeam thinks, it would be 'erroneous to impute postmodern inclinations to Oakeshott'.[66]

But what precisely does it mean to be similar to postmodernists without having postmodernist inclinations? Pilbeam's answer seems to be that Oakeshott is a conservative whose critique of modernity is not corrupted by rationalism, and his views are therefore akin to the post-modernist critique. In my view this would be an erroneous interpretation, and the analysis of what 'post-modernism' means, which is offered here, makes it clear why. It is true that 'modernism' and 'post-modernism' share in common their rejection of the unified hierarchical world-picture. Yet to reject such a picture and to recognise the conditionality of any experience does not necessarily lead to the adoption of the post-modernist view which promotes the destruction of the notions of objectivity and standards.

In his philosophy of experience Oakeshott shares the modernist conviction that there are several well-established spheres of knowledge, that these spheres are self-contained and homogeneous, that they have their own measures of objectivity and standards and that they are not going to be fragmented any further. All these premises are unacceptable to a typical post-modernist view which rejects any notion of self-sufficiency and objectivity. Moreover, as will be shown later, Oakeshott is influenced by thinkers such as Poincaré and Croce, who are alien to any post-modernist mood, and it is superficial to declare those writers 'proto-post-modernists'.

Likewise, Oakeshott builds his philosophy of society to defend the ideas of individuality and the liberal order, not to destroy them.

[64] Rorty, *Objectivity, Relativism, and Truth*, p. 197.
[65] Bruce Pilbeam, 'Conservatism and Postmodernism: Consanguineous Relations or "Different" Voices?' *Journal of Political Ideologies* 6(1), 2001, pp. 33-54.
[66] *Ibid.*, p. 44.

True, he does not speak about individuality in essentialist terms and recognises that the 'self' is an abstraction. However, for him, the 'self' is not a chimera to be deconstructed but a coherent identity valuable in itself.[67]

Yet it is not surprising why there is such a wide range of possible interpretations of Oakeshott's thought, and why many commentators see him either as a traditionalist conservative or a post-modernist. As has been shown, the idea of modernity includes features of both the pre-modern and post-modern outlook. Therefore, depending on what aspect is highlighted, modernity can be interpreted either as pre-modernity or post-modernity. Those interpreters who present Oakeshott as a traditionalist or post-modernist are not entirely wrong, they are just partially correct. Those who find in Oakeshott the combination of conservative and post-modernist critiques are even closer to the truth. Yet this is not the view that is offered in the current work, for it regards Oakeshott not as a critic, but as a defender of modernity. The affinity of his thought with some claims of pre- and post-modernists simply derives from the fact that modernity finds itself in the middle of the scale between pre- and post-modernist positions.

VI

Oakeshott, therefore, is a defender of modernity. Like many other theorists of modernity he understands it as a radical plurality resulting from fragmentation and individualisation. Yet, unlike many of them, he sees this condition as valuable in itself. The question, however, arises: by what argument can this defence of modernity be supported?

As we have seen, pessimism with regard to modernity is deeply implied within its very definition. Modernity, being both the rejection and defence of value, is unstable and self-contradictory. If this is the case, then the philosophical defence of such condition, if it is ever possible, requires a great measure of ingenuity.

I will analyse Oakeshott's position in the later parts of my book. However, some preliminary remarks may be required. As it seems, Oakeshott offers no philosophical justification for the condition of radical plurality he observes, yet he does not regard the lack of demonstrative argument as a failure. He is a philosophical sceptic who recognises the impossibility of creating a comprehensive philosophical system. For Oakeshott, the condition of plurality is just an histor-

---

[67] See ch. 3, practice, morality, individuality.

ical outcome of a series of contingent events. He does not believe that the necessity of plurality itself or of a particular form of experience can be philosophically proven. Neither does he think that philosophy is well placed to prove the very idea of irrelevance of these forms to each other. The best one can offer is not an argument, but an exposition of a certain standpoint. Philosophy can elucidate merely *what* we cherish but not *why* we cherish it.

Oakeshott's vision is, therefore, a combination of an historical claim about the existence of plurality with an implicit normative subtext asserting that in order to preserve this plurality, it is necessary to see different modes as irrelevant to each other. Yet the idea of irrelevance is merely postulated. As we shall see, for Oakeshott, maintaining modernity is not the task of modern philosophy, but of modern education which must be specifically non-philosophical.

My suggestion is that this understanding of modernity reflects the fact that Oakeshott is the heir of two very different intellectual attitudes. Oakeshott's thought is that of an English philosopher, who gets to grips with the German philosophical tradition, but who, at the same time, is able to keep his detachment from that tradition.

Oakeshott's defence of modernity is, in this sense, the response of an English intellectual to the challenge of the critique of modernity made by his continental-minded fellows. Oakeshott is an Englishman who is engaged with German philosophy and with its preoccupation with modernity. Therefore, while he is able to share this preoccupation *intellectually*, he is not ready to buy its *sentiment*. Oakeshott recognises the circumstance of fragmentation but refuses to see in it a tragedy. He does not see modernity as a project, but as his own tradition. He advocates the combination of reflexive understating of modernity with non-reflexive, 'poetical' enjoyment. What is implied here is a distinction between the intellectual and the habitual attitude towards modernity. In the speculative realm Oakeshott is a radical critic of what he affirms in the realm of practice.[68] This twofoldness is implied in his remarks which refer to 'the charm of a compromise and appeals to that love of moderation which has as frequently been fatal to English philosophy as it has been favourable to English politics'.[69] Perhaps here lies the reason why Oakeshott always thought that philosophy as an engagement of understanding was irrelevant to the pursuit of practical life. For modernity can be defended only from the practical and not the speculative standpoint.

---

[68] See, for example, ch. 2 in which it is described how Oakeshott exposes the postulates of modes of experience, while at the same time affirming the identity of each of them in the most uncompromised way.

[69] EM, p. 196.

Having grasped this, we may proceed with a detailed analysis of Oakeshott's philosophy in its two aspects — as a philosophy of experience and a philosophy of society.

Chapter 2
Philosophy of Experience

> We shall not easily forget the sweet delight which lies in the empty kisses of abstraction.
> *Experience and Its Modes*, 1933

INTRODUCTION: PHILOSOPHY AND PLURALITY

I

An inquiry into Oakeshott's philosophy of experience must start by attempting to establish its most important and original characteristic. To discover the answer to this question is already to suggest a certain interpretation in the light of which Oakeshott's entire philosophy should be understood. Yet only by grasping what is essential in his thought can we appreciate its real significance.

Different answers have been suggested by various interpreters. John Casey says that 'Oakeshott's fundamental doctrine is... about practical knowledge and practical wisdom'.[1] This view is frequently found in the literature, on account of the great attention paid to Oakeshott's essays on Rationalism and as a result of his reputation as a primarily political philosopher. This view, however, ignores the fact that many of Oakeshott's philosophical writings do not focus upon the subjects of tradition and practice, and that some of them, such as 'The Voice of Poetry in the Conversation of Mankind', even treat practice with suspicion.

Steven Gerencser suggests that the basic feature of Oakeshott's thought is its scepticism.[2] Though this view may be not entirely

---
[1] John Casey, 'Philosopher of Practice,' in J. Norman (ed.), *The Achievement of Michael Oakeshott* (London: Duckworth, 1993), p. 60.
[2] Steven Gerencser, *The Skeptic's Oakeshott* (New York: St. Martin's Press, 2000).

incorrect, the term 'scepticism' is hardly a notion which can enlighten us on any specific aspects of Oakeshott's philosophy. Whether scepticism is found in a rejection of the attempts to build an overall metaphysical system, or in an insistence on the imperfection of human beings, this view is characteristic of the twentieth century's intellectual climate. To be a sceptic these days means the same as what it meant to be a stoic in the Late Roman Empire, or utilitarian in Victorian Britain: it is more a common mood, a disposition, than a distinct philosophy. Further, Oakeshott rarely and somewhat reluctantly uses this term. Thus, in 'The Voice of Poetry' he admits very cautiously that 'a degree of scepticism' in his view 'cannot be denied'.[3] The only text where the word 'scepticism' is widely used is posthumously published *The Politics of Faith and the Politics of Scepticism*,[4] where it is specifically applied to the realm of politics. This, however, does not mean that Oakeshott's entire philosophy is 'sceptical'. On the contrary, his rigorous definition of various worldviews such as science or poetry often sounds quite dogmatic.

The interpretation offered here is different. The basic idea of Oakeshott's philosophy of experience is expressed not in a single work but throughout all of his main philosophical writings. That idea is the notion of the inherent plurality of human experience, of the variety of abstract independent worldviews, each existing for its own sake.[5] The idea of plurality is an underlying thread through all his philosophical and educational writings. This is the notion which remains consistent throughout his intellectual career. This, and not the idea of philosophy in general, is the most important aspect of Oakeshott's thought. In order to substantiate this claim, it is necessary to present in more detail the development of Oakeshott's description of the relationship between philosophy and abstract worldviews.

II

Oakeshott's intellectual career is usually divided into three periods. The main work of the early, pre-war period is a philosophical treatise, *Experience and Its Modes* (1933). The second period is marked by the publication of *Rationalism in Politics* (1962), in which ten essays, written between the forties and sixties, are included. In his late period, Oakeshott published two books: *On Human Conduct* (1975),

---

[3] 'The Voice of Poetry in the Conversation of Mankind,' RIP, p. 493.
[4] PFPS.
[5] See also Steven Grosby, 'Pluralism in the Thought of Oakeshott, Shils and Weber,' *Journal of Classical Sociology* 2(1), 2002, pp. 43-58.

which dealt mostly with the questions of practice and politics, and *On History* (1983).

All these books are seen as reflecting Oakeshott's Idealistic approach, but their concerns and styles are very different. Therefore, there is a continuous debate about whether and to what extent the general character of Oakeshott's philosophical approach changed throughout these periods.[6] W.J. Coats rightly calls this debate 'scholastic',[7] because far-reaching conclusions are usually made on the basis of a few occasional sentences extracted from Oakeshott's writings. In Coats' view, too much attention has been paid to slight stylistic modifications.

In truth, Oakeshott did not write much about purely metaphysical questions, and even in *Experience and Its Modes* the discussion about philosophy as such occupies significantly less space than the discussion about modes of experience. What, then, can be said about his few philosophical sketches? Oakeshott is certainly an Idealist, but Idealism is a broad church, and it includes many different and even contradictory philosophical approaches. All of them can be said to assert the primacy of mind, seen as the entity which does not merely reflect reality but actively creates it. On a more metaphysical level, the world of intelligibles is seen as superior to the world of unintelligibles.

Oakeshott accepted the first aspect of this view. He claimed that every experience always involves judgement and denied that sensation, perception or intuition could be seen as existing separately from thought.[8] Moreover, he accepted the coherence theory of truth and denied the existence of reality outside experience. It is difficult to say whether these claims had an ontological as well as an epistemological character. In *On Human Conduct* Oakeshott presented a very cautious point of view, analysing the character of understanding, without being concerned with the question of whether the intelligible world represents a higher form of reality.

A more complicated question concerns the specific tradition to which Oakeshott's philosophy belongs. In *Experience and Its Modes*

---

[6] See, for example, Charles Covell, *The Redefinition of Conservatism: Politics and Doctrine* (London: Macmillan, 1986), pp. 93-143; Anthony Farr, *Sartre's Radicalism and Oakeshott's Conservatism: The Duplicity of Freedom* (London: Macmillan Press, 1998); Paul Franco, *The Political Philosophy of Michael Oakeshott* (New Haven: Yale University Press, 1990); Gerencser, *The Skeptic's Oakeshott*; Robert Grant, *Oakeshott* (London: Claridge Press, 1990); John Liddington, 'Hall and Modood on Oakeshott,' *Political Studies* 30(2), 1982, pp. 177-183.

[7] W. John Coats Jr., *Oakeshott and His Contemporaries* (Selinsgrove: Susquehanna University Press, 2000), p. 48.

[8] EM, pp. 9-27.

he claims to have learnt most from Hegel and Bradley, and it is conventional to see Oakeshott's thought in the context of the tradition of Absolute Idealism.[9] There is much in his first book which makes him an heir to this tradition. He adopts the monistic view which regards experience as an interconnected system of ideas, a 'world', and he subscribes to a coherence theory of truth, according to which the only criterion of truth and reality is an achievement of such a world of ideas which would be non-contradictory and fully coherent in itself. Yet there is much more in *Experience and Its Modes* than that monism, and, as we shall see later, the theory of modes of experience comes into conflict with at least some aspects of Absolute Idealism.

Later, Oakeshott's philosophical framework and vocabulary undergo significant changes. In *Experience and Its Modes* he uses familiar quasi-Hegelian terms and distinguishes between the 'concrete', which he understands as a whole of reality, or as experience without presupposition, and the 'abstract', which is unsatisfactory, limited and defective experience, an attempt to present a part for the whole. In the essays included in *Rationalism in Politics*, and especially in 'The Voice of Poetry', the vocabulary is different. Experience becomes an activity of imagining, and modes of experience are called voices, or universes of discourse which use different idioms. Nietzsche, Wittgenstein and philosophers of language are more salient here than Hegel or Bradley. And in *On Human Conduct*, the vocabulary is mostly Kantian and neo-Kantian. The terms used are 'conditional' and 'unconditional', 'ideal characters', 'categories', 'intelligible' and 'unintelligible'.

Yet, the content of these sketches falls short of a comprehensive treatment. No metaphysical doctrine, no table of categories, no thorough analysis of consciousness are found. The excursions into pure philosophy appear more as an introduction, a convenient platform to explore the variety of worldviews, and not as an independent philosophical statement.

It is very tempting to see some frivolity in Oakeshott's approach to philosophy. The masquerade of philosophical vocabularies looks like play. And yet there is some consistency in his philosophy. This consistency and seriousness does not lie in a general philosophical system, something which is not of a great importance to Oakeshott. He was certainly opposed to any system-building in philosophy, and for him free thought meant rather intellectual curiosity than demonstration or definition. This seriousness is explicit in his deal-

[9] EM, p. 6; see David Boucher, 'The Creation of the Past: British Idealism and Michael Oakeshott's Philosophy of History,' *History and Theory* 23(2), 1984, pp. 193-214; Franco, *The Political Philosophy of Michael Oakeshott*.

ing with what he calls an 'abstraction', or a conditional mode of understanding. Oakeshott himself hints at this in one passage in 'The Voice of Poetry', where he claims that different voices of mankind meet each other in conversation. The excellence of this conversation springs 'from a tension between seriousness and playfulness. Each voice represents a serious engagement'.[10] However, in the conversation, which perhaps takes the place of a uniform philosophical system, each voice learns to be playful.

Therefore, a philosophical framework for Oakeshott is nothing other than a preface to his serious engagement, which is the analysis of different worldviews. In this engagement he proved himself to be consistent throughout his writings, although he modified his views on some points. Moreover, he apparently changed his general framework as a result of modifications in the presentation of these worldviews, and not vice versa. Thus, in his middle period Oakeshott separated 'poetry' from the practical mode of experience to which it had belonged in early writings. 'Poetry' became an activity of pure contemplation. This was indeed hardly in keeping with his previous insistence that every experience involved reflective judgement. Oakeshott then reformulated his framework referring to experience not as a thought but as an activity of imagining. Thus, contrary to the claim presented in *Experience and Its Modes*, philosophy in Oakeshott's thought became dependent on abstractions, not abstractions on philosophy.

III

Let us analyse in detail the character of the relationship between 'philosophy' and 'abstractions'.[11] According to the argument in *Experience and Its Modes*, every experience is thought, a world of ideas, which constitutes an interdependent system. The criterion of truth is the inner coherence of this world of ideas, a lack of self-contradiction. As every experience is a world of ideas, there is no such thing as complete ignorance, or complete error. Everything is true to some degree and the aim in experience is to achieve what is absolutely coherent. The whole of experience is achieved when this is experience without presupposition, experience which is fully coher-

---

[10] RIP, p. 493.
[11] In *Experience and Its Modes* Oakeshott uses the terms 'concrete' and 'abstract' in their neo-Hegelian sense, referring to 'abstract' as something which is partial, conditioned by its own postulates. A mode of experience is a limited view of reality and is therefore abstract. In Oakeshott's later writings the term 'abstract' is used less often; yet there remains the underlying idea about the conditionality of human knowledge.

ent in itself, so that it does not require any further transformation. Only experience is real, and any reality is experience. To achieve the satisfactory in experience is also to achieve the whole of reality.

Yet such completeness is rarely, if ever, achieved. Quite often experience is not pursued radically in order to achieve full coherence, but is arrested at a certain point. When an arrest happens, sometimes a homogeneous world of ideas, limited by certain presuppositions, emerges. This is an abstract world of experience, which falls short of grasping the whole of reality. This arrest 'modifies' experience, and therefore Oakeshott calls it a 'mode'. It is a homogeneous, but not complete form of experience. It is not a part of reality; it is an attempt to achieve the whole of reality, but from a limited standpoint, and therefore a failed attempt. It is dependent on concrete experience — which is the criterion of its coherence, but does not contribute anything to it. No mode of experience is necessary in order to achieve what is satisfactory in experience, and it must be either avoided or destroyed and superseded, but not incorporated. Modes of experience are irrelevant to each other, and they are also irrelevant to philosophy, which is concrete experience. Oakeshott claims that he intends to present 'a detailed criterion for determining what, in experience, is abstract' in order to overcome this abstractness.[12]

This claim is very simple, yet careful reading exposes a paradox contained in it. These ideas about the character of experience, and the fact that some forms of experience may fall short of the totality of experience, were not in themselves new. They lay within the tradition of Absolute Idealism. The criterion of the absence of self-contradiction and the idea of the modification of experience could be found in Bradley, and the map of forms of experience was developed in different ways by Collingwood and Croce.[13]

Yet Oakeshott's specific presentation of modes of experience seems to conflict with this approach. The Idealists just referred to presupposed the spiritual unity of experience. Bradley was first and foremost a metaphysician, and for him, modes, such as pleasure and pain, feeling, will etc., were merely different appearances of the Absolute. He saw each appearance as 'essential to the unity of the whole', so that 'deprived of any one aspect or element the Absolute

---

[12] EM, p. 83.
[13] F.H. Bradley, *Appearance and Reality* (Oxford: Clarendon Press, 1930); R.G. Collingwood, *Speculum Mentis or The Map of Knowledge* (Oxford: Clarendon Press, 1924); Benedetto Croce, *Logic and the Science of the Pure Concept*, trans. D. Ainsle (London: Macmillan, 1917).

may be called worthless'.[14] Collingwood also recognised a relative value of each form of experience, by which he meant art, religion, science, history and philosophy. Each form contributes to the whole. Unlike Bradley, though, Collingwood put these forms of experience in a hierarchical order, seeing them as necessary stages in the process of the development of thought. Only philosophical experience stood close to the truly absolute, and everything that fell short of it contained a necessary contradiction. A contradiction within every form of experience was quite easily identified, thus ensuring the immanent quasi-Hegelian process of the development of consciousness.

Oakeshott rejects Collingwood's view and argues, like Bradley, that there is no hierarchy of modes of experience. Yet, departing from Bradley, he does not think that any mode is essential to the whole. Although Oakeshott says that it is necessary to present a detailed and not merely general account of the criterion of these modes 'in order to overcome' abstractions,[15] this phrase contradicts what he says elsewhere. To know the detailed criterion of abstractions would be necessary if they were a necessary stage in achieving the totality of experience, but this is what he denies. Philosophy can merely pass by any abstraction. So, if there is a shorter way to the totality of experience why choose a longer one?

Moreover, Oakeshott also maintains that from another standpoint every abstract world of ideas 'is free and self-contained; it has put itself outside the main current of experience and made a home for itself'.[16] It is 'a homogeneous whole which can neither recognise nor admit anything disruptive of its homogeneity'.[17] It is true, in so far as its postulates are accepted.[18] This claim takes him very far away from the neo-Hegelian tradition, in which no homogeneity within a mode of experience is possible. Such homogeneity would contradict the claim that every form of experience is inherently contradictory. Oakeshott says that modes are independent and self-contained, but in the end they are contradictory and doomed to destruction. This rhetoric does not, however, remove the tension, if not contradiction, in his view, where abstractions and concrete experience make claims against each other. They present us with two sorts of values, but the decision of which to choose is far from being determined. For, though philosophy logically supersedes other modes, 'we are not…

---

[14] Bradley, *Appearance and Reality*, p. 404.
[15] EM, p. 83.
[16] EM, p. 75.
[17] EM, p. 327.
[18] EM, p. 77.

prevented from returning to move again in these worlds of abstract ideas'.[19] Because modes cannot contribute anything to the whole of experience, the only reason to explore them is themselves. Indeed, 'we are to live this incurably abstract life of ours'.[20] Philosophy can never take the place of this abstract life; 'it is the denial of life'.[21]

This idea becomes even clearer when Oakeshott discusses what he calls 'pseudo-modes', to which he relates ethics, theology and political philosophy.[22] They are those modifications of experience which fail to compose a homogeneous world of experience. These are abstractions, not 'as a special process, but... as a mere inadvertence'.[23] What distinguishes a mode from a pseudo-mode is that the former is self-contained, sovereign, and lies 'beyond the relevant interference of any other world of experience, so long as it confines itself within the limits which constitute its character'. Whereas the latter 'remains unprotected against interference'.[24] Thus, it turns out that an abstract mode of experience is not merely a defective attempt to achieve the whole. It has a value of its own, since, unlike a pseudo-mode, 'it has an identity to defend'.[25]

Suddenly one notices the obsession with abstraction behind the framework of Absolute Idealism. The chapters dealing with modes of experience take up more space than the description of philosophy. Despite being formally an exploration of the defectivity of modes, they instead vindicate their value, insisting on their irrelevance to other modes or to the totality of experience.

This contradiction attracted the attention of almost all the reviewers of Oakeshott's book, with the exception of L. Susan Stebbing, who took Oakeshott's claims about the defectivity of each mode at their face value and expressed the completely negative opinion, that 'those who have not been convinced by Bradley are not likely to be converted by Mr. Oakeshott'.[26] But the general tone of the reviews was that Oakeshott had developed a very original idea which went beyond his acknowledged sources of influence and came into covert conflict with them. Thus, T.M. Knox argued:

> The natural inference is that the modes are, as it were, in watertight compartments, or that they differ from each other and from concrete experience in *kind*; this seems to be at variance with the doctrine... that

[19] EM, p. 83.
[20] Ibid.
[21] EM, p. 355.
[22] EM, p. 335n.
[23] EM, p. 331.
[24] EM, p. 332.
[25] Ibid.
[26] L. Susan Stebbing, Review of *Experience and Its Modes*, in *Mind* 43, 1934, p. 405.

experience is not divisible into compartments, but that this is an inference which it is legitimate to draw seems evident from numerous passages...[27]

Knox also noticed that it is philosophy and not modes of experience which is most damaged by Oakeshott's account, since it would be worth enquiring 'what precisely philosophy is if art, religion, science, history and practical experience are all irrelevant to it'.[28] According to W.G. de Burgh, the theory of modes is 'the most striking and original feature in Mr. Oakeshott's philosophy' where he 'diverges most markedly from the Hegelian tradition'.[29] S. Lamprecht, while saying that the framework 'taken over from the traditions of absolute idealism' is 'trite', insisted that there was much more to it, referring to the theory of modes.[30] And G.O. Wood found the idea of arrested modes to be completely original, 'not merely non-Hegelian but also non-Bradleian'.[31]

In other words, most of the reviewers viewed Oakeshott's book favourably, though not without some criticism. They noticed the tension between the book's explicit claim to explore concrete experience, and the originality found in the theory of abstract modes. Whereas the general philosophical framework was not considered as particularly insightful, the idea of modes attracted great interest.

After the publication of *Experience and Its Modes* two different paths were open to Oakeshott: the philosophical pursuit of the totality of experience, or an exploration of different abstract modes. In the beginning, Oakeshott tended to choose the former. In a long essay 'The Concept of a Philosophical Jurisprudence' (1938), and in two drafts about the philosophy of politics written during the thirties and forties, he tried to reflect on the character of the philosophy of law and politics from the standpoint of concrete experience.[32] He diverged somewhat from his radical statement in *Experience and Its Modes*, that an attempt to elucidate ethics or politics from the philosophical point of view would lead to the creation of a pseudo-

---

[27] T.M. Knox, Review of *Experience and Its Modes*, in *Oxford Magazine* 52, 1934, p. 552.
[28] *Ibid*.
[29] W.G. de Burgh, Review of *Experience and Its Modes*, in *Hibbert Journal* 33, 1934, p. 147.
[30] S.P. Lamprecht, Review of *Experience and Its Modes*, in *Journal of Philosophy* 31(6), 1934, p. 163.
[31] G.O. Wood, Review of *Experience and Its Modes*, in *Times Literary Supplement*, April 26, 1934, p. 294.
[32] CPJ; 'The Concept of a Philosophy of Politics,' RPML, pp. 119-137; 'Political Philosophy,' RPML, pp. 138-155.

mode.[33] Yet it was still an explicit attempt to analyse these different aspects of reality from the philosophical point of view. Later, however, Oakeshott abandoned these attempts. He never published these essays on political philosophy, and 'The Concept of a Philosophical Jurisprudence' was never mentioned by him afterwards and was not included in *Rationalism in Politics*.

After the war Oakeshott chose the second path of elucidating various abstractions for their own sake. He was mostly preoccupied with practical life or with activities such as poetry and history. In the essay 'The Activity of Being an Historian', Oakeshott explicitly claims to have been concerned with the activity of an historian as it has come to establish itself, not with the attempt to find a manner of thinking superior to that of an historian.[34] In this essay and in 'The Voice of Poetry', the idea of the cultivation of different voices for their own sake is overtly stated. Voices participate in the conversation, but each is characterised by its own idioms irrelevant to the idioms of other voices.

In later publications, the idea that all knowledge is abstract knowledge is reinforced. Thus, in *On Human Conduct*, Oakeshott maintains that, whilst the activity of understanding is 'the unconditional, critical engagement',[35] the knowledge it produces is always conditional, being abstracted from 'the unconditional... confusion of all that may be going on'.[36] Oakeshott's concern here is theorising human conduct as 'a conditional engagement'.[37] Although he does not reject the idea of unconditional understanding altogether, it serves more as a trigger rather than as an actual experience. Already in *Experience and Its Modes* Oakeshott states that 'the supersession of the abstract by what is concrete... cannot take place in any future world of present fact, but only in the world of logical fact'.[38] In *On Human Conduct*, only the calling to theorise is 'unconditional', because any theorising necessarily takes place on some conditional platform of understanding. Thus, while the very process of thought is still understood in a somewhat Hegelian way, every achievement emerges rather as a neo-Kantian abstraction which creates its own categories, postulates and ideal characters. Finally, in *On History* he unambiguously rejects even the possibility of unconditional knowledge, saying that 'where

---

[33] EM, p. 335n.
[34] RIP, pp. 152-153.
[35] HC, p. 2.
[36] HC, p. 1.
[37] HC, p. 12.
[38] EM, p. 82.

there is no specifiable modality, there can be no enquiry and so no consequential conclusions'.[39]

Oakeshott is consistent in his emphasis on abstraction throughout all his writings. I therefore agree with Coats' view that the claims that Oakeshott significantly altered his philosophy are unproven.[40] But the argument here is the reverse of his. Coats claims that there are no indications that Oakeshott repudiated his vindication of philosophy as the pursuit of what is ultimately satisfactory in experience. By contrast, this study claims that already in *Experience and Its Modes*, Oakeshott pursues an agenda of defending abstraction against philosophy, and not philosophy against abstraction. For the 'tangible and certain satisfaction' that abstraction provides is 'one not to be despised'.[41]

IV

The assertion that the significance of *Experience and Its Modes* lies in its exploration of abstract modes, and not in the analysis of the totality of experience, can be supported by a brief look at Oakeshott's intellectual development prior to the publication of that book. It is common to refer to the period of the 1930s as the early period of Oakeshott's thought and to *Experience and Its Modes* as a philosophical expression of that early period. Yet at the time of the publication of *Experience and Its Modes* Oakeshott was a mature man of thirty two with settled intellectual habits and clear prospects for his future, as he had been just appointed a College Lecturer of History at Gonville and Caius, Cambridge.[42] Up to that time, Oakeshott had been pursuing an academic career (first as an undergraduate student and then as a fellow of the college) for more than a decade and his views must have been the outcome of his previous intellectual development.

Those who study the intellectual development of the young Oakeshott can hardly overlook two striking features of this development. One is the extent and intensity of Oakeshott's learning, his ability for hard work, the variety of his interests and his erudition.[43]

---

[39] OH, p. 2.
[40] Coats, *Oakeshott and His Contemporaries*, pp. 47-51.
[41] EM, p. 356.
[42] The appointment took effect from 1 October 1931. The appointment also included the membership in the Official Corporate Fellowship (Caius Papers, LSE Archives).
[43] 'He is very thoughtful beyond his years...' (from the reference letter by Arnold D. McNair, 9 June 1923, Caius Papers, LSE Archives); 'his capacity for work is unusual' (from the reference letter by Frank Debenham, 12 June 1924, Caius Papers, LSE Archives).

These qualities appear not only in the amount of reading that he did but also in the critical character of his studies and the independence of his mind.[44]

The other point is the central place that European philosophy occupies in these studies. This aspect of Oakeshott's education was often overlooked by those whose knowledge about his life was limited to the fact that he had graduated from the Faculty of History at Cambridge.[45] But, besides the fact that this faculty provided its students with a sound knowledge of political philosophy, one can find that Oakeshott acquired by his own effort such a level of a general philosophical education that it could have merited him another degree. Thus, as history undergraduate, he already attended introductory lectures on philosophy by J.M.E. McTaggart.[46] He spent his fourth year in the college studying ancient Greek texts.[47] And, as it appears from his writings and notes, during the twenties he acquired a profound knowledge of philosophy, both ancient and modern, including that of contemporary philosophical writings by Bergson, Husserl and Heidegger.[48]

Furthermore, one can notice that Oakeshott was youthfully, almost naïvely enamoured of philosophy. He did not yet present a finished doctrine, he often changed his opinions and his early drafts lack the famous elegance of his published writings. However all of them exhibit a deep, almost religious conviction in the crucial importance of the subject and of the purpose of philosophy: the search for truth and the attempt to understand what it means to live the good life. [49]

[44] There are a number of notebooks in which he made excerpts and notes from many books he was reading at that time, certainly a time-consuming process.
[45] Oakeshott's writing is that of 'an accomplished historian who, driven into philosophy by the problems of his own work, has found the current philosophies impotent to cope with their philosophical implications.' (R.G. Collingwood, Review of *Experience and Its Modes*, in *Cambridge Review* 55, 1934, p. 249.)
[46] Grant, *Oakeshott*, p. 13.
[47] See the register of the books borrowed by Oakeshott in 1923-24, in the possession of Gonville and Caius College's archive, Cambridge. He spent that year in Cambridge following his graduation and the award of the Christopher James studentship (Caius Papers, LSE Archive).
[48] See ERPPR; Oakeshott's Notebooks, LSE Archives.
[49] Oakeshott in his twenties seems to have been a practising and believing Christian to a large degree. He was the Chapel Clerk of the College (see the reference letter by Joseph Hunkins, 13 June 1923, Caius Papers, LSE Archives) and later participated in the 'D' society which 'was a group of around six Cambridge dons who met weekly in term-time to present theological papers to each other'. (Timothy Fuller, 'Introduction,' in RPML, p. 4n.) Many essays of this period deal with the question of religion and he also contributed reviews to

Sometimes, as in 'An Essay on the Relations of Philosophy, Poetry and Reality' he seems to be sceptical about the ability of philosophy to find such truth, yet only because there is a more certain path to it, which is poetry.[50] However, in another draft, Oakeshott reaffirms his conviction in the value of philosophy as leading us towards the knowledge of truth. The draft is named 'A Discussion of Some Matters Preliminary to the Study of Political Philosophy'. It is an attempt to mark the main parameters for the future study of political philosophy. The text is dated August 1925, that is, just before Oakeshott started his fellowship at Gonville and Caius.

This draft already possesses those qualities which distinguish a characteristically Oakeshottean way of writing: the clarity of exposition and structure and the ability to present philosophical doctrines in a concise and elegant way. Nevertheless, Oakeshott never referred to this work and did not bother to publish it. We will probably never know for sure the reasons for this, yet one suggestion can be made. This text differs significantly from the later writings in its content. Though well written, this is not an original philosophical statement but rather a synthesis of the philosophical ideas by which Oakeshott was influenced. Moreover, not only is it devoid of statements which we would recognise as originally Oakeshottean, almost all its main assumptions were later repudiated by Oakeshott himself.

One characteristic feature of this draft is Oakeshott's rigour in his insistence that the purpose of philosophy is the attainment of the total truth of things, that is of the universe. The major influences here are thinkers such as Plato, Aristotle, Spinoza, Hegel and Bosanquet. Though this rhetoric will be echoed in some later writings, this conviction will never afterwards be presented in such a forceful way without any shadow of scepticism.

---

the *Journal of Theological Studies*. Later in his life, Oakeshott abandoned at least the outward expressions of Christian belief.

[50] ERPPR. The essay is not dated, but my suggestion is that it was written in the early twenties. There is a considerable bibliography at the end of the essay. Much of it is works of French poets and philosophers, cited in their original French editions. There are only a few German works (such as Kant's *Critique of the Pure Reason* and Hegel's *Phenomenology of the Spirit*), mentioned in their English translations. Already, in his third year as an undergraduate, Oakeshott read French texts in the original language. It seems, however, that he improved his German and knowledge of German philosophy only in the middle twenties during his trips to Germany. For example, in 1926 he studied Kant's *Groundwork* in its original German edition. So it seems that the essay had been written before Oakeshott became deeply familiar with German philosophical texts.

Oakeshott argues that the task of philosophy is the knowledge of things. Words are merely significations of real things that exist in our experience. Such knowledge is achieved through the definition of a thing, but this definition is not arbitrary because some definitions stand nearer to the truth than others. The true definition is the classification through the purpose of a thing, whereby it is acknowledged as a member of a *genus*, this acknowledgement connecting a particular object of experience to a more comprehensive whole to which it belongs, and so forth until the totality of experience is achieved.[51] Thus real knowledge turns out in the end to be the knowledge of the whole.

The task of philosophy is not to change the world but to understand it. It is not a guide to practical behaviour.[52] Yet it appears that for Oakeshott, philosophy is not separated from the practical world of value as such. For, unlike history and science, which are value free disciplines concerned merely with brute facts and offering only raw material, philosophy determines judgements aiming 'at giving a final and real meaning to things by the discovery of their final and real content and value'.[53] This conclusion is not surprising, since for Oakeshott the task of philosophy is to determine the *purpose* of each thing in the totality of experience and hence give the thing its meaning.

Philosophy, then, is theorising about values within experience. It aims at the attainment of the knowledge of things through the determination of their meaning and value in terms of their purposes in the whole of experience. It is only with philosophy that real knowledge begins. History and science both present only raw material from which philosophy makes a coherent world. They are not concerned with meaning but with the sphere of cause and effect.[54] One who is searching for real knowledge cannot be content with being merely an historian or a scientist, and almost every great historian or scientist, such as Poincaré or Acton, was more than just a scientist or an historian.[55] In other words, for Oakeshott, real knowledge is a fully coherent knowledge which can be achieved only through philosophy and not other disciplines. This view, of course, is congenial with that of Absolute Idealists.

Now, if one compares these ideas with those expressed in *Experience and Its Modes* and afterwards, one can see that Oakeshott later

---

[51] DSM, pp. 12-21.
[52] DSM, p. 77.
[53] DSM, p. 52.
[54] DSM, p. 41
[55] DSM, p. 43.

repudiated most of what he had said in his early work. If in 1925 Oakeshott was still searching for the kind of intellectual activity capable of reaching the totality of experience, be it poetry or philosophy, in *Experience and Its Modes* this totality actually falls apart.

Firstly, the gap between practice and philosophy is now unbridgeable. Secondly, the role of philosophy is reduced. Now it is not the only possible way to attain real knowledge. It is indeed the way to attain the totality of experience, but this totality is now almost nothing. As we will see in the following sections, abstract modes of experience have stolen from philosophy, each in its own way, methods to build coherent worlds. Now philosophy becomes less important because history and science become more philosophical in an ordinary sense. They are not concerned with mere facts but try to build a coherent world of experience of their own.

Therefore, in *Experience and Its Modes* and afterwards, there is a real shift in Oakeshott's thinking. But this shift is often hidden behind the neo-Hegelian terminology still present in his first book. As it has been shown, this terminology creates a tension between the holistic claims of the book and the insistence on the value of abstractions. Yet one can claim that the latter element is more important because the holistic claims are those which Oakeshott inherited from his early ideas, whilst the notion of modes is new. Therefore, what is often seen as the assertion of Absolute Idealism is the remnant of the old position that Oakeshott expressed in the twenties. By contrast, the idea of the plurality of modes of experience opens a way to a significantly new philosophy, which we recognise as authentically Oakeshottean.

Experience and Its Modes, then, is just a beginning. As we have seen, Oakeshott did not completely finish his evolution there, and the work remained ambiguous. Yet it was the breakthrough, and the later intellectual development can be seen as Oakeshott's attempt to purge his own philosophy of the remnants of the old view that was rejected by him.

V

The most important and original element of Oakeshott's philosophy is, therefore, the idea of the plurality of worldviews in our experience. He maintained that in principle the number of possible abstract worldviews was unlimited, but he concentrated on what he called 'main', 'established' and 'highly developed' modes.[56] These

---
[56] EM, p. 84.

are worldviews which play a central role in establishing the character of modern civilisation. In *Experience and Its Modes* Oakeshott analysed history, science and practice. Yet while the modes of history and science fitted into his framework relatively well being convincingly described as attempts to achieve understanding from a limited standpoint, practice was a problematic mode. It seemed to be necessarily present in any other activity (a scientist trying to get funding for his new project), so that the claim that it is merely an abstract mode was more radical than the same claim with regard to science and history. Although Oakeshott recognised that practice was indispensable to any other activity, he claimed, perhaps in the attempt to refute the Heideggerian view of the primordiality of practice, that logically it was no more than a mode of experience. This attempt to put practice on the same level as other abstract modes involved a variety of problems, and Andrew Sullivan has convincingly shown that Oakeshott failed to deal with them satisfactorily.[57] I will analyse this claim in more detail in the third chapter. Meanwhile, let us notice that practice seems to be a very different mode of experience.

In 'The Voice of Poetry', Oakeshott, though mentioning practice as one of the voices, introduced some important changes. Art, which had previously been a part of practical experience, became an independent voice of poetry, and practice was reduced to utilitarian and ethical considerations. This let Oakeshott present his argument as the defence of abstract worldviews, including poetry, against the dictate of practice. In *Experience and Its Modes* Oakeshott concentrated on practice's mutual irrelevance with philosophy. In 'The Voice of Poetry' and 'The Activity of Being an Historian', the emphasis is put on the danger that poetry, science and history will be assimilated into the voice of practice. Abstract modes fight a war on two fronts: against the utopian claims of philosophy and against the appetites of practice. The emancipation of these modes from the hegemony of practice is the key moment in the development of modern Western civilisation. In an unpublished essay 'Work and Play', written apparently at the same period, Oakeshott makes this point even clearer. He describes the activities of history, science and poetry as 'play', which is free from practical considerations and is associated with 'leisure', as opposed to 'work', an incessant pursuit of the satisfaction of wants.[58]

In *On Human Conduct* Oakeshott distinguishes between three different levels of understanding. At the top, there is an activity of con-

---
[57] Andrew Sullivan, *Intimations Pursued: The Voice of Practice in the Conversation of Michael Oakeshott* (PhD diss., Harvard University, 1990), ch. 1.
[58] WP.

stant questioning of the postulates of any understanding. This is a sort of a 'philosophical' engagement. At the bottom there is an understanding of 'goings-on' as compositions of characteristics. This understanding may have a practical aim, serving as a diagnosis and being indispensable to our intelligent response to any situation. But between them, there is a sort of theorising 'poised between heaven and earth'.[59] This is an engagement of theorising ideal characters in terms of their conditions, or postulates. This is not a philosophical understanding, since it exposes postulates without interrogating them. But it is also above practical deliberations, being, in a sense, a value-free activity of pure understanding. It is not blind to the reality of its own conditionality, but this recognition does not prevent a theorist from accepting this conditionality as it is. Scientific and historical understandings are among these forms of theorising. A theorist, therefore, is engaged in an attempt to achieve an unpractical and at the same time an unavoidably abstract knowledge, which is valued for its own sake.

VI

The account of Oakeshott's philosophy of experience should, therefore, focus upon his analysis of those abstract worldviews, poised between heaven and earth, which are neither metaphysical nor practical. These worldviews can be described as homogeneous, purposeless and irrelevant to each other.

In *Experience and Its Modes* each world of ideas is described as a self-contained, homogeneous whole 'which can neither recognise nor admit anything disruptive of its homogeneity'.[60] This description reflects the contradiction implied in the existence of two different standpoints from which an argument can be pursued. On the one hand, modes of experience are regarded as being completely independent not only from each other, but also from concrete experience, so that philosophy is unable 'to take the place of any abstract world of experience'.[61] On the other hand, however, complete independence cannot be asserted, since 'no abstract world of ideas is independent of the totality of experience, for each derives its character from the whole from which it is an abstraction'.[62] Therefore, although each mode of experience is homogeneous and self-contained, it is not self-sufficient or complete, each 'constitutes a

[59] HC, p. 25.
[60] EM, p. 327.
[61] EM, p. 354.
[62] EM, p. 75.

self-contradiction'.[63] Each mode pretends to achieve concrete experience, while actually falling short of such an achievement.

Oakeshott attempts to show how these modes fail, but these excursions are usually brief and his argument is less convincing than that of Collingwood. Oakeshott's description of contradictions, at least in the case of science and history, appears more as a superficial attempt to make these modes fit the entire structure of the book, than as an absolutely necessary conclusion. Most of the analysis of these modes is dedicated to showing the validity of their claims to be able to achieve homogeneity, coherence, and perfection within their own presuppositions.

This ambiguity completely disappears in subsequent writings. In 'The Voice of Poetry', every universe of discourse is subject to a coherent system of idioms of its own. In *On History*, the postulates of historical inquiry are presented as composing a coherent system of conditions.

Further, these worldviews can be described as *purposeless*, as having no extraneous purpose or criterion. This description is, again, not completely consistent, as there are ambiguities in *Experience and Its Modes* where modes are assigned the role of attempting to achieve the whole of experience. Yet Oakeshott recognises that these abstractions may be wanted for their own sakes, claiming that 'if what we want is history, or science, or practical experience — if, that is, what we want is an arrest in experience — it is useless to go for it to the concrete totality of experience.'[64] Abstraction as such contributes nothing to the totality of experience, and, therefore, the only reason to arrest at an abstraction is to want it for its own sake. In 'The Voice of Poetry' and 'The Activity of Being an Historian', Oakeshott is again less equivocal, making it clear that science, history and poetry should be pursued for their own sake.

The modes of understanding are, then, the ends in themselves. They have no extraneous purpose, and when they meet, their society is described as a conversation and not a 'practical' engagement. Oakeshott does not use the word 'purposeless' with regard to these worldviews, but the whole argument is brought to imply this notion. Purposelessness is one of the main themes of Oakeshott's thought. In 'On Being Conservative' the most valuable activities, such as love or friendship, are described as purposeless activities, pursued for

---

[63] EM, p. 80.
[64] EM, p. 329.

their own sake.[65] And the civil association is recommended by Oakeshott because it lacks a common purpose.[66]

Oakeshott translates the ancient Aristotelian idea of good into the language of modernity. For him, as for Aristotle, the real good is a good pursued for the sake of itself. Yet he denies the existence of the highest good or of a hierarchy of goods, affirming, instead, the irreducible plurality of worldviews in the modern condition. Independent worldviews are good by virtue of their being purposeless, and are purposeless by virtue of their being good. In contrast to Hobbesian insistence that 'anything that has no purpose is Vain',[67] Oakeshott's idea can be formulated as 'everything which has an extraneous purpose is vain'.

This view itself was not original, since the idea of the plurality of values in modernity had been advanced by thinkers such as Nietzsche and Max Weber. However, their recognition of this irreducible plurality led them to adopt a very pessimistic view of the world as a battlefield on which different views clash with one another. Oakeshott was not in the mood to accept these pessimistic conclusions, since he realised that modern civilisation had been endowed with an ability to enjoy plurality without being led into self-destruction. This is because worldviews are not only homogeneous and purposeless, but also *irrelevant* to one another.

This idea of irrelevance is the most important aspect of Oakeshott's theory of modes, consistently promoted in all his writings. According to him, 'it is impossible to pass in argument from any of these worlds of ideas to any other without involving ourselves in a confusion'.[68] Thus, what is true scientifically, cannot be true or false historically, it is simply irrelevant. Irrelevance is 'the most insidious and crippling of all forms of error'.[69] The intrusion of any irrelevant argument is likely to make any process of understanding unintelligible, and irrelevance is much harder to identify and eliminate, than a mere mistake. But there seems to be a more profound reason for Oakeshott's identification of the confusion between modes as the main enemy. The preservation of irrelevance seems to be the only way to recognise the plurality of voices in modernity, to save each voice as valuable for its own sake, and at the same time to avoid the disharmony implied here, to prevent the

---

[65] RIP, pp. 416–417.
[66] HC, pp. 122-124.
[67] Thomas Hobbes, *On the Citizen*, trans. R. Tuck (Cambridge: Cambridge University Press, 1998), p. 49.
[68] EM, p. 76.
[69] EM, p. 5.

'chaos into which experience degenerates'.[70] This view is affirmed in 'The Voice of Poetry' and *On History*.[71]

Thus, Oakeshott saw abstracted worldviews as homogeneous, purposeless and mutually irrelevant. Robert Grant compared them with Leibniz's monads.[72] Yet Oakeshott's claim is more radical than that of Leibniz. In order to expel chaos from his system, Leibniz introduced the notion of a pre-disposed harmony, so that independent substances could co-exist, being set together by God in a harmonious way. Oakeshott's monads co-exist in the world without God. How, then, is harmony possible? Oakeshott might not have had a ready answer to this problem. He vindicated the plurality of abstractions despite the fact that a satisfactory logical justification for this idea is unlikely to exist. But Oakeshott rejected the possibility of an overall philosophical system. In *Experience and Its Modes* he paid lip service to the view that any diversity was impossible without unity, but his advocacy of modes made unity obsolete. Nevertheless, I think that Oakeshott had some sort of answer, but it lay outside his philosophy of experience. The answer was a certain kind of education which he advocated. This is, however, a subject which will be dealt with in the final chapter.

VII

Plurality is, therefore, the central aspect of Oakeshott's philosophy of experience. His main philosophical writings aim to elucidate the proper character of the variety of abstract worldviews as a characteristic of the modern mind. Having started with the ambitious project of finding the unity of experience, Oakeshott offered a philosophy which vindicated abstraction, hardly retaining anything of his self-proclaimed holism. He promoted the recognition of every form

[70] *Ibid.*
[71] The structure of *On Human Conduct* is more complex. Oakeshott distinguishes between two orders of inquiry. One deals with 'goings-on' perceived as exhibitions of intelligence, and the other is concerned with 'goings-on' perceived as not being exhibitions of intelligence. They are completely irrelevant to each other. Yet there are idioms of inquiry within the orders of inquiry. These idioms can be reduced to each other, but each of them is also 'capable of its own conditional perfection' (HC, p. 17). This view is somewhat different from Oakeshott's position in other writings of that period, including *On History* and educational essays. For, instead of a variety of modes, we get only two possible orders of inquiry divided into subfields. This may be explained by the fact that Oakeshott's main preoccupation in this book is not elucidating his philosophy of experience. Rather he is concerned with constructing a convenient conceptual apparatus in order to tackle his philosophy of society.
[72] Grant, *Oakeshott*, p. 39.

of knowledge, every experience, every activity as conditional, but at the same time valuable for its own sake. Modern civilisation speaks with many different languages, and the cultivation of mind consists of learning to recognise the peculiarities of each language and to maintain their purity.

The main voices of modern civilisation, which managed to establish themselves as independent worldviews acting within the system of their own postulates, are history, science, and poetry. In the following sections I intend to analyse their character in detail and show how Oakeshott defends their autonomy and integrity. Before that, several points should be emphasised.

Firstly, Oakeshott adopts those approaches which are likely to maintain the independence of each worldview in the most uncompromising manner. These are scientific positivism in science, aestheticism in poetry, and the notion of history as an unbiased narrative of past events. They emerged when each of these activities reached its maturity and was at the peak of its influence. There is always a temptation to regard Oakeshott's account of science and history merely as an Idealistic critique of positivism.[73] It will be shown that this is a very partial view, and that it puts too much emphasis on the general framework, whereas more significance should be attributed to the worldviews themselves.

Secondly, Oakeshott formulated his views in the context of the modernistic spirit of the beginning of the twentieth century. He believed in the ideas of objectivity and detachment as central values determining the mind's activities. He borrowed his ideas from a number of prominent philosophers of science, history and art, so that his views were more influenced by a contemporary intellectual context than is sometimes perceived.

Thirdly, having arrived at radical conclusions about the character of each worldview, Oakeshott did not abandon them, continuing to express and defend his ideas in an ever more relativistic and post-modernistic intellectual atmosphere. Oakeshott's main views did not change, though the climate in which he published them did.

In my account I start with science, and then turn to history and poetry, thereby departing from the order of presentation in *Experience and Its Modes*, where science comes after history. The reason for this is that Oakeshott wrote much more about history, so that the analysis of his views of this mode will be more complicated, yet his description of the character of history fits the pattern of his description of science. Therefore, it is easier to start with a more compact

---

[73] See, for example, Franco, *The Political Philosophy of Michael Oakeshott*, pp. 31-56.

presentation of science, keeping in mind that Oakeshott's defence of history proceeds along the same lines.

SCIENCE

I

Oakeshott is often regarded as an academic eccentric, preoccupied with the status of the humanities and opposed to the achievements of the new technological age. It is argued that he met science with suspicion, if not overt hostility. Thus, L. Susan Stebbing, in her review of *Experience and Its Modes* (1933), found his treatment of science 'peculiarly unsatisfying'.[74] Noel Annan, referring to Oakeshott's attitude to scientific education in universities, pointed out that 'Oakeshott distrusted science... His condescension is breathtaking; and to the scientists of his own university laughable. How scientists work and think seems beyond his comprehension.'[75]

Even the most sympathetic commentators have until recently almost completely neglected this aspect of Oakeshott's thought.[76] Today the state of research has somewhat improved and Oakeshott's philosophy of science has received more attention. Nevertheless, the main emphasis has usually been on Oakeshott's analysis of the human sciences and of social theory, rather than on his description of the natural sciences.[77] Even when this element of his thought is summarised, it is usually done under an implicit assumption that the important aspect here is the limits of scientific inquiry: not what science is, but what it is not.

This attitude towards Oakeshott is unfair. He certainly did write much more about subjects such as history, education or politics. This is not surprising, given that these were the main subjects of his interest. But what is unusual about Oakeshott is that despite his educational background he dedicated a lot of thought to modern science. He constantly insisted that science was one of the most important activities of the human mind and wrote a long chapter on the nature

---

[74] Stebbing, Review of *Experience and Its Modes*, p. 404.
[75] Noel Annan, *Our Age: Portrait of a Generation* (London: Weidenfeld and Nicolson, 1990), pp. 396-397.
[76] There are some exceptions. Thus, W.H. Greenleaf briefly analyses Oakeshott's philosophy of scientific experience, noticing similarities between Oakeshott's views of science and those of thinkers such as Russell. See W.H. Greenleaf, *Oakeshott's Philosophical Politics* (London: Longman's Green, 1966), p. 22.
[77] See an interesting study by Terry Nardin, *The Philosophy of Michael Oakeshott* (University Park: The Pennsylvania State University Press, 2001), pp. 101-40, who compares Oakeshott's ideas with those of Dilthey and of neo-Kantians such as Windelband and Rickert.

of scientific experience in his first major philosophical treatise. Oakeshott's philosophy of science is not merely a negative attempt to draw the limits of scientific activity, but a positive inquiry, the conclusions of which correspond to the views and feelings of many of his contemporary fellow philosophers and scientists.

This section, however, is not going to present a comprehensive study of science in Oakeshott's philosophy. Its aim is rather to reveal Oakeshott's understanding of science as an important autonomous voice of modern civilisation and to show that his views were shaped under the influence of scientific positivism. It will concentrate on the analysis of Oakeshott's views in *Experience and Its Modes*, simply because this is the only systematic and detailed exposition of his views of the character of scientific activity. However, it will also refer to his later works in order to show that the position outlined in his early philosophical book is preserved throughout his main writings.

II

In *Experience and Its Modes* Oakeshott presents scientific experience as 'defective experience'.[78] Scientific knowledge is hypothetical knowledge, merely 'a world of supposals about reality'.[79] Science is the attempt to discover and maintain the real world but it is unable 'to achieve the end in experience'.[80] It constitutes an abstract and limited world and therefore 'the world of science and the world of reality are, as worlds, exclusive of one another'.[81] Science is unable to achieve what it claims to achieve — the totality of experience — and when philosophy enters the scene, 'scientific experience must either be avoided or pressed beyond the borders of science, carried out of itself and seen to be an abstract world of ideas...'[82]

It is tempting to conclude from this that Oakeshott simply follows the ideas developed by Absolute Idealists, or by such thinkers as Collingwood and Croce, with regard to science and its pretence to explain the whole of reality. Science was not among the central preoccupations of these Idealists, in contrast to many philosophers of the neo-Kantian persuasion such as Helmholtz or Riehl. Some, Bradley and McTaggart among them, explored mainly metaphysical questions; others, such as Croce and Collingwood, focused on other modes of understanding such as history, which they consid-

---

[78] EM, p. 243.
[79] EM, p. 215.
[80] EM, p. 214.
[81] EM, p. 217.
[82] EM, p. 219.

ered to be more coherent. This is not to say that they did not respect modern science or did not recognise its significance. Yet they saw in science an inherently contradictory form of experience, unable to withstand the scrutiny of philosophical investigation and bound to dissolve into higher forms of experience.

Thus, they fell short of recognising it as a coherent mode of knowledge. Croce, being influenced by pragmatism, recognised science as a legitimate activity, if it did not move outside its limits, but claimed that it was not a form of knowledge at all. Scientific activity originates in practical necessity and, although this does not necessarily mean that science pursues practical ends in the vulgar sense, it is still concerned with actions, not with the quest for truth. The natural sciences for Croce are 'not knowledge of will but will; not truth, but utility'.[83]

Likewise, R.G. Collingwood rejected the positivistic concept of scientific knowledge, describing science as incoherent knowledge, because it claims to deal with general abstractions whereas, in effect, the scientist is always facing a particular event. When this incoherence between the abstract nature of scientific propositions and the historical nature of particular observed events is recognised, science is transformed into a higher mode of knowledge, which is history.[84] Science, therefore, is unable to maintain itself, and is only a stage in the process of human self-understanding.

By describing science as 'defective' experience, Oakeshott seems to concur with these views and, indeed, his analysis is usually perceived as an Idealistic critique of scientific experience.[85] However, his attitude is, in fact, far more complex. The term 'defective' is not used by him in the pejorative sense. Oakeshott also calls history a 'defective' mode, but one can hardly say that he 'distrusted' history. Certainly, Oakeshott denies that science achieves a satisfactory view of the whole of reality. However, unlike those Idealists, he does not think that science within itself is a contradictory mode of experience. On the contrary, he describes it as being able to achieve inner coherence and to maintain independence without being prone to dissolving into other forms of experience. For him, 'so long as scientific thought is engaged with what it can achieve... it remains sovereign and unassailable', and 'only scientific thinking can elucidate the world of science'.[86] Of the whole chapter on science in *Experience and Its Modes*, Oakeshott dedicates only seven pages to explaining why

---

[83]   Croce, *Logic and the Science of the Pure Concept*, p. 343.
[84]   Collingwood, *Speculum Mentis*, p. 187.
[85]   See, for example, Franco, *The Political Philosophy of Michael Oakeshott*, pp. 43–49.
[86]   EM, p. 217.

science is an abstract defective world. The rest of the chapter is concerned not with the negative but with the positive account of science, not with the scrutiny of the defects of scientific experience but with the elucidation of its character.

When Oakeshott's view is analysed carefully, it emerges that his approach lies far away from what can be recognised as the neo-Hegelian criticism of science. Oakeshott declares that the sole explicit criterion of scientific ideas 'is their absolute communicability'.[87] In order to achieve such communicability, or one could say intersubjectivity, the language of the mode of scientific experience must have common meaning for everyone: it must be stable and impersonal. The language of the senses, then, should be abandoned in favour of the language of quantities, because absolute communicability can be achieved only by adopting the quantitative form of expression. The world of science is, then, 'a world conceived under the category of quantity'.[88]

This view of the character of science was promoted by the leading philosophers of science at that period and is usually associated with what is called 'scientific' or 'mathematical' positivism. This trend is sometimes perceived as a link between Kantian philosophical tradition and logical positivism,[89] and it is represented by such philosopher-scientists as Ernst Mach, Henri Poincaré, and Karl Pearson.[90]

Antonio Aliotta called this trend the 'new' positivism as distinct from the 'old' positivism.[91] The 'new' positivists believed in the basic principles which characterised positivism in general, subscribing to the claim of phenomenalism, that scientific knowledge could account only for what is actually manifested in experience and advocating the essential unity of scientific method.[92] But in contrast to the old positivism, the new positivists abandoned dogmatic scientism and attempted to purge science of anything reminiscent of metaphysics. Scientific positivists felt that the reputation of science was so high that they could throw away any metaphysical foundations of

---

[87] EM, p. 170.
[88] EM, p. 171.
[89] See John Passmore, *A Hundred Years of Philosophy* (London: Duckworth, 1966), pp. 322-329; John Losee, *A Historical Introduction to the Philosophy of Science* (Oxford: Oxford University Press, 1993), pp. 166-182.
[90] Oakeshott explicitly mentions and quotes from works of Poincaré, Whitehead and a neo-Kantian philosopher Lotze (see EM, pp. 155, 179n, 198n).
[91] Antonio Aliotta, *The Idealistic Reaction Against Science*, trans. A. McCaskill (London: Macmillan and Co., 1914), p. 53.
[92] See Leszek Kolakowski's description of the central aspects of positivist philosophy in his *Positivist Philosophy: From Hume to the Vienna Circle*, trans. N. Guterman (Harmondsworth: Penguin Books, 1972), pp. 11-19.

science and make it stand on its own two feet. This was the way to ensure the autonomy and integrity of scientific activity.

This programme of scientific positivism found its first expression in the publications of G.R. Kirchnoff's *Principles of Mechanics* (1874) and E. Mach's *The Science of Mechanics* (1893). It was characterised by a distrust of metaphysics and an attempt to formulate rules of scientific method which would not be dependent on extraneous presuppositions. Kirchnoff and Mach saw physics as the model for all the sciences or even as the science to which all others could be reduced. Physics, they implied, was able to achieve its status due to the use of mechanical explanation. Yet the old mechanics was in an urgent need of reformulation. Concepts such as 'force' or 'absolute space' were seen as remnants of old metaphysical entities. According to Kirchnoff, mechanics is the science of motion whose object is the complete description of motions in the simplest possible manner. Science does not explain 'why' things happen and the only explanation it provides is the description of the relations between phenomena.[93]

For Mach too, explanation means description and scientific laws are just an abridged form of description.[94] The most complete world picture of our sensations is a world picture of the greatest possible stability.[95] Mach abandoned the idea of strict causality in science, insisting that 'a "causal explanation"… is nothing more than the statement or description of an actual fact or a connexion between forces'.[96] Furthermore, he rejected the idea that scientific laws were demonstrative. An economic description of connections does not apply to any particular event, for the nature of scientific law is always hypothetical.[97]

Henri Poincaré represents a less empiricist trend known as 'conventionalism', yet his approach to scientific method was similar to that of Mach. He saw scientific laws as hypothetical judgements, expressed through mathematic formulae. These laws are 'conventions' created by the scientist. 'Conventionalism' is sometimes held to be one of the expressions of the 'intuitivist' trend which became

---

[93] Passmore, *A Hundred Years of Philosophy*, p. 322.
[94] J. Bradley, *Mach's Philosophy of Science* (London: The Athlone Press, 1971), pp. 180, 207-212.
[95] John T. Blackmore, *Ernst Mach: His Work, Life and Influence* (Berkeley: University of California Press, 1972), p. 170.
[96] Ernst Mach, *The Analysis of Sensations*, trans. C.M. Williams (London: Routledge, 1914), p. 335.
[97] Bradley, *Mach's Philosophy of Science*, pp. 186-188.

influential in France in the 1890s.[98] Yet Poincaré was by no means a relativist and recognised the importance of objectivity in science. He was a conventionalist in mathematics, arguing that, in any explanation, the choice between different mathematical systems (for example, Euclidian versus non-Euclidian geometry) was arbitrary. But he recognised that hypotheses in physics could be judged as true or false. Not only was Poincaré not a relativist, but his publications actually served to popularise and defend science in a French intellectual climate in which intuitivism, associated with the name of Bergson, became a fashionable current, largely as a reaction to the domination of scientism in the previous years.[99]

Poincaré responded to two charges against science. The first claim, put forward by Catholic scientists such as Le Roy, was that science had nothing to say about the real world. These thinkers did not dismiss science itself but denied to science any objective validity with regard to reality. Against them, Poincaré defended the idea of objectivity.[100] He felt he was able to do so because he maintained what can be seen as a coherence theory of truth.[101] For him, the objective world meant not a reality separated from human perceptions but a coherent world picture common to all human beings. Scientific theory is objective because it transforms 'brute' facts into 'scientific' facts, by enabling individual perceptions to be expressed through a general and unifying language which has a common meaning for everyone.[102] For Poincaré, then, 'objectivity' stands for 'intersubjectivity'.[103]

The second charge against science was presented by those who denied it any value because of its inability to serve as a guide to a good life. Poincaré, conceding that science could not serve as a guide to practice, vigorously defended the ideal of science for its own sake, pointing out that science and art were two achievements which gave value to a civilisation. Poincaré thought that the satisfaction of the mind had a more important value than considerations of utility and

---

[98] Passmore, *A Hundred Years of Philosophy*, p. 326.
[99] On the French debates on science see Henry E. Guerlac, 'Science and French National Strength,' in E.M. Earle (ed.), *Modern France: Problems of the Third and Fourth Republic* (Princeton: Princeton University Press, 1951), pp. 81-105; Harry W. Paul, 'The Debates Over the Bankruptcy of Science in 1895,' *French Historical Studies* 5(3), 1968, pp. 299-327.
[100] Henri Poincaré, 'Sur la Valeur Objective de la Science,' *Revue de Métaphysique et de Morale* 10, 1902, pp. 263-293.
[101] David Stump, 'Henri Poincaré's Philosophy of Science,' *Study in History and Philosophy of Science* 20(3), 1989, pp. 339-349.
[102] *Ibid.*, p. 342.
[103] Kolakowski, *Positivist Philosophy*, p. 172.

suggested that the highest satisfaction was implied in the ability to construct a harmonious and economical picture of the world.[104] This construction is the source of Beauty in which the mind of a scientist finds its pleasure.[105] The emphasis on Beauty is sometimes mentioned by commentators as an 'aestheticism' implied in Poincaré's view.[106] But for Poincaré, scientific 'Beauty' means something quite different from artistic 'Beauty', and science for him is an autonomous activity worth pursuing for its own sake.

Poincaré was not a revolutionary, and despite the emphasis on the mathematical nature of scientific language he held empiricist convictions, trying to shore up conventional mechanistic physics.[107] Notwithstanding some superficial resemblance between him and later relativists such as Kuhn, his theory was very different. The idea that science was abstract and conventionalist in nature did not lead him to adopt relativism. Rather, it was a sophisticated defence of the autonomy of science. Poincaré was a thinker of an essentially conservative mentality who emphasised the accumulation of scientific knowledge was a continuous process. He stood very far from anything like the theory of scientific revolutions later advanced by Kuhn.[108]

III

Scientific positivism became one of the most influential movements in the philosophy of science at the beginning of the twentieth century. The ideas of Mach and Poincaré spread to England, where, according to Kolakowski, a trend had already developed which, under the influence of Mill and Spencer, was characterised 'by the belief that science is neutral on metaphysical questions and that it is possible to limit scientific knowledge to the symbolic record of experience'.[109] Scientists such as W.K. Clifford and Karl Pearson developed a theory of scientific method along lines similar to those of Mach. And Russell and Whitehead's inquiry in mathematics,

---

[104] Henri Poincaré, *La Valeur de la Science* (Paris: Ernest Flammarion, 1908), pp. 274-276.
[105] Henri Poincaré, *Science and Hypothesis* (London: The Walter Scott Publishing Co., 1905), pp. 22-23.
[106] Blackmore, *Ernst Mach*, pp. 195-196.
[107] Stanley L. Jaki, *Uneasy Genius: The Life and Work of Pierre Duhem* (The Hague: Martinus Nijhoff, 1984), p. 335.
[108] Andrew Pyle, 'Introduction,' in H. Poincaré, *Science and Method*, trans. F. Maitland (London: Routledge, 1996), pp. x-xi.
[109] Kolakowski, *Positivist Philosophy*, p. 121.

though aiming in a somewhat different direction, contributed to the appreciation of the role of the quantitative element in science.

Oakeshott's concept of science in *Experience and Its Modes* is deeply influenced by this positivistic trend. He mentions the danger 'of accepting too readily what scientific writers tell us about the character of scientific experience' and presents himself as analysing science from the standpoint of a philosopher.[110] Yet in his account of science he follows the ideas developed by some practising scientists of his time and even quotes such authorities as Poincaré and Whitehead.[111]

Echoing Mach, Oakeshott claims that science's 'master-conception is *stability*'.[112] And like Poincaré he argues that quantitative understanding, and not the attempt to discover facts about an 'objective', 'material', or 'external' world, is what characterises science. The reason for Oakeshott's unwillingness to use these expressions is that 'each of them introduces some notion extraneous to that of stability.'[113] Although the idea of science as discovering facts about an objective world is not completely incorrect, it is dangerous. Science can present only the quantitative description of the world, thereby leaving out what cannot be included in such a description. To claim that science represents an 'objective' reality may, therefore, either open the door to the rejection of the quantitative method, or lead to scepticism, to which Oakeshott is sharply opposed. He criticises those scientists who, having understood science as the construction of a world of ideas, concluded 'that it is consequently debarred from a true knowledge of the world of reality. Naturalism has given place to a mild and unintelligent scepticism.'[114] Furthermore Oakeshott denounces the scientist who 'takes over... what he can understand of Kant, not because his thought has followed Kant's mind to Kant's conclusions, but because the general point of view to be found in Kant's philosophy is congenial to his preconceptions.'[115]

This claim signals Oakeshott's disagreement with the views advanced by the British astronomer Arthur Eddington, whose philosophy of science was based on a Kantian epistemology that led him very close to extreme subjectivism. For Eddington, physical science represented the 'world of shadows'.[116] Several years before the publication of *Experience and Its Modes*, though, Oakeshott had

[110] EM, p. 173.
[111] EM, pp. 179n, 198n.
[112] EM, p. 171.
[113] EM, p. 172.
[114] EM, p. 174.
[115] *Ibid*.
[116] Arthur S. Eddington, *The Nature of the Physical World* (Cambridge: University Press, 1928), p. xvii.

found Eddington's account of the method and aim of modern physics 'altogether admirable' and saw it as 'applicable in principle to all the sciences'. He summarised Eddington's position as follows: 'the scientific conception of the universe is the most abstract of all conceptions, it is a universe consisting solely of physically measurable relationships, and physical science is a closed system created for the study of those relationships.'[117] This view is, indeed, in line with the main postulates of the scientific positivists.

Eddington's philosophy of science was, however, more complicated, and his attitude to positivism was ambiguous. On the one hand, he was attached to many positivistic ideas about scientific method, and his adherence to Kantian epistemology led him to distinguish between the transcendental and phenomenal worlds, claiming that science deals only with the realm of the phenomenal, and therefore science and theology cannot quarrel.[118] On the other hand, in some aspects of his thought, Eddington moved beyond positivism. Although he did not think that physics could provide us with the ultimate answers about the nature of reality, he denied that there existed strict boundaries at which physics had to stop. The world of physics was, for him, not the strictly determined world of the positivists. He discussed the idea of free will and was fascinated by new developments in physics such as the theory of relativity. Before Popper and Kuhn, Eddington argued that modern science develops through a series of revolutions which advance our knowledge, and that at each stage the ideas of what is available as scientific knowledge are likely to be reformulated. Therefore, scientific activity is open-ended and one cannot postulate finality to its development.[119]

Oakeshott, in contrast, adhered to the positivistic view of science and rejected any attempts to introduce metaphysics into science through the back door, as they would lead to scepticism and relativism. In this, Oakeshott's views differ not only from those of Eddington, but also from the later gradual abandonment of scientific positivism by Popper in his theory of scientific activity understood as an evolutionary process, and from a more radical theory of Kuhn.[120] Oakeshott never mentions the works of Popper and Kuhn,

---

[117] Review of J. Needham (ed.), *Science, Religion and Reality*, in *Journal of Theological Studies* 27, 1926, p. 318.
[118] Eddington, *The Nature of the Physical World*, pp. 351-352.
[119] *Ibid.*, p. 353.
[120] See Karl Popper, *The Logic of Scientific Discovery* (London: Hutchinson, 1959); Thomas Kuhn, *Structure of Scientific Revolutions* (Chicago: University of Chicago Press, 1970).

and it is impossible to say what precisely he thought of their philosophies. Yet the inner logic of his view stands far from their way of reasoning and is much closer to that of scientific positivism. Firstly, he did not regard science as an open-ended activity. Science for him was an activity in which progress was being made in elucidating the world under the category of quantity. He claimed that it was permissible to presuppose a final point in this undertaking, the possibility of the complete description of the world in these terms: 'it is not meaningless to speak of science approaching the stage when it will be complete'.[121] This certainly implies that scientific activity is grounded upon and directed towards the satisfaction of one unchangeable principle.

Secondly, Oakeshott did not see science as developing through paradigm changes. It is very tempting to compare Kuhn's theory of scientific revolutions with Oakeshott's philosophy of modes of experience. In some sense, as a pure analogy between Kuhn's theory of science and Oakeshott's *general* philosophy, this view can be accepted.[122] Yet it would be completely misguided to compare Kuhn's and Oakeshott's theories of science. For, while Oakeshott recognizes the existence of different paradigmatic worldviews in general, he does not admit this plurality into the analysis *within* the modes themselves. On the contrary, he uses general plurality of modes in order to shore up unity within each of those modes. A pluralist when it comes to experience in general, Oakeshott is a monistic positivist in respect of the presuppositions of the particular modes of experience.

Thus, for Oakeshott, scientific experience always deals with reality, though not with the whole of reality. This view of reality is, however, limited by the postulates of scientific understanding of the concepts of 'nature' and of 'the scientific method'. Nature and method are, in fact, not two different elements of scientific experience but represent the same whole looked at from different angles. Thus, scientific experience presupposes a specific understanding of nature which does not admit any common-sense definitions. Nature is simply 'a uniform, mathematically integrated, self-contained world of ideas'.[123] This is a world of ideas 'which admits of universal agreement',[124] and it is always static, recognising no change in time.

---
[121] EM, p. 192.
[122] But even here it should be qualified, for what is important for Kuhn is the process of change of dominating paradigms whereas Oakeshott's main preoccupation is the coexistence of varieties of experience.
[123] EM, p. 191.
[124] EM, p. 189.

This concept of nature implies the quantitative method. This method includes observation and explanation where 'all scientific observation whatever is measurement of one kind or another'.[125] This purely quantitative world of ideas is achieved in physics and therefore 'all sciences not merely resemble physics in so far as they are genuinely scientific, but tend actually to become transformed into, or reduced to physics'.[126]

According to Oakeshott, the scientific method provides a mechanical explanation.[127] He follows here the familiar line of Mach and Poincaré. 'Explanation' is indistinguishable from 'description'[128] and a mechanical explanation is the best at providing a stable explanation for the five following reasons. It is the simplest or most economical explanation; it is a general explanation; it is a quantitative explanation; all changes are explained by reference to what is closest and not what is distant; and it is an explanation in terms of motion.[129] Oakeshott even insists that in so far as science pursues an absolutely communicable world 'only a mechanistic view of the universe can succeed in satisfying it'.[130]

Scientific experience consists of several logical stages. It begins with a world of scientific ideas which is the world integrated in terms of the relations between its basic structural concepts, or 'categories' of scientific thought. This integration leads to the first type of generalisations, which Oakeshott calls 'analytic'.[131] To these he relates such generalisations as proportionality of gravity to inertia, conservation of energy and momentum, indeed all the main concepts of mechanics.[132] These concepts are the foundations of science, they are definite and invariable and they are distinct from the other kind of generalisations, termed statistical, which are based on received data.

Oakeshott's ideas here are similar to those developed by Poincaré and Eddington. Poincaré distinguished between three kinds of hypotheses — 'quite natural and necessary', 'indifferent' and 'real'.[133] Natural hypotheses are those conceptual constructions which our view of physics necessarily presupposes and without which physics would hardly be possible. Such is the theory of negli-

---

[125] EM, p. 176.
[126] EM, p. 177.
[127] Ibid.
[128] Ibid.
[129] EM, p. 179.
[130] EM, p. 180n.
[131] EM, p. 182.
[132] EM, p. 183.
[133] Poincaré, *Science and Hypothesis*, pp. 152-153.

gible influence between distant bodies or the idea that small movements obey a linear law. Indifferent hypotheses are those which are useful as a tool but whenever any of them is chosen, there is no way to disprove it. These include, for example, 'atomic' or 'aether' theories. The third kind are real generalisations. Physics is aiming towards the most stable formulations of real hypotheses on the basis of empirical observations.

Like Poincaré, Eddington distinguished between three kinds of scientific laws.[134] Identical laws are those which are imposed on the mind by the nature of subject matter, like the laws of conservation of energy and mass. Statistical laws relate to the behaviour of crowds, and their uniformity is the uniformity of averages. Transcendental laws are those which deal with basic concepts of the physical world such as atoms or quanta. Eddington realised that physics would not be able to penetrate the reality behind these laws but one can already see here a departure from positivism, as what for Poincaré were merely 'indifferent' tools of scientific research became in Eddington's vocabulary 'transcendental' laws.

By distinguishing between analytic and statistical generalisations, Oakeshott embarks upon a similar idea but with one crucial difference: he ignores the idea of the existence of 'indifferent hypotheses', or 'transcendental laws' and claims that 'all generalisations in science which are not merely analytic are statistical'.[135] Thus, he expels the last remnant of metaphysics from Poincaré's theory. The use of the word 'analytic' is hardly accidental. By stating that basic concepts can only be analytic, Oakeshott completely dismisses the possibility of a scientific *a priori* knowledge which is not analytic. This position is hardly distinguishable from that of logical positivism.

The stage which follows 'analytic' generalisations is hypothesis, and from hypothesis scientific thought proceeds to observation and experiment in order to achieve a statistical generalisation. Experiments are 'limited and controlled by hypothesis'.[136] Every experiment is a measurement of one or another kind and it must be designed in such a way that it is able to contribute to a statistical conclusion. No single measurement is important. What is important is a significant statistical generalisation achieved in the end. Such generalisations are invariable and precise, because they do not refer to any particular observation, and their uniformity is the uniformity of averages. No single event in a series should conform to this generali-

[134] Eddington, *The Nature of the Physical World*, pp. 237, 244-245.
[135] EM, p. 186.
[136] EM, p. 184.

sation: 'what is characteristic of the scientific method is not that it is inductive, but that it is statistical'.[137] This does not make such a generalisation less precise, because, with regard to the given series, statistical data is exact and invariable.[138]

The stage of statistical generalisation is, however, not final, for scientific thought also seeks generalisations which will remain relevant beyond what is actually observed. This leads to the following stage, in which the observed statistical data is extrapolated to hypothetical events in the form of probability. The idea of understanding science in terms of probability was suggested by the British scientist Karl Pearson. As editor of the journal *Biometrika* he belonged to a group of scientists who were developing statistical research methods on the questions of race, evolution and heredity. As a disciple of Mach, Pearson believed in the positivistic assumption of the basic unity of scientific method and wanted to extend the mathematical view of science to biology and the social disciplines, thereby transforming them into legitimate sciences. While the central problem with which social scientists struggled from the beginning was their inability to make good predictions, Mach's view of science seemed to point to a possible answer to that difficulty. We have seen that, according to Mach, scientific method means the economical description of perceived phenomena and not the formulation of categorical statements about what is not immediately observed. From this Pearson concluded that any scientific statement about the future may be formulated only in terms of probabilities.[139] Therefore, he and his colleagues placed particular emphasis on the theory of probability in statistical research, playing a significant role in the development of the quantitative method in the social sciences.[140]

Like Pearson, Oakeshott says that to apply the data of a statistical generalisation to unobserved events is to extend it in terms of probability. Then, 'what is true categorically of the observed series... can be shown to be relatively true of any member of the series and of what may lie altogether outside the observed series itself.'[141]

This view has a crucial implication for the possibility of the social sciences. Because 'exact' sciences such as physics come up with almost deterministic generalisations, the question of the nature of

---

[137] EM, p. 185.
[138] EM, p. 187.
[139] Karl Pearson, *The Grammar of Science* (London: Adam and Charles Black, 1911), pp. 139-142.
[140] Scott Gordon, *The History and Philosophy of Social Science* (London: Routledge, 1991), pp. 529-532.
[141] EM, p. 188.

their laws, whatever its theoretical importance, is not likely to halt their development or shake their self-confidence. For the social sciences, in contrast, the idea of probability became a window of opportunity. Social phenomena are characterised by relatively low uniformity but they can be described in terms of probability.

Thus, Oakeshott maintains that a scientific generalisation is a statement of probability, that this probability is always quantitative, and that 'any specific probability is both definite and invariable'.[142] Therefore, from the point of view of scientific experience, it is absolutely unimportant what the specific predictability of any event is. The probability of, say, 0.3 (such correlation is regarded as quite a good result in modern sociology) is no less stable and exact a result than that of 0.99. The lack of high uniformity in the subject matter of a certain science does not make this science less 'scientific'.

This approach enables Oakeshott to defend the positivistic idea of the unity of all sciences, of which physics, which has achieved the highest level of quantitative abstractness, is a model. Though he does not call 'for the immediate reduction of sociology to physics', he insists on the logical unity of all sciences, which is 'the life and inspiration of every science'.[143]

Oakeshott recognises that outside of physics his view of scientific experience seems to be contradicted by the reality of the scientific practice. Thus, some sciences are not sufficiently quantitative. For example, geology or zoology may have an appearance of being natural histories which study an actual change in the world of perception. But this 'arises from the fact that the present world of science is imperfectly scientific'.[144] Although there are many scientists who want to make an exception in favour of this or another particular science advocating 'vitalism in biology and philosophism in psychology', these approaches appear to be 'anachronistic, if not absurd… Instead of making these sciences less abstract compliance with these demands will succeed only in making them less scientific.'[145] Scientific theories are fruitful so long as they can be formulated according to scientific method and in terms of purely scientific abstractions. Thus, 'biological evolution refers to the phylogeny of the race, and the "race" is not an historical fact, or something that can be seen, it is a scientific abstraction. The theory of evolution is, of course, insecure

---

[142] *Ibid.*
[143] EM, p. 246.
[144] EM, p. 192n.
[145] EM, pp. 180-181.

and unscientific in so far as it falls short of a statistical generalisation expressed mathematically.'[146]

The social sciences are 'scientific' if they acquire a quantitative character. Oakeshott agrees that psychology and economics are candidates for being regarded as legitimate sciences. In the case of economics, Oakeshott mentions the challenges that it is not an 'exact' science, that it is concerned with behaviour, that experiments are impossible in it, and so on.[147] But he does not face serious difficulties in dealing with these claims. Although economics has not yet achieved the same success as the natural sciences, it is already a developed science and is capable of reaching valid generalisations, in so far as it is concerned not with subjective motives of the behaviour of human agents, but with abstract scientific concepts such as supply, demand, price, utility etc. Only quantitative economics is a scientific economics.[148] This does not necessarily mean that such economics is more useful. 'This interest in practical life is not... illegitimate; it is merely dangerous from the standpoint of scientific thought.'[149]

Psychology is a less developed science than economics, yet there is nothing that would prevent it from becoming a fully legitimate science, in so far as it limits itself to measurable phenomena such as stimuli and reactions. Although Oakeshott criticises the founder of behaviourism, J.B. Watson, for what he sees as an attempt to reduce psychology to physiology,[150] this is a criticism from an even more positivistic view. Such reduction presupposes the distinction between mind and matter where the mind is conceived as an unobservable entity so that the only thing that a psychologist can do is to observe physiological phenomena. But for a consistent positivist there are no unobservable phenomena in principle. This is why Mach was opposed to Watson's behaviourism.[151] According to Oakeshott, if such concepts as 'imagination' or 'memory' can be conceived quantitatively they will be completely legitimate. Nevertheless, it is clear from Oakeshott's discussion that if any approach has any chance of becoming a scientific psychology, it is the behaviouristic approach, and not Freudian or 'cognitive' psychology. Such psychology, indeed, 'has nothing to offer us in the way of a

[146] EM, p. 192n.
[147] EM, pp. 223-228.
[148] EM, p. 232.
[149] EM, p. 233.
[150] EM, p 236.
[151] Blackmore, *Ernst Mach*, p. 70. Today behaviourism is usually recognised as denying the distinction between mind and matter. Mach and Oakeshott can be seen as criticising Watson for not being consistent enough in his behaviourism.

knowledge of human life',[152] for human life is by definition beyond scientific knowledge.

In the chapter on history, Oakeshott also evaluates anthropology as a possible science but his conclusions are less optimistic. He does not deny that scientific anthropology is possible in principle, for one can try to work out a purely quantitative model of man, society, civilisation, moral development and religion. But, firstly, it would be difficult to form a scientific conception of man or society sufficiently different from that of biology, psychology or economics, and, secondly, there would be relatively few measurements to take. Thus, 'a scantiness of data will certainly render scientific generalisations insignificant', and therefore such a science 'would be relatively unimportant'.[153] No anthropologist will actually be willing to accept this scientific mode of explanation. This is why anthropology, so long as it is a serious discipline, is none other than an historical inquiry. For Oakeshott, a scientific study of society is not impossible, but simply uninteresting.

Oakeshott denies that the social sciences can combine features of both natural sciences and humanities and deal both with quantitative data and with the interpretation of meaning. So long as the social disciplines intend to become real sciences they should purge themselves of everything that contradicts their scientific nature. This view leads Oakeshott to advocate a view of the social sciences as value-free disciplines, based purely on quantitative methods of research, which is the only valid method of reaching scientific knowledge.

Thus, Oakeshott adopts towards science the most rigid norms advanced by scientific positivism, despite the claim that he merely gives an account of scientific experience as it actually exists. His description of scientific experience does not only show what it is, but also what it ought to be. In this positivistic outlook, Oakeshott differs significantly from other Idealists. Collingwood argues that the view of science as hypothetical is partial and self-contradictory, and claims that 'a tissue of hypotheses cannot be a self-contained and autonomous organism'.[154] Contrary to this, Oakeshott completely agrees with scientific positivists who insist on the hypothetical nature of science. He maintains that because the end product of science is generalisations in terms of probabilities, 'all scientific generalisations are hypothetical, and not categorical statements about the

---

[152] EM, p. 241.
[153] EM, p. 163.
[154] Collingwood, *Speculum Mentis*, p. 183.

real world'.[155] Although Oakeshott also holds the view that the hypothetical aspect of scientific experience presupposes its abstract character, he claims that this world of hypothetical quantitative judgements is a self-contained and autonomous world of ideas.

Furthermore, Collingwood denies the possibility of a unified science, or the reduction of all sciences to an ordered whole, saying that 'there cannot possibly be a system or world of the sciences'.[156] By contrast, Oakeshott insists that such logical unity is both possible and necessary. Scientific experience is 'a single, specific mode of experience'.[157] It achieves 'a homogeneous and coherent world of experience'.[158] When seen within itself, this mode of science is not in danger of disintegration. It is self-contained, absolutely non-contradictory, and has very rigid limits. Science can be seen as an incoherent mode only when it is investigated from outside, but a dedicated scientist would hardly need to worry. As his world is completely self-contained, there is no urgent logical need to supersede it.

Thus, on the one hand, Oakeshott inserts the scientific mode into an Idealistic framework, yet, on the other hand, he uses this framework to assert the absolute integrity of scientific method. He insists on the complete separation of science from practice and is not bothered by the fact that science cannot explain everything or be a guide to life. Science merely provides us with knowledge of reality from a certain standpoint. This knowledge is stable and impersonal and it is what we can call objective knowledge.

By subscribing to scientific positivism, Oakeshott affiliates himself with the view which more than any other approaches symbolises the influence and popularity which science achieved in the consciousness of modern civilisation. In the beginning of the twentieth century scientists felt confident enough to expel all remnants of metaphysical justifications and present their activity as being completely independent, and subject to a rigorous method of its own. At the same time, positivistic methodology made it possible to separate science from other forms of experience. In the positivistic period, religion, if it wanted to defend itself against the claims of science, somewhat paradoxically had to adopt the far-reaching conclusions of positivism about the irrelevance of metaphysics to science.[159] Then, no finding of science could be seen as contradicting religious truth, for science and religion were regarded as two mutually irrele-

---
[155] EM, p. 211.
[156] Collingwood, *Speculum Mentis*, p. 191.
[157] EM, p. 243.
[158] EM, pp. 214–215.
[159] Blackmore, *Ernst Mach*, p. 167.

vant spheres of understanding. Many religious scientists of this period such as Pierre Duhem or Ivan Pavlov readily embraced positivistic methodology as a way to reconcile their scientific pursuits and religious convictions.

For Oakeshott too, the description of scientific experience as an experience limited by the category of quantity serves to leave other forms of experience free from the dictates of science. At the same time, his position is an attempt to defend the integrity of scientific activity itself and its purposeless character. Science, he insists, is 'the creation of the scientific mind for the sole purpose of satisfying that mind'.[160]

IV

After *Experience and Its Modes*, Oakeshott did not discuss science in detail, and it is hardly possible to reach an unequivocal conclusion as to whether and to what extent he modified his view. But one can still find indications of Oakeshott's position in those short pieces of his later work which contain some reference to science. There are some changes in the way he describes scientific activity, due to the changes in the structure of his view and its vocabulary. At the same time, the content of his view remains essentially the same. Throughout his writings Oakeshott still maintains the definition of scientific activity as a self-contained quantitative world.

Thus, in his review of Herbert Butterfield's *Origins of Modern Science* (1949), Oakeshott repeats his main idea of science as 'a body of knowledge which is in the highest degree communicable, not resting upon the personal idiosyncrasies of the individual scientist, but based upon the sure foundation of measurement and expressed in the impersonal language of mathematics'.[161] The social sciences are not intrinsically impossible and the main thing which impedes their development is the lack of 'a scientific opinion'.[162] This idea of the importance of existing 'scientific opinion' emerges later (1958) in Oakeshott's review of Michael Polanyi's *Personal Knowledge*. He seems to have adopted this idea from Polanyi's previous publications,[163] and he treats Polanyi's book with respect. Yet he expresses doubts in the author's central argument about the importance of the 'personal coefficient' in scientific knowledge, since 'to call for the

---
[160] EM, p. 193.
[161] Review of H. Butterfield, *The Origins of Modern Science, 1300-1800*, in *Times Literary Supplement*, November 25, 1949, p. 761.
[162] *Ibid.*, p. 762.
[163] See reference to two publications of Polanyi in SS, p. 692n.

recognition of this component is not itself to have formulated a theory of scientific knowledge.'[164]

In 'The Voice of Poetry in the Conversation of Mankind' (1959) there is a short section describing the place of 'science' in this conversation. The description differs somewhat from the earlier view. Firstly, science is called not a homogeneous world of experience, but an activity, springing from an impulse, 'a way of imagining and moving among images'.[165] Secondly, Oakeshott insists that 'so-called "methods" of scientific investigation emerge in the course of the activity', and that 'in advance of scientific thought there are no scientific problems'.[166] But one would be mistaken to suppose that Oakeshott adopts the view of science as a completely open-ended activity the character of which is determined and reformulated every time scientific knowledge advances. For he repeats the familiar definition of science, according to which the world of science is understood independently of our practical desires, and it necessarily invokes exactness of communication. It excludes 'whatever is private, esoteric, or ambiguous'. Thus, 'images become measurements according to agreed scales, relationships are mathematical ratios, and positions are indicated by numerical coordinates: the world of science is recognised as the world *sub specie quantitatis*.'[167]

Oakeshott emphasises even more strongly the value of science as an independent activity when he speaks about science as achieving an 'emancipation from the authority of practical imagining'.[168] Science exists only when the impulse for rational understanding is 'cultivated for its own sake', and when 'the products of this engagement... are what is valued, and are valued only for what can be contrived from them'.[169]

In *On Human Conduct* we encounter science again, not as 'an activity of imagining', or 'a mode of experience', but as 'an order of inquiry'. This is an order of inquiry the aim of which is to make 'intelligible' those 'goings-on' which are themselves understood as not being an 'exhibition of intelligence'.[170] The only way to understand them is to put conditions which somehow 'determine' them, for example through such concepts as 'laws' and 'causality'. They are always understood in terms of the determined process. This order of

---

[164] Review of M. Polanyi, *Personal Knowledge*, in *Encounter* 11(iii), 1958, p. 78.
[165] RIP, p. 505.
[166] RIP, p. 506.
[167] RIP, p. 508.
[168] RIP, p. 507.
[169] RIP, p. 506.
[170] HC, p. 13.

inquiry is categorially distinct from the one that theorises those identities which are themselves understood as 'intelligent' and which require exploration of motives in terms of 'practice'.

There are two respects in which Oakeshott deviates from his early view. First, he seems to have retreated from the new positivistic approach to the basic Kantian position defining science with the notions of laws and causality. This impression is, however, illusory. Though Oakeshott evokes the vocabulary of 'process' and 'causality', it soon becomes clear that the mathematical character of science is still its distinct characteristic. Thus,

> the notion that the categorial gap is narrowed or even bridged when relationships between identities are understood in terms of probabilities is, of course, an illusion. A relationship may be understood as a probability only when the identities concerned are already recognised as the components of… a 'process'. A probability is no more "uncertain" than the most determinate casual relationship.[171]

Further, while claiming that psychology has developed into a mature science, he says that it 'has acquired scales of measurement and its theorems are such that they may be plotted on graphs and displayed in diagrams or mathematical equations'.[172]

Secondly, Oakeshott does not insist any more that the world of science is a single world, and recognises that an order of inquiry can consist of many various 'idioms of inquiry' by which he means particular sciences. Each science is autonomous and 'is capable of its own conditional perfection'.[173] However, the idioms of inquiry within the same order of inquiry are not exclusive of one another and may suffer reduction. Moreover, Oakeshott still seems to see unity as the logical foundation of science. Arguing in favour of scientific psychology he makes the point that, like other sciences, 'it is also unable to resist hypotheses which ally it to what began by being somewhat different investigations… and thus to prefigure the "reduction" of the terms in which its theorems are formulated to the categorially similar terms of chemistry and physics'.[174]

As in *Experience and Its Modes*, Oakeshott is not opposed to the human sciences *per se*, in so far as they are 'truly scientific' and concern themselves only with what is understood as a part of a process. Earlier he suggested that psychology would develop into a fully legitimate science. Now he says that it has actually achieved this stage. It should just be cautious enough to recognise its own limits

---
[171] HC, p. 14n.
[172] HC, p. 21.
[173] HC, p. 17.
[174] HC, p. 21.

and understand reality in such terms as 'instinct, drive, reflex, valence, latency, threshold' and not 'wanting, believing, playing' and so on. In other words, a truly scientific psychology is a kind of behaviourism which does not pretend to achieve knowledge about human conduct, understood as a meaningful interaction of human agents. Oakeshott also discusses sociology in terms similar to his early book, in which he discussed anthropology. According to Oakeshott, 'whether or not a "general sociological theory" is made to emerge from the engagement to understand "social processes", it is remote from anything recognisable as an engagement to theorise human conduct'.[175] Again, he does not deny that scientific sociology is possible, but only doubts that such a discipline would have any value.

There is, then, no substantial change in Oakeshott's view on the nature of scientific activity. He rejects any hermeneutic or relativistic approaches to science. The modernistic ideas of scientific mathematical positivism as they emerged in the writings of the scientists at the beginning of the twentieth century remain for him the best way to present and defend modern science as an independent activity, existing for its own sake.

Oakeshott values science as an important intellectual activity, and he is always at pains to stress that his criticism of 'Rationalism', and especially of 'Rationalism in politics', is not directed against modern science. Contrary to the myth that Oakeshott was a critic of modern scientific civilisation, he never missed the opportunity to emphasise his respect for scientists. Thus, in his famous essay 'Rationalism in Politics' (1947), Oakeshott denies that 'we owe our predicament [that is, the prevalence of the Rationalistic mode of thinking] to the place which the natural science and the manner of thinking connected with them has come to take in our civilisation.' Although some scientists are infected with the Rationalistic way of thinking, 'the influence of the genuine natural scientist is not necessarily on the side of Rationalism.'[176] The trouble starts only when 'the scientist steps outside his own field', and the prestige of the Rationalist disposition of mind 'is the work, not of the genuine scientist as such, but of the scientist who is a Rationalist in spite of his science'.[177]

In another essay (1947), Oakeshott defends scientific inquiry from the accusation of Hans Morgenthau that it brought about attempts to introduce 'scientific politics'. The pursuit of scientific inquiry and a belief in the omni-competence of scientific understanding are not the

---
[175] HC, p. 25.
[176] RIP, p. 34.
[177] RIP, p. 35.

same thing. In fact, '"scientism" is a superstition about scientific inquiry'. The problematic belief in the modern world is 'not the faith that the natural scientist has in his own methods of inquiry, nor even the belief (in Mill's words) that "the methods of physical science are the proper model for political", but the belief that the problems of practical politics are, in the strict sense, scientific problems'.[178]

In yet another publication, 'Science and Society' (1948), Oakeshott goes further, claiming that 'a well-ordered society may be supposed on occasion to use its customary or legal authority of control, not merely by way of limitation but also by way of the promotion of the application of scientific discovery to human affairs'.[179]

This shows that Oakeshott's attitude towards modern science was respectful, the attitude that we would expect from a Cambridge scholar. Moreover, far from being 'laughable' to the scientists of his own university,[180] this view seems to have been widespread among Cambridge scientists of his time. At least, this can be inferred from C.P. Snow's famous lecture on *The Two Cultures*. Snow can hardly be called an admirer of Oakeshott's Idealism, and Oakeshott would have regarded him as a 'Rationalist'. Yet, referring to his experience as a young scientist in Cambridge in the early thirties, Snow claimed that pure scientists of that time had been isolated from industry and tended to see their research as an intellectual activity: 'We prided ourselves that the science we were doing could not, in any conceivable circumstances, have any practical use'.[181]

V

To conclude, Oakeshott did not write much about science, but he was very interested in this form of human activity, and considered it to be of value. He was opposed to science's attempts to present itself as the dominant worldview, but he also wanted it to preserve its own integrity. His Idealistic framework of thought did not lead him to reject science or to adopt a form of relativism. On the contrary, it enabled him to present the view which emphasised the values which modern science itself preached at the peak of its influence, such as objectivity and detachment. Oakeshott's view developed under the influence of the scientific positivism of the beginning of the twentieth century, and he pushed these positivistic claims to their extreme.

---

[178] 'Scientific Politics,' RPML, p. 99.
[179] SS, p. 693.
[180] See note 75.
[181] C.P. Snow, *The Two Cultures* (Cambridge: Cambridge University Press, 1993), p. 32.

Oakeshott regarded science as a legitimate voice of the modern age. His rejection of the claims, which presented science as the dominant activity, did not lead him to reject modernity, for he thought it would be wrong to equate modernity with the hegemony of science. As he pointed out, 'the Scientific revolution did not in fact succeed in shouting down the voices of religion and poetry, and its repercussions in the minds of men such as Pascal, Lichtenberg, Blake and Goethe… are a significant part of the history of the impact of the scientific revolution upon European history.'[182] All these personalities succeeded in sharing their scientific interests with literary activities, without confusing them with each other.

For Oakeshott, a truly scientific mind is one that rigorously adheres to the presuppositions of scientific knowledge but recognises their limits and is able to combine the scientific thought with a wider humane outlook, understanding that there are questions which science cannot and should not ask.

HISTORY
I

R.G. Collingwood, in his review of *Experience and Its Modes,* praised Oakeshott's philosophy of history as 'the most penetrating analysis of historical thought that has ever been written, and will remain a classic in that hitherto almost unexplored branch of philosophical research'.[183] There is no doubt that the philosophy of history was one of Oakeshott's central preoccupations throughout his life.

Oakeshott was no stranger to the world of history. In Cambridge he studied history as an undergraduate and then taught it for many years. As a professor of Political Science at LSE he used to give lectures on the history of political thought; and his writings show great familiarity with contemporary historical research and philosophies of history.

For quite a long period of time Oakeshott's philosophy of history received relatively little attention. In the last two decades, however, there have been some important studies which elucidate its character and intellectual context. Thus, David Boucher undertook a thorough investigation of the origins of Oakeshott's philosophy of history within the tradition of British Idealism. He pointed to similarities and differences between Oakeshott and authors such as

---
[182] Review of Butterfield, p. 763.
[183] Collingwood, Review of *Experience and Its Modes*, p. 250.

Bradley, Collingwood, and also compared him with Croce.[184] The most comprehensive research has been carried out by Luke O'Sullivan who presented in detail the main developments of Oakeshott's philosophy of history and also widened its intellectual context by comparing Oakeshott's views with those of German thinkers such as Droysen and Dilthey, and 'narrativists' such as Danto and Gallie.[185]

This section does not attempt a full exposition of Oakeshott's philosophy of history. Firstly, such exposition would require a book-length treatment and, secondly, the existing research absolves me from the need to analyse all aspects of Oakeshott's view. The aim here is more modest: it is to present Oakeshott's defence of historical experience as an independent mode which refuses to be incorporated into a monistic system but is also immune to the attacks of relativism. My focus is therefore on Oakeshott's defence of the objectivity and autonomy of the historian.

II

According to the view presented in *Experience and its Modes*, the historical past is not the past that 'really happened'. This past is constructed by an historian; it does not exist apart from the historical investigation. This view is often interpreted as an attack on historical positivism and realism. Oakeshott is seen as adopting the constructionist view of history, according to which the aim of an historian is

---

[184] Boucher, 'The Creation of the Past'; 'Human Conduct, History and Social Science in the Works of R.G. Collingwood and Michael Oakeshott,' *New Literary History* 24, 1993, pp. 697-717; 'Overlap and Autonomy: The Different Worlds of Collingwood and Oakeshott,' *Storia, Antropologia e Scienze del Linguaggio* 4, 1989, pp. 69-79.

[185] Luke O'Sullivan, *Oakeshott on History* (Thorverton: Imprint Academic, 2003); 'Michael Oakeshott on European Political History', *History of Political Thought* 21(1), 2000, pp. 132-151. On Oakeshott's philosophy of history see also William H. Dray, 'Michael Oakeshott's Theory of History,' in P. King & B.C. Parekh (eds.), *Politics and Experience* (Cambridge: University Press, 1968), pp. 19-42; W.H. Walsh, 'The Practical and Historical Past,' in *ibid.*, pp. 5-18; Gertrude Himmelfarb, 'Supposing History Is a Woman – What Then?' *American Scholar* 53(4), 1984, pp. 494-505; Preston King, 'Michael Oakeshott and Historical Particularism,' *Politics* 16(1), 1981, pp. 85-102; Christopher Parker, *The English Idea of History from Coleridge to Collingwood* (Aldershot: Ashgate, 2000), pp. 135-160; Nathan Rotenstreich, *Philosophy, History and Politics: Studies in Contemporary English Philosophy of History* (The Hague: Martinus Nijhoff, 1976), pp. 111-131; Thomas W. Smith, 'Michael Oakeshott on History, Practice and Political Theory,' *History of Political Thought* 17(4), 1996, pp. 591-614; Roy Tseng, *The Sceptical Idealist: Michael Oakeshott as a Critic of the Enlightenment* (Thorverton: Imprint Academic, 2003), pp. 213-274.

not to reconstruct the course of real past events but to build a narrative of his own. Thus, Oakeshott follows Croce and Collingwood in his critique of positivism and realism, a critique which is in many aspects similar to today's post-modernist theories of history.[186]

To what extent is this view correct, and how far can it be pushed? In order to answer this question, it is necessary to see the context in which Collingwood and Croce formulated their philosophies of history. Their criticisms were directed against two different trends — positivism and empiricism which had a 'realistic' epistemology in common. These two trends were often mixed together and sometimes the latter was regarded as a form of 'positivism' by its critics. But there is an important difference between the two.

The positivistic view in a narrow sense is that history should adopt a 'scientific' method and be regarded as a 'science' which differs from natural sciences only in degree. Oakeshott refers to two French historians, Charles Langlois and Charles Seignobos, as advocates of such an approach.[187] This is a view of the historical method as a collection of facts and a search for scientific causes on the basis of the information that these facts provide. A similar view is presented by J.S. Mill, although in a more moderate form.[188] Even the young Bradley in *The Presuppositions of Critical History* saw the historical method as similar to that of scientific inquiry.[189] He was criticised by Collingwood for not having freed himself completely from the influence of positivism in this essay.[190] Oakeshott refers also to Carl Hempel and Karl Popper as the proponents of 'scientific' understanding of history in terms of 'laws' and causal explanation.[191] Thus, Hempel advanced the claim that the task of the historian is to explain events in terms of general laws by means of the preceding occurrences as necessary causes of the subsequent ones.[192]

Yet there emerged another view of the character of historical studies, which lacked a coherent philosophical doctrine behind it but

---

[186] See, for example, Smith, 'Michael Oakeshott on History, Practice and Political Theory,' p. 601. Even Boucher ('The Creation of The Past,' p. 206), though offering a different interpretation, calls Oakeshott's view 'relativistic'. On the postmodernist theories of history see, for example, Beverly Southgate, *History: What and Why? Ancient, Modern and Postmodern Perspectives* (London: Routledge, 1996).
[187] EM, p. 96.
[188] OH, p. 93n.
[189] F.H. Bradley, *The Presuppositions of Critical History* (Don Mills: J.M. Dent & Sons, 1968), pp. 96-99.
[190] R.G. Collingwood, *The Idea of History* (Oxford: Clarendon Press, 1993), p. 139.
[191] OH, p. 83.
[192] Carl G. Hempel, 'The Function of General Laws in History,' in *Aspects of Scientific Explanation* (New York: The Free Press, 1965), pp. 231-243.

was more readily accepted by professional historians, especially in the Anglo-Saxon world. It was sometimes called 'diplomatic', or 'political' history. More generally it can be called the 'empiricist' approach. This view implies that history is an objective discipline which studies the past 'as it really was' concentrating on the careful analysis of the available, preferably written, evidence.

This view was developed by empirically-minded British and American historians who interpreted literally the famous Ranke phrase that the task of an historian is to describe events 'as they really happened'. The idea of history as a professional disinterested study of the past was introduced in America by scholars who had been trained in Germany. Many of them were Ranke's students who had been fascinated by his erudition and ability to present an account of events in an apparently unbiased way.[193] A new literary modernistic style such as that of Flaubert, where a narrator adopts an ironic, detached attitude to his characters, was accepted as the most appropriate way of describing past events.[194] Likewise, British historians such as Stubbs and Maitland established the form of historical research based on a careful analysis of the historical evidence. The rejection of an ideological bias in historical writings by the next generation of historians is reflected in Herbert Butterfield's famous attack against what he called 'the Whig interpretation of history'.[195] Oakeshott was educated within this tradition of historical research. He was on friendly terms with Butterfield, mentioned Maitland as an example of a true historian, and admitted that his view of European history owed much to Ranke.[196]

It is plain why this view appealed so strongly to professional historians who wanted to establish history as a solid discipline. It claimed that history was an objective field of study and, at the same time, it preserved history's autonomy because it did not require historians to adopt 'scientific' methodology. It is true, though, that Rankeans regarded themselves as proponents of the 'scientific method' in history. Yet by this they did not mean that history should

---

[193] Peter Novick, *That Noble Dream: The "Objectivity Question" and the American Historical Profession* (Cambridge: Cambridge University Press, 1988), pp. 26-31.
[194] On the influence of Flaubert's fiction see *ibid.*, pp. 40-46.
[195] See Herbert Butterfield, *The Whig Interpretation of History* (London: G. Bell and Sons, 1931). On the development of British historiography at the 19th and the beginning of the 20th century see P.B.M. Blaas, *Continuity and Anachronism: Parliamentary and Constitutional Development in Whig Historiography and in the Anti-Whig Reaction Between 1890 and 1930* (The Hague: Martinus Nijhoff, 1978); also John Kenyon, *The History Men: The Historical Profession in England since the Renaissance* (London: Weidenfeld and Nicolson, 1993), pp. 149-208.
[196] 'The Activity of Being a Historian,' RIP, p. 173; HC, p. 286n.

become a kind of scientific enterprise directed to the search of laws and causes. Rather, as Peter Novick argues, they advocated 'a rigidly empirical approach: "observations" were sacred'.[197] They also did not follow the path of the neo-Kantian critics of positivism such as Windelband who, by including history among other moral disciplines, presupposed that it would deal with the question of values. History thus stayed outside the moral and the scientific worlds.

This approach was often referred to by its critics as a form of positivism.[198] This is not correct but it makes sense from a certain point of view, for this trend plays in history a similar role to the one played by positivism in science. Positivism purged science of all remnants of metaphysics, proclaiming its objectivity and autonomy. For the same reason the objectivistic, empiricist approach delivered history from the shadows of science, philosophy and morality.

Croce and Collingwood were opposed to both the positivistic and empiricist approaches to history, regarding them as philosophically unsound. They rejected the epistemological premises on which these views were based, such as the presupposition that there is a world of isolated historical facts that an historian can collect in order to reconstruct the real course of events. An historian is not one who simply retells the historical chronicle; he is rather involved in the critical interpretation and construction of history itself. For both Croce and Collingwood, history is a higher form of experience than science. Thus, according to Croce, 'science' is not a form of knowledge at all.[199] Collingwood introduces history as a form of experience into which science is dissolved when it recognises its own incompleteness.[200]

Yet there are also some differences between them. Croce insists that history is driven by an interest in the present life.[201] For chronicle merely is a 'dead history'.[202] But he is also careful to stress that this interest in the present means not the biased perception of historical events or the demand for a moral judgement but rather the reflection of the development of the Spirit. Collingwood, on the contrary, claims that the task of an historian is to re-enact the thoughts

---

[197] Novick, *That Noble Dream*, p. 34.
[198] Thus, François Furet once mentioned the idea of 'historical event' as positivistic. See F. Furet, 'Quantitative History,' in F. Gilbert & R. Graubard (eds.), *Historical Studies Today* (New York: W.W. Norton & Company, 1972), p. 47.
[199] Croce, *Logic and the Science of the Pure Concept*, p. 343.
[200] Collingwood, *Speculum Mentis*, p. 187.
[201] Benedetto Croce, *Theory and History of Historiography*, trans. D. Ainsle (London: George G. Harrap & Co., 1921), p. 12.
[202] *Ibid.*, p. 19.

and the intentions of the historical actors. This re-enactment is the way to link the present and the past, to construct a 'living' past.[203]

Neither of them, however, attempted to 'deconstruct' history. Their purpose was rather to provide history with a better philosophical grounding, given that in the interwar period the idea of historical objectivity came under a serious attack from relativists.[204] Thus, Croce recommended the view of the 'present' past because he realised that the 'realistic' epistemology was self-defeating. As it is impossible to acquire certain knowledge of what actually happened in the past, 'realism' is likely to provoke deep scepticism. But, if what is important in history is the living present, then this objection is not valid. Similarly, Collingwood supported the ideas of the objectivity and autonomy of history. In *The Idea of History* he seems to be convinced that historians are able to form correct judgements about the past on the basis of the available evidence.[205] In other places Collingwood sounds much more sceptical. As Allan Megill points out, Collingwood's rapprochement between philosophy and history, and his idea of 're-enactment' carry potentially subversive consequences for his ideas of objectivity and autonomy.[206] Oakeshott himself once pointed out that 'almost imperceptibly, Collingwood's philosophy of history turned into a philosophy in which all knowledge is assimilated to historical knowledge, and consequently into a radically sceptical philosophy'.[207] Be that as it may, Croce and Collingwood were concerned not with undermining the distinctness of history but rather with offering it a more satisfactory philosophy.

To see Croce and Collingwood as proto-post-modernists is to present a view which is as partial as one which sees Poincaré as a predecessor of Kuhn. All artificial similarities notwithstanding, these theories, being elaborated in different periods and contexts, aimed at two opposite directions. One was a defence of the objectivity of science and history. The other led to relativism and scepticism.

---

[203] Collingwood, *The Idea of History*, pp. 282-302, 334.
[204] See, for example, Novick, *That Noble Dream*, pp. 133-167.
[205] *Ibid.*, pp. 249-282.
[206] Allan Megill, '"Grand Narrative" and the Discipline of History', in F. Ankersmit & H. Kellner (eds.), *A New Philosophy of History* (London: Reaktion Books, 1995), pp. 162-163.
[207] Review of R.G. Collingwood, *The Idea of History*, in *English Historical Review* 62, 1947, p. 85.

III

In *Experience and Its Modes* Oakeshott, like Croce and Collingwood, rejects both positivism and empiricism. Yet, as Boucher has shown, his view of history is significantly different.[208]

Oakeshott regards his task as that of a philosopher who analyses the historical mode of experience from outside. He is concerned with elucidating the postulates under which historical inquiry is performed. History is sharply distinguished from philosophy. The historian is not the best judge of what history is simply on the grounds of being an historian.[209] This is contrary to Collingwood's view that only one who is an historian himself can properly understand the character of historical experience.[210] Oakeshott avoids Collingwood's rapprochement between philosophy and history, and thus lays the foundation not only for criticism of history from the philosophical point of view but also for the integrity of history itself. Oakeshott claims that he offers 'neither a description of how history has been written, nor advice as to how it ought to be written'.[211]

Oakeshott argues against the presuppositions of many historians as to the nature of their activity. The historian sometimes 'sets before himself the task of constructing an unbiased account of the course of events'.[212] This often leads to a confused view according to which the aim of history is the collection of facts uninfluenced by experience. He believes in the past which really happened.[213] In other words, most historians profess a sort of philosophical 'realism' and 'empiricism', believing that their propositions must correspond to some real events which took place in the past. Oakeshott rejects this view. Yet he does not advocate its abandonment by historians. He calls it the past '*for* history': the past which 'the historian is accustomed to believe, and it is difficult to see how he could go on did he not believe his task to be the resurrection of what once had been alive'.[214] This concept of the past for history must remain intact. Oakeshott is not concerned with undermining the traditional concept of historical research as a disinterested search for true historical facts. He is

---

[208] See Boucher, 'Human Conduct, History and Social Science in the Works of R.G. Collingwood and Michael Oakeshott'; 'Overlap and Autonomy: The Different Worlds of Collingwood and Oakeshott'.
[209] EM, pp. 86-87.
[210] Collingwood, *The Idea of History*, p. 7.
[211] EM, p. 88.
[212] EM, p. 94.
[213] EM, p. 106.
[214] EM, p. 107.

rather aiming at providing a philosophically sound view of historical activity.

In Oakeshott's view, 'realism' supplies historical experience with a shaky philosophical ground on which to base its claims for independence. What Oakeshott is worried about is that, similarly to the naïve realism in scientific experience, realism in history opens the door to scepticism. Indeed, history used to be regarded as a defective discipline for what was seen as its inability to provide certain knowledge. Oakeshott admits the strength of these criticisms, pointing out that 'a fixed and finished past, a past divorced from and uninfluenced by the present, is a past divorced from evidence... and is consequently nothing and unknowable.'[215] For Oakeshott, any experience is always present experience. If the past does not belong to the present world of experience, history is impossible. If the study of past is to make sense, it should be formulated as a certain form of present experience. Oakeshott's answer is radical. For him, the past is the present. The past in history is not concerned with the discovery of a 'real course of events'. The basic element of this past is not what happened but the present evidence. What is known in history is not 'what was' but 'what the evidence obliges us to believe'.[216] And history 'is the historian's experience,' based on his belief in the truth of the present evidence.[217]

Oakeshott's rejection of the notion of history as telling 'what really happened' is not supposed to express his scepticism or relativism. On the contrary, this is the way to defend historical experience from scepticism. One can see that the expression, 'what the evidence obliges us to believe', does not contradict the practice of history aiming at presenting the objective course of past events. When Oakeshott rejects the term 'objective' experience, he means the experience 'untouched by thought or judgement'.[218] He does not mean that this experience is arbitrary. History is 'objective not because it is free, or comparatively free from the "inference" of thought, but because it is what the historian as such is obliged to think'.[219] Notwithstanding all his claims that the historian constructs the historical past, Oakeshott thinks that the historian is strictly limited in what he is allowed to say. The fact that history is constructed in the historian's mind does not leave him free in his judgement for, again, 'the past in history is not whatever enters the historian's head, it is what

---

[215] Ibid.
[216] EM, p. 108.
[217] EM, p. 99.
[218] EM, p. 93.
[219] EM, p. 100.

he is obliged to believe'.[220] Or, in other words, 'the past in history is not a merely fancied past... it is categorical and not merely apodeictic'.[221]

This view is based on Oakeshott's coherence theory of truth, according to which truth is achieved when experience is coherently organised and not when the mind's ideas correspond to the facts of outside reality. This view, when applied to historical experience, eliminates scepticism because the belief in truth here is based on the coherent interpretation of the available evidence, not on the question of whether this evidence corresponds to what really happened. Oakeshott follows in general the ideas developed by F.H. Bradley, in his mature period, about what constitutes belief in testimony and authority.[222] But he certainly supersedes the ideas of the young Bradley found in the *Presuppositions of Critical History*. Bradley claimed that the only criterion of history is the historian himself who should reject even the most authoritative testimony if it contradicts his experience.[223] However, he described two steps in the critical assessment of any evidence — the authority of the evidence, and its ability to be accepted by the historian on the basis of his own experience. Oakeshott goes further, claiming that 'the grounds of our historical belief are not two — conformity with our own experience and the testimony of others' experience — they are our single world of experience taken as a whole'.[224]

Oakeshott's dissatisfaction with philosophical 'realism' is that it cannot fight scepticism. Croce and Collingwood were driven by a similar dissatisfaction. But their solutions were less radical and, therefore, more prone to turn into a form of relativism. This is especially true for Collingwood whose idea of the 're-enactment' of the past sounds not dissimilar to various hermeneutic approaches. Croce is more radical and his views on history are more akin to those of Oakeshott. Without mentioning Croce by name, Oakeshott refers favourably to the view according to which 'the present dominates the past; all history is contemporary history.'[225] However, he finds this view to be not radical enough since 'behind it lies the notion of a complete and virgin world of past events which history would discover if it could, but which it cannot discover on account of some

---

[220] EM, pp. 110.
[221] EM, pp. 102.
[222] EM, pp. 115.
[223] Bradley, *The Presuppositions of Critical History*, pp. 106-107.
[224] EM, p. 116.
[225] EM, p. 109.

radical defect in human knowledge.'[226] This leads to the idea of contemporary history which presupposes that some contemporary present interest is implied in it. But such interest contradicts the character of the past in present historical experience as 'the past for its own sake'.[227]

This concept of the past for its own sake is what defines the historical past and distinguishes it from other forms of past, such as the past which is understood only in relation to the present, which Oakeshott calls 'practical' past. The historian is interested in 'a dead past; a past unlike the present'.[228] This view is indeed very different from those of Croce and Collingwood who tried to advocate a 'living' past in different forms: Collingwood by re-enacting the past in the mind of the historian, Croce by assimilating it to the present. Oakeshott's more radical epistemology enables him to maintain the integrity of the historical past. Historical experience is present because nothing is real except the present, but this is a very specific attitude towards the present, an attitude in which everything is regarded as potential evidence about the past.

Thus, Oakeshott maintains the idea of the objectivity of an historical inquiry, although he avoids the term 'objectivity' itself. He defends objectivity in both senses, as a lack of bias and a lack of arbitrariness. There is no arbitrariness in historical experience because the historian is not trying to discover the vanished past but rather to say what the evidence obliges him to think. There is no bias because the historian avoids practical considerations in his research and regards the historical past as the past for its own sake. One can argue that Oakeshott does not solve the problems of historical methodology, for the question is precisely how to know what the evidence obliges us to think and how to weight different interpretations of the same evidence against each other. But Oakeshott does not try to provide the answer to this question. His aim is to present a philosophical argument against scepticism, leaving the questions about the practical methodology to historians themselves. Besides, Oakeshott, who was educated as an historian and who was strongly influenced by such historians as Maitland, seems to have never doubted the ability of a good historian to construct a narrative which is not arbitrary or biased.

Another vindication of the autonomous character of historical experience is found in Oakeshott's treatment of historical explanation. History presupposes an explanation different from that of

[226] EM, pp. 109-110.
[227] EM, p. 106.
[228] Ibid.

other modes of experience. The historical explanation can be described as 'the attempt to account rationally for historical change', being, then, 'an explanation of the world in terms of change'.[229] But what is the method which best suits this task?

One will be hardly surprised to find out that Oakeshott rejects altogether the idea of cause in the historical explanation. Cause belongs to the world of science referring to the minimum conditions required to explain the observed result. In history it would mean an attempt to eliminate all causes except those of existing effects, and this will fall short of the full account of the past as the evidence presents it. Moreover, 'the historian would find himself obliged to consider (by a kind of ideal experiment) what *might* have happened as well as what the evidence obliges him to believe did happen.'[230] In other words, instead of maintaining the character of history as a 'science', the explanation in terms of causes will distract the attention of the historian from the quest for the past for its own sake. The only meaning of cause which preserves the integrity of history is one where 'the emphasis is placed upon the *complete* antecedent course of events'.[231] This meaning, however, has nothing in common with what is usually associated with the word 'cause', which requires the separation and a relative isolation of cause and effect.

The concepts of chance or divine providence are no less irrelevant to history than scientific explanations. By being used indifferently to explain everything, they in the end will explain nothing. This means not that these explanations may not be true in some sense but only that they stand outside of history.[232] Neither are practical considerations relevant to historical experience. Nothing can be learned from history: '*die Weltgeschichte* is not *das Weltgericht*'.[233] And indeed, the attempts to formulate a 'philosophy of history', whether they mean the search for general laws which govern the whole course of history, or 'a kind of general review of the course of human life', or the elucidation of the plan or plot of history, are misconceived. They either introduce extraneous and irrelevant considerations into an historical inquiry, or are indistinguishable from history as such.[234]

Oakeshott also rejects some other ideas which look more plausible to many historians themselves. Thus, he objects to the idea of the historical explanation in terms of great, decisive events, or turning

---

[229] EM, p. 125.
[230] EM, pp. 127-128.
[231] EM, p. 132.
[232] EM, pp. 126-127.
[233] EM, p. 158.
[234] EM, pp. 154-155.

points because this view implies the distinction between essential and incidental events. This is, according to Oakeshott, 'a monstrous incursion of science into the world of history'.[235] The same is true about the attempts to explain history in terms of personal character or 'motive'.[236] For Oakeshott, Collingwood's idea of re-enactment is hardly able to enlighten our understanding of the past. For what is important is not the ideas and intentions of historical actors but the events themselves. Finally, Oakeshott is critical of the idea of contingency advanced by J.B. Bury. According to this view, many historical events are a result of a co-incidence of several independent series of events. The clash of these series, which is contingent itself, sometimes contributes to an important historical development. Oakeshott finds this view more plausible, and discusses it at length, but in the end he feels obliged to reject it.[237] This interpretation still retains the elements of scientific explanation although in a compromised form. It still preserves the idea of 'normal' course of events or 'cause' within a series of events, while supplementing it with the idea of accident when two independent chains of events meet at some point. This compromise makes this theory sound more plausible but, in fact, it is based on two already rejected ideas: 'cause' and 'accident'. Their combination does not create any logical unity.

What could a more satisfactory concept of an explanation look like? Oakeshott's view is that no additional concept of explanation is required. 'Change in history carries with it its own explanation'.[238] Oakeshott seems to mean by this a complete account of events in which every different event is presented in the context of the continuous description of the past. Thus, 'the only explanation of change relevant or possible in history is simply a complete account of change... The relation *between* events is always other events, and it is established in history by a full relation *of* the events.'[239] A full account of change is actually the explanation of this change. Nothing in the world of history is non-contributory and there are no events in the past which are mere errors, or which can be judged as accidents from the point of view of our present preoccupations. History is 'a positive unity' and this implies that 'such negative concepts as "evil", "immoral", "unsuccessful", "illogical", etc., have, as such, no place at all'.[240] This is reminiscent of Croce who thought in a

---

[235] EM, p. 129.
[236] EM, p. 131.
[237] EM, pp. 133-141.
[238] EM, p. 141.
[239] EM, p. 143.
[240] EM, p. 142.

quasi-Hegelian manner that history is the positive development of the Spirit and that it recognises no explanation in terms of struggle of 'good' and 'evil' but rather presents a gradual development of humankind from 'good' to 'better'.[241] But Oakeshott's approach is very different again. For Croce, this is an important philosophical reflection about the meaning of human history, elaborated in the later writings as the story of liberty.[242] Oakeshott simply means that history should be presented as it actually is, regardless of the importance of particular events to our present interests. History must not be read backwards.

This view implies that at least in principle, if not in practice, one can imagine an history which would fully present a single course of events. History does not repeat itself and there are neither two parallel courses of events in historical experience, nor two different narratives about the same events representing different points of view. The postulates of historical experience 'determine the only course of events known in history'.[243]

History is, then, 'a homogeneous, self-contained mode of experience'.[244] It, however, falls short of self-completeness because it represents an arrest in experience, which must be superseded by philosophy in order to achieve experience satisfactory to itself. So far, this view is parallel to Oakeshott's account of scientific experience. But there emerge here some differences which make Oakeshott's treatment of history less coherent than his treatment of science.

Oakeshott's criticism of history from the standpoint of the totality of experience is longer and more substantial than his criticism of science. The reason for this is perhaps that Oakeshott's knowledge of scientific method was mostly based on the acquaintance with the secondary literature written by practising scientists. In the case of history he was more familiar with historical practice and philosophies of history, and this makes his account of history more critical. He presents two arguments in favour of the view that history is an arrest of experience. The first is that the very character of historical experience, as the present seen under the category of the past, is self-contradictory. Here the form contradicts the content; the character of history as present experience contradicts its self-presentation as an account about the past. History is, therefore, limited by its own

---

[241] Croce, *Theory and History of Historiography*, pp. 83-93.
[242] Benedetto Croce, *History as the Story of Liberty* (Indianapolis: Liberty Fund, 2000).
[243] EM, p. 168.
[244] EM, p. 156.

postulates, and first of all by the category of past.[245] This argument does not yet make the world of history incoherent. Scientific experience is also conditioned experience limited by the category of quantity. Yet science is seen as an experience which is able to achieve inner coherence. A limited world of experience can still be a homogeneous world. However, there is another argument which degrades history's claims for self-completeness. Historical experience consists of historical individuals, by which Oakeshott means events; things (institutions); or personalities as subjects of historical inquiry. Neo-Kantians, such as Windelband or Rickert, argued that history deals with individual events whereas science deals with generalities. This view is unacceptable from Oakeshott's point of view because the attempt to present individuality as mere singularity ends up in an infinite regression in the pursuit of a completely isolated entity. Secondly, even a brief look at history will show that there are no isolated individuals in history. The Roman Empire is not a single thing which is identical to itself during its whole history; nor can it be satisfactorily distinguished from its environment. The same applies to historical events, or even to historical personalities. Therefore, an historical individual is a combination of particular and general. It is established by 'the double conception of continuity and discontinuity' where 'its beginning is marked by an apparent break in the continuity of what went before, and because, having once been established, it could maintain a continuous existence'.[246] This individual is in some degree separable from its environment, but it cannot be absolutely clear and coherent. Thus, an individual, though always designated, falls short of the satisfactory definition.[247] History begins with a world of presupposed individuals, but in the attempt to make an individual more coherent, 'there is a constant temptation to abandon the terms of the presupposition... Historical experience, like all abstract experience, is always on the verge of passing beyond itself.'[248]

However, we have seen that scientific experience is not described as giving the same impression. Oakeshott presents the world of historical experience as less self-sustainable than the world of science. While opposing scepticism, he introduces it through the back door. This may place Oakeshott closer to Collingwood, in whose opinion modes of experience, being internally incoherent, necessarily pass beyond themselves in experience. This view makes his whole

---
[245] EM, p. 148.
[246] EM, p. 121.
[247] EM, p. 148.
[248] EM, p. 122.

approach more satisfactory from the vantage of Absolute Idealism, but also makes it less Oakeshottean.

Yet these sceptical claims co-exist with claims of another kind. Historical individuals, Oakeshott says, although 'themselves the product of generalisation, do not admit of further generalisation'.[249] Once an individual is established, it is, for history, absolute, though 'not in the sense of being ultimately complete and self-sufficient'.[250] Designation of an individual is never arbitrary and, when it is established, the individual should be stable and consistently adhered to. In fact, a practising historian has no problem with the designation of relevant individuals. Thus, for Gibbon, 'barbarism and religion are... easily distinguished from their environment, and his business is merely to make sure that the distinction he works with is consistent.'[251] Oakeshott, therefore, does not apply his scepticism to the actual work of an historian.

Thus, two different directions of thought are implied in Oakeshott's description of history in *Experience and Its Modes*. One sees history as a homogeneous mode of experience; the second is much more sceptical, regarding history as an incoherent world of experience which is in danger of passing beyond itself. There is no formal contradiction between these two claims; indeed, the same argument is presented with regard to scientific experience. But in fact, the nuanced analysis shows that Oakeshott finds more internal tension in history than in science. This tension is almost unavoidable, since, after all, history is less certain knowledge; and one who is keen on defending the integrity of historical inquiry will hardly find it easy to ignore this fact. Therefore, some scepticism enters even Oakeshott's thought, but nevertheless, his defence of history against the claims of practice, science and philosophy is more radical and consistent than that of Collingwood and Croce. While radicalising their Idealism, Oakeshott reaches the conclusion which favours a view of history as a search for the past 'as it really happened', though he bases this view on completely different epistemology. The historian builds 'a specific and homogeneous world of ideas'.[252] He is looking in history not for 'what must, or what might have taken place, but solely what the evidence obliges us to conclude did take place'.[253]

---

[249] EM, p. 160.
[250] EM, p. 161.
[251] EM, p. 120.
[252] EM, p. 144.
[253] EM, p. 139.

IV

There are different opinions among commentators as to whether, and to what extent, Oakeshott's views on history changed after the publication of *Experience and Its Modes*. Gertrude Himmelfarb and Robert Grant point to the amazing continuity in Oakeshott's writings on history, whilst Luke O'Sullivan and Terry Nardin emphasise the changes in some of Oakeshott's ideas.[254] Yet these two views do not necessarily exclude each other. And for the purpose of the current discussion it will be argued that Oakeshott's views on the autonomous character of history remained basically the same in his later writings. Despite some changes of emphasis and vocabulary, Oakeshott continued and even strengthened his advocacy of history as an autonomous and objective discipline.

In the context of Oakeshott's middle period, the central work for his discussion of history is an essay 'The Activity of Being an Historian' (1955) which reiterates, in general, the view presented in *Experience and Its Modes*. History is one of the voices in the conversation, which is independent and cannot be assimilated to other voices. Yet there are two changes in emphasis. Firstly, *Experience and Its Modes* reflected the tension between two contrary aims: on the one hand to affirm the independence of the historical inquiry from the intrusion of other modes of experience; on the other hand to show the incompleteness of history which is to be superseded by philosophy. Now, as Oakeshott's preoccupations with metaphysics completely vanish, the first aspect becomes central. Oakeshott does still point out that it is possible to generate the definitive character of historical activity and that such an inquiry would be superior to history in its present condition and capable of taking its place.[255] Yet in the essay he is concerned only with a general description of history 'as it has come to establish itself'.[256] In other words, Oakeshott is now completely preoccupied with the character of historical experience as it exists *for* history. The voice of the professional historian is dominant here.

Secondly, in *Experience and Its Modes* one of the main adversaries is a scepticism which insists on the arbitrariness of history. This scepticism was rebuffed with the theoretical claim about the character of the historical past as the present. Here, Oakeshott concentrates his efforts on the attempt to defend unbiased, 'objective' history against relativism. In this undertaking he uses an idiosyncratic language of

---

[254] Himmelfarb, 'Supposing History Is a Woman'; Grant, *Oakeshott*, p. 99; O'Sullivan, *Oakeshott on History*; Nardin, *The Philosophy of Michael Oakeshott*, pp. 141-181.
[255] RIP, pp. 152-153.
[256] RIP, p. 153.

his own. Yet Oakeshott's main ideas were not eccentric, fitting well into the general intellectual climate of his time and corresponding to the concerns of many other historians at the period. As Novick points out, the insistence on the character of science and history as a disinterested search for objective truth had become 'the distinctive epistemological posture of the Free World' for many intellectuals in the fifties.[257] Indeed, Oakeshott expressed this thought in a more detached language but he made clear that the idea of autonomous history was one of the most important achievements of modern Western civilisation. According to him, the specification of historical activity was achieved in modern Europe 'in a process of emancipation from the primordial and once almost exclusive practical attitude of mankind'.[258] This implied that those attacking the idea of historical detachment were undermining one of the assets of modern European civilisation.

According to Oakeshott, the historical attitude towards the past is one in which past events are understood 'in respect of their independence of subsequent events or present circumstances or desires, and are understood as having no necessary and sufficient conditions'.[259] An historical interest is an interest in the past for its own sake, which is independent from practical considerations. In this sense Oakeshott finds similarities between science and history because the aspiration to see the world independently from our desires is also present in scientific activity. Both attitudes 'have emerged together, and with some interdependence, in modern Europe',[260] and in some general sense, history can be said to advocate 'a "scientific" attitude towards the past'.[261] Oakeshott does not confuse the two. For him, historical and scientific activities are very different voices, and yet they are both children of modernity. The purpose of this essay is to defend them against practice as their common adversary which denies to them the right to be cherished for their own sake. Yet, while science is able to defend itself relatively easily, history stands on more shaky foundations, for it is 'an immensely difficult achievement' — to free oneself from an attitude which regards past choices and actions of mankind 'as if they were present'.[262] The practical attitude always stands in the way of the appearance of the 'historical' past. History is a fragile world of expe-

---

[257] Peter Novick, *That Noble Dream*, p. 295.
[258] RIP, p. 171.
[259] RIP, p. 174.
[260] RIP, p. 171.
[261] *Ibid.*
[262] *Ibid.*

rience and therefore needs to be defended more vigorously than science.

In this description of the character of historical activity, Oakeshott follows the main ideas outlined in *Experience and Its Modes*. The historian is preoccupied with the historical past which is distinguished from the practical past by being a past for its own sake, and not with respect to our present desires. This past is determined by the present evidence, and 'everything that the evidence reveals or points to is recognised to have its place'.[263] There are no 'non-contributory' events; no event can be explained backwards; every event is neither accidental nor necessary.[264] The historian is not supposed to express his judgements about these events. He explains events by means of other events and this explanation makes an event an intelligible occurrence.

Oakeshott does not accept Collingwood's view that the task of an historian is to re-enact the past.[265] Nor does a wide sympathy with all the persons and interests engaged turn an account of the situation into an historical account.[266] In a book review published several years earlier, Oakeshott criticised E.H. Carr for attempting to write an history of the Bolshevik Revolution by entering into 'the intention of his subjects',[267] which he saw as a mistake since the historian is the maker of his events. To reveal merely what historical persons thought about themselves and their contemporaries 'is to show an imperfect mastery' of characters.[268] As Bolshevik leaders spoke an extraordinary private language, to try merely to re-enact their thoughts and their interpretation of events leads to both an incomprehensible account and a false view of what really happened. This is a typically Oakeshottean argument, for he emphasises the view that the historian is the master of his characters only to show later that such mastery is required in order to present the objective account of events.

Thus, history is not a re-enactment, and it lacks a unity which may characterise the analysis of ideas. Yet, even without a feeling of unity, an historical account of events is clearly distinguished from other accounts. Although Oakeshott does not use the phrase 'an account of events as they happened', his description of the voice of history as one in which, in contrast to a drama, 'events have no

---

[263] RIP, p. 169.
[264] RIP, p. 172.
[265] RIP, p. 179.
[266] RIP, p. 177.
[267] 'Mr. Carr's First Volume,' *Cambridge Journal* 4(6), 1951, p. 344.
[268] *Ibid.*

over-all pattern or purpose, lead nowhere... and support no practical conclusions'[269] is hardly distinguishable from this common sense view of history.

Oakeshott admits this when at the beginning of the essay he mentions various definitions of history, such as the claim that an historian deals with what *did* happen, not with what must or might have happened; that he is concerned with human actions and not natural processes; that he is not looking for 'origins' and is not concerned with moral rightness and wrongness.[270] He rejects these reflections on the nature of historical activity as unsatisfactory but he does not find them entirely wrong. Indeed, these suggestions were designed in order to insulate historical activity from the claims of practice. The only problem is that these reflections 'have often been supported by irrelevant reasoning'.[271] Oakeshott thinks that his theory supplies historians with a more plausible view of their activity.

Yet his criteria of what it is to be an historian raise again the tension between the allegedly descriptive character of his essay and its seemingly strong normative content. As in the case of science, Oakeshott provides the most rigid criteria for what is to be regarded as historical in order to distinguish it from the practical. Thus, even such common expressions as 'the death of William the Conqueror was accidental', or 'the evolution of Parliament' are excluded by him on the grounds that they introduce irrelevant concepts of accident and evolution.[272] This sounds controversial because hardly any historian can be found who has managed to avoid all these kinds of unhistorical statements. To this, Oakeshott replies that, although all sorts of unhistorical statements are sometimes made by historians, only historians and nobody else express a 'historical' attitude towards the past.[273] But the rhetoric of the essay gives a strong impression that Oakeshott tells us not only how history is written but also how it ought to be written, if it is to maintain its character as an independent activity, or a world of experience.

V

The sixties and seventies presented new challenges to the ideal of history as a disinterested study of the past, especially when this ideal was articulated in terms of empirical political and constitutional his-

---
[269] RIP, p. 182.
[270] RIP, pp. 155-156.
[271] RIP, p. 175.
[272] RIP, pp. 162-163.
[273] RIP, p. 168.

tory. Firstly, the very pre-eminence of this field of study was criticised by proponents of new approaches in history, many of whom were influenced by American, and especially French currents, such as structuralism and the *Annales* school. There were calls for a synthesis of history and social sciences in an attempt to develop what was called 'social history'.[274] This combination of science and history would certainly be an anathema in Oakeshott's eyes, providing a clear example of *ignoratio elenchi*, or the error of irrelevance.

The popularity of social history was, however, relatively short, and in Britain it never fully established itself.[275] A more damaging attack was waged from the opposite direction, and with more lasting consequences. It challenged the liberal Cold War consensus with regard to historical objectivity, undermining the stance of history as an autonomous and objective discipline.

Various arguments would be later employed by radical thinkers in order to present a far more relativistic approach to history. Yet doubts about the idea of objectivity were expressed not only by radicals. Thus, E.H. Carr, in his influential series of lectures *What is History?*, argued that a completely unbiased and objective history was impossible. Historians actively choose and interpret different historical facts, thereby introducing an element of subjectivity into historical research. Nevertheless, Carr did not advocate relativism. He believed in the integrity of his profession and insisted that there are limits to subjectivism for, in his opinion, the historian is constrained by the existing facts and evidence.[276]

Yet the following generation of more radical critics was not easily satisfied with this limited admission of the subjective element into the work of an historian. Different theories appeared which used new approaches of literary criticism and deconstruction to undermine history's claims for objectivity and autonomy. Thus, following Hayden White, a view emerged that history was nothing but a form

---

[274] See Lawrence Stone, *The Past and the Present Revisited* (London: Routledge & Kegan Paul, 1987), pp. 17-44; John Stevenson, 'Social History,' in L.J. Butler & A. Gorst (eds.), *Modern British History: A Guide to Study and Research* (London: I.B. Tauris, 1997), pp. 207-217; Kenyon, *The History Men*, pp. 291-298. On *Annales* see Peter Burke, *The French Historical Revolution: The* Annales *School, 1929-1989* (Cambridge: Polity, 1990).
[275] See Stone, *The Past and the Present Revisited*, pp. 74-96.
[276] Edward H. Carr, *What Is History* (London: Macmillan & Co., 1962). On the complexity of Carr's views see Jonathan Haslam, *The Vices of Integrity: E.H. Carr, 1892-1982* (London: Verso, 1999), pp. 192-217.

of literary narrative.[277] By assimilating history to either poetry or practice this view completely denied its autonomy. A subjectivist claim was put forward that an objective past did not exist and that an historian just wrote a narrative of his own. The moderate, modernistic position of Carr was also rejected and turned into a post-modernistic denial of history.[278] Whatever the professional historians thought about such theories, only a few of them such as G.R. Elton were ready to defend the traditional view of history in an uncompromising way. It is interesting to note that Elton's defence of history was in many aspects similar to that of Oakeshott. Thus, Elton emphasised that history studies only 'the present traces of the past' according to the surviving evidence, that it deals first of all with events, and that events and facts are always particular and never identical to other entities of a similar kind.[279] He was also hostile to broader generalisations, and, as Richard Evans points out, he 'inveighed against the use of concepts such as "factors", "forces" and "trends" in the search for causes because, he thought, they removed agency from history.'[280] In general, he 'believed that history should be studied for its own sake and had no cultural or political value in the present.'[281] In addition, most of Quentin Skinner's recent criticisms of Elton's views, such as the latter's insistence that 'true historians... are not marked by "the problems they study" but "by the manner of their study",' can be equally directed against Oakeshott.[282]

Although Oakeshott did not engage directly in the hot controversies on the proper character of historical study, he continued to reflect intensely on the nature of historical experience, with his ideas finding a theoretical expression in *On Human Conduct* (1975) and *On History* (1983). *On History* sprang from discussions at the seminars on the history of political thought which Oakeshott organised at LSE in the sixties and the beginning of seventies, the time when he was

---

[277] Hayden White, *Metahistory: The Historical Imagination in Nineteenth-Century Europe* (Baltimore: John Hopkins University Press, 1973); Dominic LaCapra, *History and Criticism* (Ithaca: Cornell University Press, 1985).
[278] See Keith Jenkins, *On "What is History": From Carr and Elton to Rorty and White* (London: Routledge, 1995), p. 6.
[279] See G.R. Elton, *The Practice of History* (London: Methuen and Company, 1967), pp. 9-11.
[280] Richard J. Evans, 'Afterword,' in G.R. Elton, *The Practice of History* (Oxford: Blackwell, 2002), p. 184.
[281] *Ibid.*, p. 189.
[282] Quentin Skinner, 'Sir Geoffrey Elton and the Practice of History,' *Transactions of the Royal Historical Society* 7, 1997, p. 312.

writing *On Human Conduct*.[283] Thus, both books belong to the same period.

On Human Conduct contains little theorising on the nature of history. An historical mode of understanding is analysed only in so far as it is regarded as the best way to grasp substantive performances in human conduct. *On History*, by contrast, contains three long essays which deal exclusively with history, discussing such concepts as historical past, event and change. But here the analysis will be limited only to Oakeshott's defence of history as an autonomous and objective world, a defence which is found in both books.

In *On Human Conduct* Oakeshott uses the classification of orders and idioms of inquiry instead of that of modes of experience. There is, indeed, a close link between 'historical experience' and the 'order of inquiry' of intelligible occurrences, but they are not identical. The order of inquiry concerned with 'goings-on' identified as an exhibition of intelligence includes such idioms as ethics, jurisprudence and aesthetics.[284] The understanding of the postulates of human conduct is not an historical understanding either. Only when substantive performances of human agents are involved, the best way to understand them is through historical understanding.[285] This means not that only history deals with intelligent goings-on but that historical understanding is extremely suitable for theorising substantive performances. In *On History* Oakeshott deals with what he calls an historical 'universe of discourse' in general terms without relating it necessarily to human conduct.[286]

Oakeshott says that historical events are 'contingently' related but he uses this term differently from Bury whom he criticises in *Experience and Its Modes*. However, it is not easy to define 'contingency' precisely. Oakeshott argues that the relationship between historical events must be a 'significant' relationship and that the contingent relationship is a sequential relationship of intelligent individual occurrences.[287] The historian is concerned with distinguishing between significant and insignificant antecedents, and he is not looking 'for the total of all antecedents'.[288] Thus, Oakeshott may be seen as supporting the view that history is preoccupied with elucidating the meaning of an intelligible context. However, such an interpretation of his position would be not quite right. In *On History*

---

[283] Timothy Fuller, 'Foreword,' in OH, p. xvi.
[284] HC, p. 17.
[285] HC, p. 107.
[286] OH, p. 28.
[287] HC, pp. 103-104.
[288] OH, p. 93.

Oakeshott gives three characteristics to the concept of 'contingency'.[289] Firstly, the contingent relationship is an 'immediate relationship' which is the relationship of events themselves without support from any external concept. Secondly, this is a 'circumstantial relationship', that is, there is 'evidential contiguity' between two events. Thirdly, this is a significant relationship because when one event 'touches' another it imparts not itself but a difference. In other words, a contingent relationship is one where a subsequent event is different from the antecedent but is not regarded as a necessary outcome of this event. 'Significant' means something rather more simple than the context of meaning: it means only that a subsequent event is different from the antecedent. Thus, for the historian to give an account of only significant events simply means to eliminate those antecedent occurrences which do not impart difference to the following ones.

In *On Human Conduct* the thought is similar. The relationship of 'touch' means 'the absence of interval' since in a contingent relationship 'there is only unbroken continuity of occurrences'.[290] And the idea of the intelligibility of such relationships is stressed not in order to emphasise that history is looking for the hermeneutical explanation but rather just to show why such relationships are contingent. According to Oakeshott, intelligible 'goings-on' do not determine subsequent occurrences. Intelligibility means that outcome is neither necessary nor merely accidental. When an outcome is of such a character one can speak about 'contingency'. As intelligibility is inherent in human conduct, and as contingency belongs to the historical world, this explains why the historical understanding fits best with the theorising of substantive performances. Contingency thus understood elucidates, but does not change, the character of the historical explanation as a complete account of change, presented in *Experience and Its Modes*. The only difference is that in *On History* Oakeshott is clear that the relationships analysed are not mutual. A subsequent event is to be understood in terms of antecedent ones, but antecedent events cannot be explained by the subsequent. In this too, his ideas on the character of historical explanation concur with those of Elton who argued that the historian means by cause:

> those antecedent events, actions, thoughts, and situations which can be proved, by demonstration and inference, to have influenced the coming about of the event which he is trying to explain. In order to discover

---
[289] OH, p. 102.
[290] HC, p. 104.

them, he works from the event to be explained... to the explaining events...; that is, he deduces the cause, not the consequences.[291]

But nothing here contradicts Oakeshott's early ideas either. Although in *Experience and Its Modes* Oakeshott spoke in terms of 'a world of ideas' and not 'a series of events', nothing in his description of historical explanation lets us presume that he allowed an explanation of some events by their consequences. Oakeshott was always opposed to reading history backwards.

Oakeshott sounds more moderate about the categorical character of historical experience where the evidence obliges us to understand the past in a specific way. He is aware that evidence can be ambiguous and that every occurrence may become subject to different kinds of historical inquiry.[292] Yet he continues to defend vigorously the idea of the independent and objective character of an historical inquiry. History is an independent world of understanding which cannot be assimilated to another world of understanding, determined by different modal conditions.[293] The historical past should be distinguished from the practical past as the past for its own sake. This past is present experience (for every experience is present) in which everything is seen as a survival from the vanished past, and therefore, potential evidence. The historical past is something which is inferred from evidence and exists only in history books.[294]

Oakeshott continues to reject Collingwood's idea of the re-enactment of the past, by arguing that:

> the theorist is not concerned to re-enact in his own imagination the performance of an agent or to rehearse it in terms in which it was performed. His engagement is to enlist whatever evidence he can find in order to take hold of a performance and to endow it with a conditional intelligibility of which he is the author.[295]

This engagement includes among other things 'an exact appreciation of [an action's] provenance and circumstances' and a criticism of a variety of contingent relationships, 'each sustained by a reading of the evidence'.[296] History is concerned not with dispositions and

---

[291] G.R. Elton, *Political History: Principle and Practice* (London: Allen Lane, 1970), p. 137. We should not be misled by the fact that Elton uses the word 'cause', which Oakeshott would rather avoid as confusing.
[292] OH, pp. 34-35, 56.
[293] OH, p. 26.
[294] OH, p. 36.
[295] HC, p. 106.
[296] *Ibid.*

intentions but with 'the unintended eventual by-products of such transactional engagements'.[297]

Thus, in his later writings Oakeshott adheres to the same idea of history as an independent unbiased activity. Moreover, he abandons the criticism of history as a 'defective' mode of experience altogether, and the latest writings represent a clear and radical defence of history. Oakeshott agrees that history 'has remained a somewhat uncertain and confused engagement'.[298] But precisely because of this it is important to elucidate the true character of history and prevent it from being confused with other modes of understanding.

VI

Collingwood praised the profundity and originality of Oakeshott's philosophy of history; yet he did not find any philosophical justification for the existence of history in Oakeshott's treatise. He was puzzled by this and was not content with what he regarded as an attitude to historical activity which saw it as just playing a game.[299]

This section can be seen as an attempt to answer this question. The argument here is that the failure to explain why history should be practised is not a failure at all but the intrinsic feature of the whole of Oakeshott's approach. For Oakeshott, the ability to recognise and cherish the purposeless character of different worldviews is the central feature of modern Western civilisation. History has no extraneous purpose and therefore its existence cannot be philosophically justified. It is one of the voices of modernity which must be cherished for its own sake.

Oakeshott's view of history is sometimes seen as resembling post-modernistic attacks on 'positivism' and 'empiricism' but, in fact, Oakeshott's purpose is precisely the opposite. He is trying to defend the notion of history as a constructed but not fictional exposition of events of the past for the past's sake. His rejection of various 'realistic' and 'empiricist' approaches is driven by the same dissatisfaction which makes him reject 'realism' in science. To base philosophy of science and history on the correspondence theory of truth means to open the way to scepticism and relativism. Thus Carr, who assumed that the historian's work was to find real historical facts, could not ignore the objection that the choice and interpretation of facts were dependent on the historian himself. And thus, he presented a moderately sceptical view in which the historian's subjec-

---

[297] OH, p. 71.
[298] OH, p. 127.
[299] Collingwood, *The Idea of History*, p. 156.

tivity was tempered by the existence of real facts. In Oakeshott's view, such moderation leads to a disaster, being unable to offer a coherent concept of history, protected from more radical relativistic claims.

Oakeshott's way to defend history was to adopt a seemingly contradictory philosophy. He claimed, firstly, that the historical past is not about the events that really happened but about what the evidence obliges us to believe and, secondly, that historical understanding was sharply distinguished from all others, especially from practical understanding. Thus, Oakeshott could defend the autonomy and 'objectivity' of historical activity. Quite paradoxically, his philosophical path was more radical than that of Croce, but at the same time it led to conclusions which did not differ much from the views of a defender of traditional historical professionalism such as Elton.

POETRY
I

Oakeshott's thought is often portrayed as having a strong aesthetic dimension. Thus, the influence of the Renaissance and Romanticism on his worldview is emphasised, he is sometimes compared with European existentialists, and one commentator even described his life as 'poetic, not prosaic'.[300]

There are, however, relatively few studies outlining the development of Oakeshott's aesthetic theory.[301] These are usually found in short chapters in general surveys of Oakeshott's philosophy. Thus, W.H. Greenleaf analyses Oakeshott's theory of aesthetics in the context of the Idealistic tradition exemplified by Hegel, Croce and Collingwood; Robert Grant discusses and rejects what he sees as the deceptive parallels between Oakeshott and the Bloomsbury group, and Andrew Sullivan argues that an aesthetic dimension is present in Oakeshott's concepts of practice and politics.[302] Yet no compre-

---

[300] Andrew Sullivan, 'Taken Unseriously,' *The New Republic*, May 6, 1991, p. 42. See also Coats, *Oakeshott and His Contemporaries*, pp. 15-27; Colin Falck, 'Romanticism in Politics,' *New Left Review* 18, 1963, pp. 60-72; Kenneth Minogue, 'Oakeshott's Idea of Freedom,' *Quadrant*, October 1975, pp. 77-83; Glenn Worthington, 'Michael Oakeshott on Life: Waiting with Godot,' *History of Political Thought* 16(1), 1995, pp. 105-119.

[301] For the only journal article focusing on Oakeshott's theory of aesthetics see Howard Davis, 'Poetry and the Voice of Michael Oakeshott,' *British Journal of Aesthetics* 15(1), 1975, pp. 59-68.

[302] Greenleaf, *Oakeshott's Philosophical Politics*, pp. 30-35; Grant, *Oakeshott*, pp. 104-110; Sullivan, *Intimations Pursued*.

hensive analysis of the development of Oakeshott's philosophy of aesthetics has yet been published.

One of the reasons for this may lie in the fact that Oakeshott wrote little about aesthetics and, moreover, he was very ambiguous in his views on the character of this form of experience. As we have seen, he formulated his views on science and history relatively early and never departed from them afterwards. In contrast, it took him a long time to elaborate a coherent theory of aesthetics.

This theory, however, occupies a central place in Oakeshott's mature philosophy as he radically defends 'poetry' as one of the independent worldviews which constitute the character of modern experience. The purpose of this section is to present the development of Oakeshott's view of the autonomy of aesthetic experience within its intellectual context.

II

Oakeshott's interest in art is visible in his early publications, in which he tends to recognise the independent character of aesthetic experience. Oakeshott makes clear the attitude towards art he is defending in his first student article, which discusses the character of Shylock in Shakespeare's drama. Oakeshott is attracted by Shakespeare's ability to describe a villain as a character and by his capacity for sympathy for a personality, some of whose traits he may have loathed. That such sympathy does not imply any absolute moral standard, makes Shakespeare's description more profound, for 'life is more complex than to foster heroes and villains of the conventional type'.[303]

Oakeshott is opposed to the vulgar moralisation of art, and argues that the artist is able to present a deeper and more complex view of life where all characters 'have some intrinsic value of their own'.[304] In the inter-war period in which artists were often demanded to serve one or another social cause this position was not as commonplace as it is now. Oakeshott aligned himself with the trend usually called 'aestheticism' in England or *l'art pour l'art* in France, which had been at the peak of its influence at the end of the nineteenth and the beginning of the twentieth century, and while still quite popular in the twenties, was being challenged from many directions.

Aestheticism insists on the independent character of artistic activity and artistic perception which are driven by the 'love of the things

---

[303] SJ, p. 61.
[304] *Ibid.*

of intellect and imagination for their own sake'.[305] Some of its proponents, such as Pater, introduce a strong subjectivist element into aestheticism, by denying that beauty belongs to an object as the objective quality, and concentrating on aesthetic experience.[306] Aestheticism puts itself into an opposition to the practical attitude to art and advocates the independent value of aesthetic experience and of artistic creativity. It looks for sources of inspiration in the Renaissance and in the Romantic movement; it is closely connected with artistic movements such as Decadence and Symbolism, and its exponents include names such as Ruskin, Pater and Wilde in Britain, and Flaubert, Mallarmé and Proust in France. At the beginning of the twentieth century the ideal of art for art's sake transformed itself into formalism and found its best expression in the theories of 'significant form' of Clive Bell and Roger Fry.

Oakeshott's aesthetic tastes lie within this cultural tradition. He was fascinated by the Renaissance; Montaigne was one of his favourite authors; and he liked the Romantic notion of adventure. Pater was one of the writers he warmly recommended and he appreciated the talents of some of the figures of the Bloomsbury group such as Virginia Woolf.[307] In one of his juvenile works, Oakeshott also admits the influence of Bergson's philosophy on him.[308]

The term 'aestheticism' is, however, ambiguous and can be used to indicate various, even contradictory, approaches towards art. It can be interpreted both as the consequence of the industrialisation and division of labour in modern society, in which the artist becomes a professional, and as a protest against rationalisation and alienation in modern industrial civilisation.[309] It can be seen as an escape from life, a disenchantment from Nature and attempt to find a shelter in the artificial world of beautiful things.[310] But some of its proponents

---

[305] Walter Pater, *The Renaissance: Studies in Art and Poetry* (London: Collins, 1967), p. 33.
[306] *Ibid.*, pp. 27-32.
[307] See Sullivan, *Intimations Pursued*, p. 281n; Grant, *Oakeshott*, p. 106.
[308] ERPPR. The draft is apparently written in the early twenties. Oakeshott is here under the influence of Bergson's intuitivism, and claims that while both philosophy and poetry attempt to reach the knowledge of reality, the poetical insight is a shorter and a more certain way to the truth than the philosophical investigation. Although many claims of this work are later abandoned by Oakeshott, the essay is the evidence of his early interest in the questions of aesthetics, and of his attachment to the genre of poetry.
[309] Arnold Hauser, *Sozialgeschichte der Kunst und Literatur* (München: C.H. Beck, 1972), pp. 771-772.
[310] *Ibid.*, pp. 944-945.

have presented it as an endeavour to render life in its fullness.[311] One can even argue that aestheticism bears in itself the seeds of its own destruction, since its insistence on the irrelevance of moral values comes into conflict with the tacit criticism of modern society implied in aestheticism's rejection of reality and concentration on artificial beauty.[312]

As for aestheticism's insistence on the irrelevance of morality, Monroe Beardsley distinguishes between two different arguments. The first is what he calls 'an argument from Innocuousness', in which there is an implied optimism about the potential of aesthetic education. A proper education in art is supposed to teach the right way to respond to aesthetic objects, while preventing people from confusing artistic and non-artistic discourse. Though moral considerations are irrelevant to art, this will not lead to immoral conduct. The other argument is 'an argument from Aesthetic Primacy', where an aesthetic attitude is perceived as the supreme attitude towards life, and where it demands the rejection of all moral considerations if they stand in the way of the pure aesthetic experience.[313] The intimations of such view can be found, for example, in Bell's presentation of art as the highest good.[314]

In other words, two contradictory tendencies exist in aestheticism. One insists merely on the autonomous character of art; the other presents the aesthetic as the highest form of a good life, however immoral such a life may seem from the point of view of a conventional morality.

This ambiguity is not peculiar just to the realm of aesthetic, and the modern philosophies of science and history contain the same contradictory tendencies. Thus, one can see in scientific positivism either merely a method to preserve the independent character of scientific experience with respect to other modes, or the supreme form of understanding of any aspect of reality. Philosophies of history, while aiming to defend its autonomy, may end up as well describing history as the superior form of understanding.[315] Already in his early writings Oakeshott, in order to defend the autonomy of science and history, argues against their claims for supremacy; yet his view

---

[311] Albert Cassagne, *La Théorie de l'Art Pour l'Art: En France chez les Derniers Romantiques et les Premier Réalistes* (Seyssel: Champ Vallon, 1997), pp. 401-402.
[312] Ralph-Reiner Wuthenow, *Muse, Maske, Meduse: Europäischer Ästhetizismus* (Frankfurt am Main: Suhrkamp, 1978).
[313] Monroe C. Beardsley, *Aesthetics: Problems in the Philosophy of Criticism* (Indianapolis: Hackett Publishing Company, 1981), pp. 561-563.
[314] Clive Bell, *Art* (Oxford: Oxford University Press, 1987), pp. 106-117.
[315] As in Lord Acton's phrase that 'history rescues us from transient', cited by Oakeshott in EM, p. 149.

on the autonomy of art is more ambiguous. In his occasional remarks on art, Oakeshott seems to sympathise with the view that art, being seemingly detached from the world, expresses the true value of life.

Thus, in one of his book reviews, Oakeshott distinguishes between three different notions of culture which shape our civilisation. The first sees in culture 'the indiscriminate acquisition of knowledge of whatever sort'.[316] Its opposite pairs are Culture and Ignorance. This activity is, however, 'pathetic' and 'febrile', containing 'a fanatic, breathless view, totally out of harmony with the real conditions of human life: it has no answer ready for death'. The second notion associated with Matthew Arnold and T.S. Eliot, calls us back to the past by creating standards coined by 'the classics' of literature, the 'great men' of history, or 'the masters' of art. Its pairs are Culture and Anarchy. Oakeshott finds it unsatisfactory, though to a lesser degree, because this view ignores life by looking into the past in the quest for a 'classic' permanence. Not unlike Bell, he is opposed to the concept of culture as the cultivation of the standards of taste.[317]

Oakeshott recommends the third view, which he calls 'a personal criterion for culture'. This notion's pairs are Culture and Despotism, and the representatives of 'culture' in this sense include Epicurus and Montaigne. It is characterised by 'an improvident desire for freedom, integrity', where the only thing which is essential is 'an integrated self, whose purpose is... to live a life contemporary with itself', a life of one's own, in which personal integrity in the present is valued above all. 'What is valued is not the fruit of experience, but the flower — something we know only in a present enjoyment and cannot garner.'[318]

The emphasis on personal integrity as a condition of human freedom, the radical insistence on the importance of the present, and the idea of an aesthetic resignation from the endless process of satisfactions of desires are characteristic of the views which Oakeshott advocated in the early thirties. He praised those who had embraced 'a radical, an Epicurean individualism'.[319] According to him, the real meaning of life lies not in the pursuit of external rewards, which makes one a slave to the future and past, but in the integrity of the self. Such integrity is achieved when life is conducted in the present. For Oakeshott, art is one of the activities which reflect this profound condition of human life in which integrity of character can only be

---

[316] Review of J.C. Powys, *The Meaning of Culture*, in *Cambridge Review* 51, 1930, p. 367.
[317] See Bell, *Art*, pp. 267-273.
[318] Review of Powys, p. 367.
[319] JL, p. 73.

achieved, if it is pursued entirely in the present regardless either of the past or of the future. 'The length of art does not dismay us, for we are not conscious of the briefness of life.'[320]

In Oakeshott's view, art's role in life was akin to that of religion. He saw religion as 'practical experience in its fullest'[321] and claimed that 'culture is... a way of life, a religion'.[322] The character of religion is twofold. It rejects the world composed of an incessant satisfaction of desires, where what is valued is the external result, but at the same time, this rejection gives an inner value to life, thus endowing it with a real significance.[323] Similarly, an artist is independent of society, but also involved in it up to his neck. In *Experience and Its Modes* Oakeshott claimed that 'the most thoroughly and positively practical life is that of the artist or the mystic.'[324] Art, music, poetry are not an escape from life, since in them 'we are wholly taken up with practical life'.[325]

Collingwood's *Principles of Art* (1938) presented Oakeshott with another opportunity to reflect on the role of art and of the artist. Collingwood saw artistic activity as a process of creation by which the artist expresses his emotions. This creation involves an activity of imagination in which an emotional state is raised to the level of consciousness. Thus, what is expressed is not an immediate feeling of emotion which vanishes, but a conscious reflection about this emotion. By expressing his emotions the artist also compels a society to be more deeply conscious of itself. Therefore, the content of art is of no less importance than its form. As Collingwood points out, 'subject without style is barbarism; style without subject is dilettantism. Art is the two together.'[326]

In his review of this book, Oakeshott did not spare his praise of Collingwood, saying that this was 'the most profound and stimulating discussion I have ever read of the question, What is art?' This is 'a

---

[320] 'Religion and the World,' RPML, p. 34.
[321] EM, p. 294.
[322] Review of Powys, p. 367.
[323] On Oakeshott's view of religion see Maurice Cowling, *Religion and Public Doctrine in Modern England* (Cambridge: Cambridge University Press, 1980), pp. 251-282; Glenn Worthington, 'Michael Oakeshott and the City of God,' *Political Theory* 28(3), 2000, pp. 377-398.
[324] EM, p. 296.
[325] EM, p. 297.
[326] R.G. Collingwood, *Principles of Art* (Oxford: Oxford University Press, 1958), p. 299.

book which anyone who can take pleasure in a profound and critical piece of philosophical thinking will find a delight'.[327]

It is not hard to see what so attracted Oakeshott in Collingwood's treatise. Affirming Oakeshott's own intuitions, Collingwood succeeded in constructing a philosophical view in which he preserved the relative autonomy of art but at the same time afforded it the noble role of raising modern society's consciousness of itself. Unsurprisingly, Collingwood's influence is salient in Oakeshott's short essay 'The Claims of Politics', published a year later. There he argued against the claim that politics was the central expression of social sensibility, insisting that it was a relatively unimportant realm of social activity. A political system serves for the protection or modification of the legal and social order, but it lacks the ability to contribute to the permanent recreation of a society. This function can be fulfilled only by literature, art, and philosophy, and, paradoxically, in order to perform this role, an artist and a philosopher should abstain from any political activity. In a Collingwoodian manner, Oakeshott describes their task as mitigating 'a little their society's ignorance of itself'.[328] They are active not in the political sphere, 'but in another and deeper sphere of consciousness'. As 'the last corruption that can visit a society is a corruption of its consciousness', their role is to make a society become 'conscious and critical of itself'.[329]

III

Oakeshott, however, was not entirely satisfied with these views on the character of artistic activity. In the early post-war years he still saw art as a reflective activity. In the essay 'Rational Conduct' (1950) he mentioned the artist alongside the historian, the cook, the scientist and the politician as one 'engaged upon answering questions of certain sort'.[330] Yet there are already indications that Oakeshott is less certain about this claim, because he sometimes advances a rather different view which denies reflectivity to 'poetry'. This appears in the essay 'The Tower of Babel' (1948), where poetry is likened to what is called 'morality of custom'. Sounding here more like Nietzsche than Collingwood, Oakeshott argues that 'a poem is not the translation into words of a state of mind. What the poet says and

---

[327] Review of R.G. Collingwood, *The Principles of Art*, in *Cambridge Review* 59, 1938, p. 487.
[328] RPML, p. 96.
[329] RPML, p. 95.
[330] 'Rational Conduct,' *Cambridge Journal* 4(1), 1950, p. 16. Oakeshott deleted 'artist' when he published this essay in *Rationalism in Politics*. See Greenleaf, *Oakeshott's Philosophical Politics*, p. 33n.

what he wants to say are not two things, the one succeeding and embodying the other, they are the same thing… Nothing exists in advance of the poem itself, except perhaps the poetic passion.'[331]

Moreover, his previous views seemed to entail a certain tension. On the one hand, he sympathised with the view of art as an autonomous activity, but on the other hand he recognised the importance of the link between art and society, thus being led to include art in practical experience. This tension seemed to weaken his general idea of the existence of absolutely independent and homogeneous modes of experience.

These doubts led Oakeshott to review his views on the nature of artistic activity in the essay 'The Voice of Poetry in the Conversation of Mankind' (1959), where he for the first time presented an elaborate aesthetic theory. This essay was later included into *Rationalism in Politics*. As Oakeshott said in the preface to this volume, 'The Voice of Poetry' was 'a belated retraction of a foolish sentence in *Experience and Its Modes*'.[332] There, as we have seen, the life of an artist had been described as 'most thoroughly and positively practical'.[333] In 'The Voice of Poetry', Oakeshott completely abandoned this view and presented an opposite claim: poetry is an independent voice in the conversation of mankind, irrelevant to the considerations of the practical voice.

Oakeshott's ideas here seem to be shaped under the influence of Edward Bullough who taught at Cambridge in the first decades of the twentieth century. Oakeshott published a long obituary of Bullough after his death in 1934, in which he mentioned all Bullough's major works, including those concerned with aesthetics.[334] Bullough is primarily known in the history of aesthetics because of his concept of 'psychical distance' as the main characteristic of aesthetical experience.[335] Yet even before introducing this term, Bullough presented a coherent theory of aesthetical experience in his lectures, which, as Oakeshott tells us, he delivered in Cambridge annually from 1907 until shortly before his death.[336] It is quite likely that Oakeshott attended one of these courses of lectures and also had an opportunity to consult them again when they and the

---

[331] RIP, p. 479.
[332] RIP, p. xi.
[333] EM, p. 296.
[334] EB.
[335] Diané Collinson, 'Aesthetic Experience,' in O. Hanfling (ed.), *Philosophical Aesthetics: An Introduction* (Oxford: Blackwell, 1992), pp. 158-161.
[336] EB, p. 2.

article on 'psychical distance' were republished in 1957, just two years before the publication of 'The Voice of Poetry'.

In the lectures Bullough, like many other theorists of art for art's sake, rejected the concept of beauty as an objective essence, and argued for the psychological analysis of aesthetic perception. He distinguished between four sorts of experience: practical, scientific, ethical and aesthetic, each determined by its own set of conditions and independent from the others. Aesthetic experience is characterised by detachment and contemplation in which aesthetic delight is achieved.[337] This view is presented later as the idea of psychical distance. The distance is between the self and its affections, so that the phenomenon is perceived in a detached form — a fog at sea does not raise anxiety or terror but merely a contemplative pleasure. The artist creates through this experience of detachment, which is not reflective. 'The genuine artist appears to have no deliberately elaborated intention in producing his work.'[338]

Oakeshott, like Bullough, distinguishes between four completely independent forms of experience, which he calls 'voices'. Every voice is constituted through the partnership of an active self and the images it constructs, and each of them creates different kinds of images.[339] There are some differences between Oakeshott and Bullough with regard to the classification of voices. Oakeshott adds an historical voice not mentioned by Bullough and, as in *Experience and Its Modes*, he unites 'practical' and 'ethical' within the same voice. 'Practical' is characterised by two parallel pairs of images, those of desire and aversion, and those of approval and disapproval. Yet even Bullough's taxonomy itself crops up once, when Oakeshott mentions the difference between 'poetic' delight and 'pleasure or virtue or knowledge', so that it is obvious that 'pleasure' stands for practical, 'virtue' for ethical, and 'knowledge' for scientific experience.[340]

Oakeshott calls aesthetic experience a 'poetic' activity, and defines it in terms of 'contemplating' or 'delighting'. Its images are not concerned with making propositions and are individual and unique, because they cannot change or be destroyed. They exist only in the present, and no image can take the place of another one. The combination of these images does not constitute an argument, and their composition has no premeditated end or conclusion. The voice of

---

[337] Edward Bullough, *Aesthetics: Lectures and Essays* (London: Bowes and Bowes, 1957), pp. 66-79.
[338] *Ibid.*, p. 85.
[339] 'The Voice of Poetry in the Conversation of Mankind,' RIP, pp. 495-497.
[340] RIP, p. 540.

poetry is not concerned with the images of the practical voices such as desire or aversion, approval or disapproval, and 'fact' or 'non-fact'. As Oakeshott says:

> images in contemplation are merely present: They provoke... only delight in their having appeared. They have no antecedents or consequents; they are not recognised as causes or conditions or signs of some other image to follow, or as the products or effects of one that went before; they are not instances of a kind, nor are they means to an end; they are neither 'useful' nor 'useless'.[341]

By presenting the idea of 'contemplation' as irrelevant to practical considerations, Oakeshott associates himself with the respectable modern philosophical tradition which sees in 'disinterestedness' the central feature of aesthetic experience. Aesthetics as a distinct field of philosophical inquiry, like the term 'aesthetics' itself, is a peculiar development of eighteenth century European philosophy. From the beginning, the concept of 'disinterestedness' played a key role in it, becoming especially associated with the Kantian idea of the 'beautiful' outlined in his *Critique of Judgement*.[342] According to Kant, the judgement of the beautiful arises from a disinterested delight. This delight is distinct from the pleasure derived from what is agreeable and what is good. The pleasure from the agreeable implies some practical interest in the object of pleasure, whereas the judgement of taste is contemplative, thus being indifferent to the existence of an object. Kant insists that judgements of beauty are categorically distinct from judgements involving practical and moral considerations, treated by Oakeshott as images of desire and aversion, or approval and disapproval.

Thus, for Oakeshott 'poetry' is a sort of a disinterested activity, and this preconditions the kind of questions that can be appropriately asked about poetic images. For example, it is irrelevant to consider them in terms of 'fact' and 'non-fact'. It is irrelevant to inquire whether Anna Karenina's words were accurately reported by Tolstoy, or what was Hamlet's normal bed-time. They cannot exist apart from the poetic images in which they are presented, so that 'what Anna said on any occasion could not have been misreported by Tolstoy because she is incapable of speaking any words which he

---

[341] RIP, pp. 509-510.
[342] Immanuel Kant, *The Critique of Judgement*, trans. J.C. Meredith (Oxford: Clarendon Press, 1978), part 1. See also Dabnew Townsend, 'From Shaftesbury to Kant: The Development of the Concept of Aesthetic Experience,' in P. Kivy (ed.), *Essays on the History of Aesthetics* (Rochester: University of Rochester Press, 1992), pp. 205-223.

has not put into her mouth. Hamlet never went to bed…'[343] We are usually held back from approving or disapproving of the conduct of such characters as Anna Karenina, because we recognise them as poetic images. Finally, these images do not evoke pleasure or pain, for those are partners of desire, which is absent in contemplation. 'Pleasurable or painful situations in poetry are alike delightful.'[344]

This view causes Oakeshott to oppose some other explanations of the character of poetic activity. One is the view that a poetic image represents some 'poetic truth' which is deeper than other manifestations of truth. This cannot be correct, as 'truth', in Oakeshott's view, implies making certain propositions, while poetic images are never of this character, because the concepts of 'fact' and 'non-fact' are alien to them.[345] Another view describes poetic activity as one which sees things 'as they really are', but it is similarly unsatisfactory, for it presupposes either the world of independent facts or the Platonic theory of 'permanent essences', which is rejected by Oakeshott. He also distances himself from Schopenhauer's interpretation of contemplation as an achievement of the highest reality by escaping the domination of an irrational will.[346] For him, the fact that aesthetic imagining is different from the practical does not make the former superior.[347]

A third view is that poetic images represent the expression of the poet's feelings or emotions. According to this view, 'poetry begins with an emotional experience undergone by the poet himself… this emotional experience is then contemplated, and from this activity of contemplation a poetic image is generated which is an "expression" of an analogue of the original emotional experience…'[348] Oakeshott presents Wordsworth, Sidney and Shelley as proponents of this view, and one can also notice the similarities between it and Collingwood's understanding of art as the creative expression of an artist's emotions. Here Oakeshott rejects it completely, pointing out that this implies the belief that 'poetry must be supposed to provide information or instruction of some sort'.[349] This, however, would contradict the view of poetry as a contemplative activity. Oakeshott follows Bullough, denying that the process of the poetic creation consists of several stages, and says that there is no deliberately set

---

[343] RIP, p. 519.
[344] RIP, p. 520.
[345] RIP, p. 522.
[346] RIP, p. 511.
[347] This position is also a retraction of Oakeshott's own early view outlined in the aforementioned essay ERPPR (see note 9).
[348] RIP, p. 524.
[349] *Ibid.*

end in the poetic activity. The poet 'does *one* thing only, he imagines poetically'.[350] Furthermore, this theory assumes that the poet is pre-eminently a man of feeling and emotion, whereas Oakeshott thinks that it is not necessary to have experienced the emotion in order to contemplate it. Moreover, 'it would seem that the spectator-like mood of contemplation would be more likely to establish itself if the emotion had *not* been experienced'.[351] This view does indeed correspond to Bullough's idea of psychical distance.

Thus, Oakeshott presents a radical view of the nature of aesthetic experience, which he sharply distinguishes from other forms of experience. He unequivocally defends the independence of aesthetic activity and advocates the view of art for art's sake. At the same time, this radical separation enables him to reject his previous view, according to which aesthetic experience somehow represents a higher form of human life. Oakeshott even further distances himself from any accusations of providing aesthetic justifications for ethical nihilism, by stressing that, in the social discourse, certain images 'are more readily and more unmistakably recognised as poetic images because of the circumstances in which they appear'.[352] These images are called works of art. Of course, no work of art is absolutely protected from being read in an unpoetical manner, and every work of art can be subject to a scientific, historical or practical inquiry. Yet the circumstantial frame in which a work of art appears, be it a theatre, a picture gallery or the covers of a book, significantly protects its character as a poetic image and points to the kind of questions which can relevantly be asked about it. Oakeshott adopts here what Beardsley calls 'an argument from Innocuousness' about the relation between art and morality, claiming that the framework of art is likely to prevent it from being confused with the voice of practice.

Thus, Oakeshott finally distinguishes between the aesthetic and other forms of experience, although he limits aesthetic experience primarily to recognised forms of art. Poetry is a completely independent voice, and together with science and history is one of the most important activities in modern civilisation. A poetical imagining is not 'a naïve and a primordial activity'.[353] Poets, indeed, existed in the ancient world, but their activity did not acquire a peculiar aesthetic character, being confused with the wisdom of a magician or the entertainment of a gleeman. The emancipation of poetic activity

---
[350] RIP, p. 525.
[351] RIP, p. 524.
[352] RIP, p. 517.
[353] RIP, p. 529.

from the authority of practical imagining is a much later development. 'Properly speaking, it never took place in ancient Greece; a glimpse of it is to be found among the Romans; and subsequently in Europe it has been slowly and uncertainly achieved.'[354] A purely aesthetic attitude emerged later as a result of a gradual circumstantial change in which surviving works of art were detached from their religious and practical context thereby inviting the attitude of contemplation and making a poetic outlook on art possible. This attitude of detachment is a specific feature of modern European civilisation, and therefore it is 'a comparatively new and still imperfectly assimilated experience'.[355]

Oakeshott is not alone in his view of aestheticism as a trend exclusively characterising modern Western sensibility. As Gene Bell-Villada points out, art for art's sake is 'a specifically Western notion, generated on European soil by European writers', with 'no major, vital resonances or academic standing outside Western (and Westernised) societies'.[356] Moreover, Oakeshott is attentive to the underlying tendencies of his time, for when he was writing 'The Voice of Poetry', aestheticism again became an influential and fashionable view. In the forties such prominent figures as E.M. Forster and the literary critic Lionel Trilling protested against the over ideologisation of art and defended the autonomous character of aesthetic experience.[357] In the fifties, the view of art for art's sake acquired a new popularity, when the New Criticism, which rejected any external criteria for judging works of art and advocated criticism from within as the only appropriate form of aesthetic judgement, became the pre-eminent doctrine on U.S. campuses.[358] Moreover, in the context of Cold War liberalism, the idea of art for art's sake was regarded as an alternative which preserved the freedom of artistic expression in opposition to Communist ideological suppression.[359]

Poetry, then, finally captures in Oakeshott's thought the place of one of the corner-stones of Western modernity, being a completely autonomous voice, along with science and history. Yet even here

---

[354] RIP, pp. 530-531.
[355] RIP, p. 532.
[356] Gene H. Bell-Villada, *Art for Art's Sake and Literary Life* (Lincoln: University of Nebraska Press, 1996), p. 3.
[357] See E.M. Forster, 'Art for Art's Sake,' in *Two Cheers for Democracy* (London: Edward Arnold & Co., 1951), pp. 98-104; Lionel Trilling, *The Liberal Imagination* (New York: Doubleday, 1953).
[358] Bell-Villada, *Art for Art's Sake and Literary Life*, p. 254.
[359] *Ibid.*, p. 254. See also Eva Cockroft, 'Abstract Expressionism, Weapon of the Cold War,' in F. Frascina & J. Harris (eds.), *Art in Modern Culture* (London: The Open University, 1992), pp. 82-90.

Oakeshott's attitude towards poetry is ambiguous, as he attempts to qualify his insistence on the absolute irrelevance of poetry to practice. In this, however, he exposes the complexity of the idea of 'disinterestedness' itself within the philosophy of aesthetics.

Thus, Kant sees judgements about what is agreeable, beautiful and good as distinct from each other, and therefore maintains the autonomy of beautiful. At the same time, he thinks that delight in the beautiful may serve as a passage from the agreeable to the good, because the experience of the beautiful somehow intimates in itself the experience of the good. Morality, according to Kant, is the realm of freedom. Because in the experience of the beautiful, intuition and thought engage in a 'free play of imagination', without forming some 'determinate concept', this experience symbolises the freedom of the moral law, and thus beauty can be called a 'symbol of good'. Paradoxically, the realm of the beautiful is independent, but this independence serves the interests of practical reason in the long run.[360] Friedrich Schiller applied this view to his social concerns, seeing the aesthetic education of man as a necessary stage in social progress. In order to serve the practical interest, aesthetic experience should remain independent, being only indirectly linked to the realm of morality.[361] Paul Guyer calls this view a 'dialectic of disinterestedness'.[362]

Likewise, Bullough indirectly connects aesthetic experience with certain practical aspects of life, notwithstanding his affirmation of its independent character. For him, one who has an aesthetic ability to see his own actions as well as those of others in a detached light is likely to contrive conduct which will provoke admiration, behaving according to duty and not sensual pleasure. This leads Bullough to the assertion that aesthetic experience is conducive to individualism, which he ardently supports since he thinks that the social significance of the individual is superior to that of the community.[363]

This ambiguity is present in Oakeshott's essay as well. Although he separates poetry from practice, he still thinks that there are some intimations of poetry in the practical life. Oakeshott rejects any straightforward relation of art to society, yet he states that some of the ideas about such a relation 'may not be ill-observed or untrue'.[364]

---

[360] Kant, *The Critique of Judgement*.
[361] Friedrich Schiller, *On the Aesthetic Education of Man*, trans. E.M. Wilkinson & L.A. Willoughby (Oxford: Clarendon Press, 1967).
[362] Paul Guyer, *Kant and the Experience of Freedom* (Cambridge: Cambridge University Press, 1993), pp. 50, 96.
[363] Bullough, *Aesthetics*, p. 85.
[364] RIP, p. 534.

It is possible to speak about the role of art in a society, if the society is understood not in terms of an engagement in practical enterprise, but as a society of conversationalists. Then, 'Schiller's thoughts on the usefulness of a "useless" activity' are not altogether incorrect.[365] The metaphor of conversation lets Oakeshott say that idioms of each voice are irrelevant to the arguments of other voices and, at the same time, claim that different voices may recognise each other and understand the idiom in which everyone is speaking. Therefore, although practice and poetry are, strictly speaking, irrelevant to each other, there are still in practical activity 'intimations of contemplative imagining capable of responding to the voice of poetry'.[366] Among the examples of such intimation are relationships of friendship, which are 'dramatic, not utilitarian', or of love, whose object is 'individual and not concretion of qualities'. Friends and lovers are not concerned with what use they can make of each other, but 'only with the enjoyment of one another'.[367] Although these are not strictly speaking contemplative activities, 'they are at least ambiguously practical activities' which constitute a channel of common understanding between poetry and practice'.[368] Or, Kant-like 'moral goodness', in which an action is detached from usefulness and external achievement, can also be seen as an intimation of poetry.[369]

At the same time Oakeshott denies that, by virtue of this fact, poetry can be understood as superior to other voices. The attempt to base the conduct of life on an aesthetic dimension is folly since by its own nature poetry is elusive and transient. 'There is no *vita contemplativa*; there are only moments of contemplative activity abstracted and rescued from the flow of curiosity and contrivance.'[370]

IV

This newly formulated view of the independence of poetic activity presented, however, some problems for Oakeshott's general position. As we saw earlier, in *Experience and Its Modes*, Oakeshott, following the Idealistic tradition, emphasised the significance of reflective thought and postulated that every experience involves

---

[365] RIP, p. 534n.
[366] RIP, p. 536.
[367] RIP, p. 537.
[368] RIP, p. 538.
[369] *Ibid.*
[370] RIP, p. 541.

judgement.[371] The inclusion of art into practical experience as a reflection of consciousness of some sort fitted well into this structure. But now, as Greenleaf points out, Oakeshott presented a poetic imagination as a sort of experience from which thought, which is concerned with making propositions, was absent.[372]

This involved a significant change in Oakeshott's description of the character of mental activity. Not every act of thinking is reflective, and alongside reflective thought there is an unreflective imagination. This new understanding of the mental activity corresponded to the general spirit of *Rationalism in Politics*. In essays such as 'Rationalism in Politics' and 'The Tower of Babel' Oakeshott placed an unreflective, poetic-like mental activity (called 'practical' knowledge, or 'morality of custom') in opposition with that which included reflective thought ('technical' knowledge or 'reflective morality') and gave precedence to the former. This distinction invited accusations of irrationalism and 'revulsion' from thought.[373] These were not always fair since, for Oakeshott, the distinction between the reflective and unreflective was analytical, and he recognised that, in actual activity, both kinds are involved to some degree. Yet there was some truth in these claims, because the general mood of Oakeshott's essays of that period seemed to be hostile to reflective thought. Even Peter Winch, who was quite sympathetic to many of Oakeshott's ideas, found this aspect of his thought unsatisfactory.[374]

Oakeshott seems to have taken these criticisms seriously. In *On Human Conduct* he attempts to present such a view that would emphasize again the importance of reflection and judgment in human experience, thus offering a framework which cannot be interpreted as the rejection of thought. He makes clear that any experience involves reflection. He distinguishes between practical conduct and understanding of this conduct, but points out that even conduct itself involves 'deliberating' as one of its postulates.[375] This view is, however, presented at the expense of 'poetry'. Oakeshott builds an appropriate theoretical framework for the analysis of practical conduct, distinguishing between two orders of inquiry, those of intelligent and non-intelligent goings-on. But in this new framework, which emphasises reflection, he can barely find a place for

---

[371] EM, pp. 9-27.
[372] Greenleaf, *Oakeshott's Philosophical Politics*, pp. 33-34.
[373] M. Postan, 'The Revulsion from Thought,' *Cambridge Journal* 1(7), 1948, pp. 395-408.
[374] Peter Winch, *The Idea of Social Sciences and Its Relation to Philosophy* (London: Routledge & Kegan Paul, 1958), pp. 62-65.
[375] HC, pp. 43-46.

poetry, which appears only a few times in the book. Firstly, aesthetics is mentioned alongside ethics and jurisprudence as one of distinguishable idioms of the order of inquiry concerned with intelligent 'goings-on'.[376] Yet here aesthetics seems to be mentioned in its common meaning as a theoretical activity which analyses art. Secondly, in his account of religion Oakeshott mentions the 'poetic quality' of its images, but it is not clear from this phrase if 'poetic' stands here in the relation of 'conversation' to practice, or whether this is a return to the earlier view from *Experience and Its Modes*.[377] The description of 'self-enactment' and of an 'individual' can be seen as intimating some 'poetical' quality.[378] Yet I tend to think that Oakeshott still considers 'poetical' experience to be irrelevant to practical conduct. He analyses human conduct in terms of the relationships between human agents, and distinguishes between 'acting' and 'fabricating'. In 'acting' the agent is looking for a response from other agents, while in 'fabricating' the imagined outcome is an artefact. Fabricating is usually understood as a performance in 'acting' made in order to evoke a certain response in the conduct of other agents. Only when an artefact is 'recognised as a work of art',[379] is it taken exclusively as the product of fabricating. It follows from this that Oakeshott believes that artistic activity as such does not belong to the realm of 'human conduct'. However, all these brief remarks in *On Human Conduct* hardly say anything substantial about the mode of poetry as such.

In *On History* Oakeshott hints that he still holds the view that poetry is a distinct universe of discourse 'governed by delight'.[380] At the same time, the ambiguity is present in his remarks as he speaks about 'the poetic terms of affection, friendship and love'.[381]

Thus, after the publication of 'The Voice of Poetry' Oakeshott did not publish anything significant on this subject. It seems that his views on the character of poetry still remained ambivalent. Nevertheless, he never repudiated the view expressed in 'The Voice of Poetry', according to which 'poetry' is an autonomous human activity which deserves to be cherished for its own sake.

---

[376] HC, p. 17.
[377] HC, p. 86.
[378] See Worthington, 'Michael Oakeshott on Life.'
[379] HC, p. 35.
[380] OH, p. 26n.
[381] OH, p. 14.

V

To conclude, aestheticism is an ambiguous phenomenon, much harder to grasp than the idea of science for science's sake or history for history's sake. From his early writings, Oakeshott intuitively felt sympathy for the idea of art for art's sake, but did not avoid the ambiguities, uncertainties and contradictions which characterised this view. However, towards his middle period he worked out a view of aesthetic experience, in which he defended its autonomous character. He argued that poetry was one of the important voices of modernity, but at the same time denied it any claims of supremacy to ethics. Poetry is an autonomous activity establishing criteria of its own, but in society it is usually put within an appropriate framework such as a theatre performance.

Oakeshott did not abandon completely the view that life could have aesthetic overtones, which endowed it with a unique value, but realised that these overtones were only 'a brief enchantment'.[382] An intelligent aesthetic education is supposed to teach us how to recognise 'poetry' as an independent world, and not to confuse it with ethical discourse. Poetry, like science or philosophy has nothing to teach about life, it is merely 'a dream within the dream of life'.[383]

CONCLUSION

I

We have now arrived at a clearer view of the character of Oakeshott's philosophy of experience as a philosophy of abstraction. Oakeshott started his intellectual career by publishing a book of which the explicit aim was to explore the character of what is satisfactory in experience. Yet this book entailed an unavoidable contradiction, for its holistic framework concealed, in itself, a sentiment which presupposed a different line of thought. It was not a possible logical unity of knowledge that attracted Oakeshott's attention but a diversity of worldviews in modern society. Pretending to have attempted to disclose the partiality of these worldviews, Oakeshott ended up by vindicating the value of abstraction. He could not hope to find the unity which would provide a justification for the existence of these abstractions. According to Oakeshott, modes of experience must be either superseded or avoided, if the totality of experience is to be achieved. Therefore, abstract worldviews have no

---

[382] 'The Voice of Poetry in the Conversation of Mankind,' RIP, p. 540.
[383] RIP, p. 541.

option except standing on their own feet and proclaiming their own value for the sake of themselves.

His later writings made explicit what had been implied in *Experience and Its Modes*: his preference for abstraction and his defence of it. The ability to understand and accept an abstraction as it is, bears witness both to the dignity and the humility of the modern mind. Humility, because it has abandoned the vain search for the absolute knowledge; dignity, because the recognition of the value of abstraction has freed the mind from the fear of its own inadequacy. Scepticism, which is nothing other than a sign of the lack of self-confidence, can be avoided only if there is the courage to recognise that the abstract is valuable for its own sake.

II

Oakeshott faced, however, some difficulties in attempting to determine the precise character of each worldview. Two modes, philosophy and practice, appeared to be especially problematic, for they might pretend to carry some basic element of unity from which diversity originated. The claims of philosophy were more easily discharged, by ignoring them. Having paid lip service to the totality of experience in *Experience and Its Modes*, Oakeshott dedicated himself to the exploration of abstractions. In 'The Voice of Poetry' he turned philosophy into a 'parasitic' voice and in *On Human Conduct* almost avoided it. By contrast, practice appeared to be a more difficult adversary since it claimed to be present in every human activity. As the analysis of practice in *Experience and Its Modes* was not satisfactory, Oakeshott attempted to find a place for it, without destroying the independence of other modes, in the distinction between the level of understanding and the level of doing that he drew on in *On Human Conduct*.

Nevertheless, between practice at the bottom and philosophy at the top, modern experience developed independent activities such as science, history, and poetry. Their abstract character was easily recognised but because of this they needed protection from the claims of practice. Attempting to protect each of these worldviews, Oakeshott pushed to the extreme the most radical available approaches which supported their claims for independence in the purest form. He adopted the most extreme positivistic view with regard to science, attributing to it an uncompromisingly quantitative character; he saw history as the narration of change in which what is known is what the evidence obliges us to believe; and he found poetic delight to be the exclusive feature of aesthetic experience.

Oakeshott rejected any attempts to combine the claims of each mode for objectivity and detachment with the recognition of the subjective element in them. This attempt, undertaken by Carr in history and Eddington in science, would ultimately destroy the integrity of a mode instead of saving it. When the consistent view is compromised, nothing can prevent the argument being pressed to its conclusion, thus resulting in relativism.

Oakeshott, therefore, adopted positions similar to those of Poincaré in science, of Collingwood and Croce in history and of Collingwood and then Bullough in poetry, because they appeared to be radical vindications of these worldviews. Poincaré was not a 'predecessor' of Kuhn's relativism but rather a defender of the idea of scientific 'objectivity' and science for science's sake. Croce and Collingwood are often seen as 'proto-post-modernistic' critics of history but their efforts were directed to the affirmation of history; and notwithstanding the pragmatism present in Collingwood's view of art, he is at pains to free the artist from short-term social duties.

Moreover, when adopting these radical approaches, Oakeshott tends to formulate them in an even more radical form. Thus, he moves beyond Poincaré when he ignores the alleged existence of 'indifferent' hypotheses in science, claiming that any scientific statement which is not analytic must be statistical. With regard to science, his rejection of metaphysics is uncompromising and reminiscent of that of logical positivism. Likewise, he goes further than Croce or Collingwood, claiming that historical experience is present experience, but precisely because of this, it is certain experience. The historian says only what the evidence obliges him to believe. In his aesthetic theory, Oakeshott abandons the view that the artist in some way contributes to society's self-consciousness, and adopts, though not without some doubt, the complete separation between aesthetic and moral or scientific considerations.

If Oakeshott's statements are taken apart from the logic of his own thought and outside the intellectual context of his time, this may lead to a confused attempt to perceive Oakeshott's views as close to the post-modernistic deconstruction of scientific and historical objectivity and of aesthetic detachment. Yet this would be a grave misrepresentation. A relativist, finding science and history to be not exact representations of the outside reality but mental constructions determined by conventional paradigms, throws doubt on the claims for the independence and integrity of their method. Oakeshott, on the contrary, finds here the only way to save these worldviews from self-destruction. When he insists that history does not show the past *wie es gesentlich gewesen*, he does not reject the methodology of the professional study of history associated with this view. He only means that this phrase is ill-conceived and that a less vulnerable vindication of this methodology can be found in his own philosophy of history.

III

This radical theory of modes is the most important and original element of Oakeshott's philosophy of experience. This philosophy quite surprisingly turns out to be lacking a metaphysics of its own, as the general framework is lost in the analysis of different worldviews.

Each mode is understood to be an end in itself, yet it is important to avoid the danger that after achieving inner coherence within its own system of postulates, each worldview might try to claim to be the truest expression of the whole of experience, thus committing the sin of *superbia*. This fault would be dangerous not only to the freedom of other modes but also to the purity of the dominant mode itself. For, while the claims of each mode are infallible when taken within postulated limits, they would be ridiculous and open the way to scepticism and relativism when seen as the whole truth. For example, scientific understanding is always quantitative understanding, but if science pretends to be the truest representation of reality, it comes under attack which it is unable to withstand because a quantitative description cannot explain the totality of experience.

A proper consciousness is one in which each voice recognises itself within its own limits and does not move beyond them. Each mode is required to demonstrate the capacity for rigid self-discipline and the ability to enjoy its own nature without imposing itself on others. In *Experience and Its Modes* there is no direct relation between modes, and philosophy is one which is able to elucidate the character of each of them from the standpoint of the totality of experience. But this view involves a serious difficulty, for philosophy cannot help rejecting and superseding these modes so that any exposure of a mode to a consideration from outside destroys it. The change of the framework in 'The Voice of Poetry' helps to solve this problem. The voices are completely independent but they are engaged in a certain kind of relationship which is the relationship of 'conversation'. Each voice has an ability to understand the idiom of another. There are 'innate tendencies towards barbarism' in some voices.[384] Yet when voices meet, they are able to be 'kindled by the presence of ideas of another order'.[385] Being engaged in such a kind of relationship, voices seem to be able to limit themselves to appropriate idioms of their own, recognising these idioms as essential for the preservation of their integrity. The civilised mind is one which avoids confusion and maintains the proper conversationalist relationship between its worldviews. Therefore, 'it is the ability to participate in this conversation, and not the ability to reason cogently, to make discoveries about the world, or to contrive a better world, which distinguish the human being from the animal and the civilised man from the barbarian.'[386] And such a civilised mind is an essentially modern mind.

Furthermore, mind always comes into contact with a society, and without such contact it would be empty. The conversation 'goes on both in public and within each of ourselves'.[387] Science, history and poetry may exist as worldviews within a particular mind. But they are also disciplines in university education. Furthermore, on an even larger scale, science, history and poetry are social activities. So long as the members of a society have developed the principles of civility within their minds, they are likely to maintain the conversation between themselves in a society and preserve the independence and flourishing of every activity.

The only society which has achieved a great measure of the recognition of the conversational character of relationships between its activities is, in Oakeshott's view, modern Western society. By virtue of a long historical process such activities succeeded in emancipating themselves from the dictates of the practical voice, and declared their independence. What is valuable in our civilisation is to a large extent the result of this process of emancipation. Modernity thus gives us a unique opportunity to value things for what they are and not for what effect they will have.

This view entails an unavoidable problem since, although modern Western society may differ from all others by the fact of the plurality of worldviews it maintains, this plurality is incomplete, and some confusion between different worldviews is rarely avoided. As a result, there is tension between Oakeshott's claim that he describes modes as they are, and the strong normative aspect of his philosophy. He establishes strict criteria for every voice but, having done so, he analyses not the activities as they are actually pursued but their

---
[384] RIP, pp. 491-492.
[385] RIP, p. 489.
[386] RIP, p. 490.
[387] *Ibid*.

ideal types. Many sciences are in this sense imperfect sciences and many historical inquiries are biased inquiries. Oakeshott admits this in 'The Activity of Being an Historian'. Moreover, he himself does not avoid the overlap between modes, and sometimes, as has been shown, makes connections between, say, poetry and practice. But at the same time he intends to show that the recognition of plurality is the peculiar feature of our civilisation and it is this which makes it valuable. Its plurality, however imperfect in reality, must be preserved and, when explored theoretically, radically affirmed.

This radical plurality leads, however, to another difficulty which can hardly be avoided. Oakeshott effectively denies the existence of some underlying principle behind this plurality. The voices do not compose any logical system and nothing extraneous to them can serve as a philosophical justification of their existence. What, then, can prevent them from disintegrating? This radical plurality seems to be logically unsustainable because, in the absence of some fundamental principle, it is likely to lead to a further disintegration, thus making rigid adherence to the character of each mode impossible. This is why those philosophers who feared disintegration invested so much in looking for an idea which would serve as a basic point behind this diversity. Oakeshott does not look for such system and, for him, a rational justification is impossible. The preservation of plurality cannot be based on a logical argument. This conclusion affects Oakeshott's view concerning the kind of education which he thinks to be appropriate in the modern condition. But before we present this view, it is necessary to discuss Oakeshott's philosophy of society as such and to deal with the mode of practice and his later explorations of social, moral and political issues which have been left untouched in this chapter.

Chapter 3
Philosophy of Society

> Political philosophy may be understood to be what occurs when this movement of reflection takes a certain direction and achieves a certain level, its characteristic being the relation of political life, and the values and purposes pertaining to it, to the entire conception of the world that belongs to a civilization.   'Introduction' to *Leviathan*, 1946

INTRODUCTION
I

In the previous chapter I have attempted to unravel Oakeshott's philosophy of experience and its particular aspects such as philosophy of science, history and poetry. Yet my main preoccupation in this study has not been these various branches of philosophy as such, but rather their significance from the standpoint of Oakeshott's thought as a whole, the vision behind it, and its impact on our understanding of the modern human condition. As we have seen, Oakeshott's philosophy of experience provides a map of self-understanding of our civilisation. In particular, it helps to establish the freedom and integrity of various intellectual activities, as these relate to the important controversies of the age.

Now we reach the other part of Oakeshott's thought which can be called philosophy of society. It is directly preoccupied with social life, and its subject-matter is not an intellectual adventure in understanding the world but the question of human relationships in a society. Before embarking on a discussion of its character, it is necessary to make some preliminary remarks about the method of exposition.

II

It has already been stated that Oakeshott's philosophy of society and his philosophy of experience are understood here to be two aspects of his thought, different in subject-matter but analogous in the character of their argument. Towards the end of this chapter hopefully it will become clear where this analogy lies and how the structure of the philosophy of experience helps to elucidate some aspects of the philosophy of society. However, the method of the presentation here will be different from the previous chapter and it is necessary to explain in what respect and why.

Oakeshott's philosophy of experience represents an almost accomplished whole from the outset. His basic views are clearly present in his first major work *Experience and Its Modes* and they remain the same in his later writings, notwithstanding some qualifications and differences of approach which modify the major framework but do not destroy it. My presentation of that part of his thought has been structured accordingly in a relatively simple way. The major postulates are explained in general terms in the introduction and conclusion whereas the sections in the middle serve to exemplify the points which have been asserted.

This is not the case with Oakeshott's philosophy of society. *On Human Conduct*, which is his major work in this sphere, is an outcome of a long intellectual development. Oakeshott's early views are indeed connected with *On Human Conduct* for there is a strong continuity in his thought, and various claims elaborated philosophically in the later treatise are already implicitly present in many of his earlier writings. Yet the difference between the early and later writings is not small and it is impossible to appreciate the significance of *On Human Conduct* without first trying to understand the intellectual development that precedes it. Therefore, unlike the previous chapter, this one has to present Oakeshott's philosophy of society gradually, paying attention to some views which are rejected later and elaborating on some nuances, the significance of which will become clear only towards the end of the discussion. There is, it is hoped, an inner logic in this exposition but it can only be revealed in a gradual way.

Furthermore, social and political thought was the subject of Oakeshott's own teaching, on which he wrote quite a lot and, paradoxically, this requires a more cautious approach. For Oakeshott's writings on other philosophical subjects are few in number but at the same time they are carefully thought through, offering a more or less considered view and representing only what is really important to him. In the sphere of the philosophy of society, however, the collection of his writings is more miscellaneous. While some are genuine philosophical works, others are occasional pieces which reveal Oakeshott's preoccupations but do not necessarily contribute to the coherence of his thought. Some judgement with regard to the importance of different works is required but it would be unwise to disregard minor writings completely for, even if they do not necessarily lead us towards understanding the general character of Oakeshott's philosophy, they reveal nuances of his thought and problems with which he was preoccupied. Therefore, the form of the analysis of Oakeshott's philosophy of society is bound to be less coherent.

At the same time, I will try not to lose the thread completely and to accentuate those aspects which are important for understanding his philosophy of society as a whole, and the order of priorities here does not necessarily correspond with that of many other commentators. Oakeshott became known as a political philosopher before the publication of his principal tract *On Human Conduct* and, therefore, for many years the study of his thought focused on those aspects which were not necessarily the central part of his philosophy. For example, as it will be shown, the preoccupation with his critique of Rationalism is exaggerated and often leads to a misleading interpretation of the rest of his thought. The hope is to keep these aspects in proportion, without neglecting them.

Finally, there is a question of the role of the contemporary intellectual context in both parts of Oakeshott's thought. The relations of elements of his philosophy of experience to intellectual trends of the period are relatively straightforward and articulating them is indispensable for the correct understanding of his thought. For example, without grasping that Oakeshott's philosophy of science is an exposition of the doctrine of scientific positivism in its most uncompromised form opposed to any kind of relativism, it is impossible to understand what he wants to say in the philosophy of experience. However, the contemporary context of the philosophy of society is less direct, for his thought here is more transformative and it absorbs a great number of different intellectual influences. Oakeshott was, of course, influenced by his contemporaries and by some, such as Hayek or Jouvenel, more than others.[1] But the transformation of these influences into a significantly more esoteric philosophy makes them a less certain guide, for similarities here are often deceptive and the more philosophical Oakeshott's thought

---

[1] See Oakeshott's Review of B. de Jouvenel, *Sovereignty*, in *Crossbow* 1, 1957, pp. 43-44; letter to F.A. Hayek, April 30, 1968, Hoover Institute Archives.

becomes, the less significant the immediate context appears to be. I will try to reveal some possible parallels and influences — especially in the third section where the development of Oakeshott's social and political views is discussed. However, where his writings are more philosophical, it is more important to pay attention to the inner logic of his ideas.

III

There is an additional possible source of confusion which is a tendency to characterise Oakeshott's thought as mainly 'political philosophy'. This term may be misleading because of the legacy of the separation of various social sciences in which 'political' refers to the study of government and political institutions. Oakeshott would regard this separation as artificial. There is no Oakeshott political philosophy in this narrow sense. For Oakeshott, politics is an integral part of the relationships between human beings within the human collective. His thought continues the nineteenth-century tradition of human studies, thus regarding the questions of morality, laws and institutions to be merely parts of social theory as a whole. In this sense, Oakeshott is close to what is known as the tradition of classical sociology which can be traced from thinkers such as Montesquieu, Hegel and Tocqueville to Weber and Jouvenel. His study of society is therefore a study of the basic postulates of human relationships and it is 'political' only if it is understood as 'the study of all agencies tending to establish and develop the conditions of fruitful co-operation between them'.[2] Or, as the young Oakeshott said himself, explaining his dissatisfaction with how politics was taught at Cambridge when he was an undergraduate in the twenties: 'I desired to know what I ought to think about our life as human beings in society.'[3] He pointed out that genuine political philosophy deals first of all not with institutions but with men.[4] Oakeshott, therefore, never concentrated on the study of institutions as such but always considered them in the context of the beliefs and habits of human beings whose actions had led to the appearance and preservation of these institutions. For him, the question of the character of the state and government is intrinsically linked to the analysis of the character of the society, morals, and individuals composing a state. Oakeshott's philosophy of society includes not only what is

---

[2] Bertrand de Jouvenel, *Sovereignty: An Inquiry into the Political Good*, trans. J.F. Huntington (Indianapolis: Liberty Fund, 1997), p. 359.
[3] CSPS, p. 4.
[4] CSPS, p. 12.

regarded as a 'proper' political philosophy but also a philosophy of practice and morality.

Therefore, the structure of this chapter is as follows. The next section will present the development of Oakeshott's views with regard to human conduct and morality in general. It will be shown how Oakeshott's views develop from the early presentation in *Experience and Its Modes* towards *On Human Conduct*. The third section will explore Oakeshott's more political writings, pointing to their affinity with the sentiments of some trends of European liberalism. And the fourth section will explore Oakeshott's peculiar theory of the civil condition which lies at the heart of *On Human Conduct*. This theory is founded on the assumptions of Oakeshott's philosophy of conduct and it incorporates his earlier liberal sentiments, thereby completing his philosophy of society. It will also be explained how his philosophy of society corresponds with his philosophy of experience.

PRACTICE, MORALITY, INDIVIDUALITY
I

Oakeshott's philosophy of practice and morality has attracted significantly more attention than his philosophy of science, history or aesthetics. Many commentators have come to see Oakeshott mainly as a philosopher of 'practice' or of 'practical knowledge',[5] and as a representative of an alleged tendency of British conservatism to treat 'intellectualism' with suspicion.

The reasons for this attitude are obvious. Firstly, the interpretation of Oakeshott's ethical–moral views was seen as a necessary stage in the understanding of his political philosophy. Secondly, Oakeshott published much more on this subject than on such topics as science or art. The questions of practice and morality occupy the central role in his most famous essays such as 'Rationalism in Politics' and 'The Tower of Babel'.

However, this relatively large number of published writings bears witness to the complexity of the subject. Usually, Oakeshott chose to publish his works only when he thought he had reached a more or less comprehensive and satisfactory understanding of the problems

---

[5] On Oakeshott as a philosopher of 'practice' see, for example, Josiah Lee Auspitz, 'Individuality, Civility, and Theory: The Philosophical Imagination of Michael Oakeshott,' *Political Theory* 4(3), 1976, pp. 261-294; John Casey, 'Philosopher of Practice,' in J. Norman (ed.), *The Achievement of Michael Oakeshott* (London: Duckworth, 1993), pp. 58-66; Andrew Sullivan, *Intimations Pursued: The Voice of Practice in the Conversation of Michael Oakeshott* (PhD diss., Harvard University, 1990).

he was dealing with. Yet he published a significant number of essays concerned with conduct and morality, constantly modifying his views, and approaching the subject from different angles. This suggests that it took him more time and effort to reach a fully satisfactory view.

This fact, combined with the tendency of commentators to focus exclusively on Oakeshott's practical philosophy, led to the perception of him as an unsystematic thinker. Yet it seems that there is a logic behind the evolution of his views, and that the changes in his practical philosophy are not accidental but reflect an attempt to reach a coherent theoretical position, which would conform to the underlying vision of his entire philosophical project. Such a position is in fact formulated in his later book *On Human Conduct*.

The purpose of this section is to analyse the major changes in Oakeshott's philosophy of practice and to show what was achieved in *On Human Conduct*. The evolution of Oakeshott's views will be dealt with in three different aspects: the practical mode of experience, the notion of morality, and the idea of self and individuality. As I did in the previous sections, I do not intend to write a comprehensive summary of Oakeshott's works but to provide a general framework for a better understanding of his main concerns.

II

In the previous chapter we have seen that one of the central aspects of Oakeshott's thought is the conditionality of human experience and understanding. Our experience consists of a variety of homogeneous worldviews which can exist only within the system of their own postulates. The confusion between them leads to the logical error of irrelevance.

We have already analysed three such worldviews: science, history, and poetry. In addition to these Oakeshott describes another voice which he calls 'practical experience' in *Experience and Its Modes*, or 'the language of practice' in 'The Voice of Poetry'. In his first presentation of practice in *Experience and Its Modes* Oakeshott claims that it is an abstract mode of experience, and he analyses it in a way similar to his analysis of other modes. He defines its presuppositions and explains why they turn 'practice' into an abstraction irrelevant to concrete experience or to other abstract modes.

Given this structure of argument, one would expect a certain symmetry between 'practice' and the other modes. For example, practice could be presented as a homogeneous world of experience, valuable in itself. In his dealing with history and science Oakeshott employed the most radical philosophy available to him in order to assert their autonomy, while at the same time disclaiming their claims to superiority. With regard to the conduct of life there was no shortage of contemporary theories which would serve Oakeshott's purpose to maintain the exclusivity of practice. It could be found in the philosophy of life of Bergson and Eucken, or in some trends of pragmatism. One of the most radical versions of the primacy of 'life' was perhaps promulgated by Albert Schweitzer in his *Civilization and Ethics*.[6] Oakeshott was familiar with Schweitzer's writings and he mentioned this particular book on several occasions.[7]

Schweitzer's view can be described as the defence of life for life's sake. Following the intellectual mood of his age he understood the condition of Western civilisation as a tragic fragmentation of our knowledge and experience. Having lost a comprehensive worldview, modern Western civilisation found itself 'devoid of any world-view at all, therefore of any civilization.'[8] To find such an ideal should be the main task of Western civilization if it wants to survive. And where others found this ideal in science, history, or art, Schweitzer found it in life and ethics. Our civilization should be based on an adherence towards an ethical ideal which is called 'reverence for life'. Yet this ideal cannot be supported by philosophy. Philosophers tried to find the knowledge of ethics and failed for the reason that there is the 'dualism of world-view and life-view, of knowledge and volition'.[9] The two cannot be reconciled, they cannot live in harmony with each other, and we are, therefore, 'obliged to make up our minds to give preference to the latter'.[10] Like other modernist intellectuals Schweitzer despaired of the attempt to find a comprehensive worldview which would incorporate ethics, and therefore insisted on the full independence and primacy of the ethical realm.

In a certain sense Oakeshott uses this sort of view in a way familiar to us through his philosophies of science, history and poetry. Like Schweitzer, he maintains that practice is completely independent from philosophy, but nevertheless valuable as an abstraction. Philosophy cannot be of any relevance to life, for 'from the standpoint of practical experience there can be no more dangerous disease than the love and pursuit of truth in those who do not understand, or

---

[6] Albert Schweitzer, *Civilization and Ethics: The Philosophy of Civilization Part II*, trans. J. Naish (London: A. & C. Black, 1923).
[7] ERPPR ; DSM, p. 182.
[8] Schweitzer, *Civilization and Ethics*, p. viii.
[9] *Ibid.*, p. xiv.
[10] *Ibid.*, p. xv.

have forgotten, that a man's first business is to live'.[11] And the character of reflection employed in practical experience in order to lead the examined life has no relation whatsoever to the quest of philosophy.[12] Yet unlike Schweitzer Oakeshott rejects the view that it is a mode of experience which should possess superiority. Practice should not attempt to impose itself on other, non-practical modes, since such an attempt will lead to nothing but confusion and irrelevance.

This position, however, leads to serious difficulties which did not arise in the case of science or history. These difficulties are analysed in detail by Andrew Sullivan in his description of Oakeshott's approach towards practice in *Experience and Its Modes*. According to Sullivan, these difficulties derive partly from Oakeshott's unwillingness to separate completely practice from philosophy, notwithstanding all the claims to the contrary. Sullivan argues that for Oakeshott, practice is a privileged mode in comparison with other abstract modes, and that its relationship with philosophy is one of tension in which there is both the 'conviction of the separateness of philosophy and practice and yet also of their inescapable entanglement'.[13] In my analysis of practice I will follow some of Sullivan's insights, but at the same time reach different conclusions. I agree that practice is a different sort of mode, yet I do not believe that, for Oakeshott, it is a 'privileged' mode of experience.

Oakeshott's view of practice may be briefly described as follows. Practice is a world of experience. It is not 'a tissue of mere conjunctions',[14] but a world, an attempt to achieve what is satisfactory in experience, that is, concrete experience. Like every experience, it unavoidably involves thought and judgement, since 'volition is itself thought and not the mere result of thought.'[15] This experience is based on certain presuppositions. It postulates the world understood under the category of change. Practical experience is always an action, directed to the alteration of existence, and even the activity of preservation is actually an alteration. Therefore it involves the discrepancy between what is here and now, and what is yet to be.

These 'here and now' and 'yet to be' are moments of two distinct worlds within the world of practical experience: the world of practical fact and the world of what 'ought to be', in other words the world of value. These two worlds within the world of practical experience

---

[11] EM, p. 320.
[12] EM, p. 303.
[13] Sullivan, *Intimations Pursued*, p. 81.
[14] EM, p. 250.
[15] EM, p. 252.

possess presuppositions of their own. Thus, the world of 'here and now' has its own explicit concepts of fact, truth and reality. This is the world of the present as such which lacks internal stability. What is true now can be untrue later, the fact of today is a 'non-fact' of tomorrow. It always presupposes a situation which is subject to change, and the achievement of a certain outcome just creates a new situation demanding an alteration. It is a world of separate selves which are recognised as possessing independent wills and acting under the category of freedom.

The other world is the world of valuation. It is an independent mode of experience which cannot be reduced to 'what is' as a mode. Yet it does exist in a certain sense. The world of 'ought to be' belongs only to practical experience, because whatever is regarded as a value is recognised not as a fancy, but as something which is capable of existing here and now. It is 'a world of being'.

In practical experience there is an attempt to reconcile 'what is' and 'what ought to be', but not theoretically, not between the two worlds as worlds (it would be impossible as those are two different abstract worlds), but between two particular instances of 'what is' and what is 'not yet'. And if the future state of things appears to possess 'superior coherency', this specific action becomes a duty or obligation.[16] Yet the category of duty cannot serve as the most concrete reconciliation because 'every achievement brings with it a new view of the criterion, which converts this momentary perfection into imperfection.'[17] Reconciliation is achieved only in religion which is regarded as 'the form of practical activity in which this attempt is carried furthest ... it is merely practical experience at its fullest.'[18] Religion is seen not as a system of dogmas, not as a theology, but as a conduct, in which the integrity of self is achieved through the focus on the devotion to one's own way of life. The conduct of life is 'a rare and peculiar genius which enables a man to see clearly what belongs to his life and to follow it without reserve, unhindered by the restraint of prudence or the impediment of doubt'.[19] Here Oakeshott follows Bradley, according to whom religion transcends the self-contradiction of 'is' and 'to be' inherent in morality, so that the ideal self is 'considered as realised and real'.[20] However, there are limits to the extent of integration that even religion can achieve, and certainly it never achieves what is satisfactory in experience. It is still

[16] EM, p. 280n.
[17] EM, p. 291.
[18] EM, p. 292.
[19] EM, p. 295.
[20] F.H. Bradley, *Ethical Studies* (Oxford: Clarendon Press, 1927), p. 319.

subject to the practical presuppositions of change, finality and the permanent discrepancy between 'is' and 'ought'.

There are several things to be said about this view, and the most salient is that there is no symmetry between the character and status of the mode of practice and that of other modes. Firstly, the practical mode seems to be much more incoherent than either science or history. We have already seen that Oakeshott considered both history and science to be homogeneous modes of experience, which, while being incapable of achieving the ultimate satisfaction in experience, are nevertheless self-contained and autonomous. The argument about their inner defectiveness is relatively brief and looks somewhat artificial. In contrast, practical experience seems to be inherently discrepant and incoherent. The very presupposition of practice as the never ending attempt to reconcile what 'is' with what is 'not yet' implies such a discrepancy.

Moreover, the practical mode of experience itself consists of two modes of experience, each with presuppositions of its own. The reconciliation is attempted between specific moments of 'what is' and 'what is ought to be', and not between the two worlds as worlds, since 'the world of value and the world of practical fact are two worlds, and to pass directly from one to the other, or to attempt an explanation of one in terms of the character of the other, must always involve an *ignoratio elenchi*.'[21] Yet it is unclear how this assertion fits into Oakeshott's framework. Nowhere do we find a discussion of whether a specific reconciliation may be just an aspect of the confusion between these worlds. But, even granting this point, the difficulty is still present, since Oakeshott elsewhere claims that two different abstract modes must be completely irrelevant to each other, and this is obviously not the case about the relations of either of these two worlds to the world of practical experience. They are necessary parts of this world.

Secondly, while being a less homogeneous world, practice is at the same time the most unavoidable. For it seems to be present in every activity, including that of philosophy, science and history. How history can be an abstract world of experience is clear, for one can perhaps have an experience of life without ever making a judgement recognised as historical. But one cannot live without making a practical judgement. Oakeshott recognises this distinct feature of practice, and his answer is that, although practice may be unavoidable, it does not possess a logical priority. Practical judgement is not the only criterion of judgement, and if practice cannot be avoided, it

---

[21] EM, p. 284.

'must be superseded'.[22] But this still leaves many questions open, as, for example, whether practice possesses, even if not the whole truth, at least a larger degree of truth in comparison to science and history.

Practice, then, is presented as both more and less of a world than history and science. It seems to be less coherent, and at the same time more basic. This asymmetry leads Sullivan to suggest that practice is in some sense a privileged mode. He even argues that Oakeshott may have considered the world of 'value' to stand close to the world of philosophy, since other forms of experience such as science and history can in principle be subject to the criticism of the world of value.

The interpretation here is different. It seems that Oakeshott regards practice not as a more privileged world but as a more threatening one. It is true that he defends the identity of practice, but this point is similar to science and history.[23] The difference lies in his emphasis on the defects of this world of experience, and on its obvious lack of coherence, which is not the case with other modes. Precisely because practice seems to be omnipresent, Oakeshott is much more concerned with combating its claims to represent the concrete truth. A Heideggerian notion of 'being' would be fully rejected by him. The entire argument of *Experience and Its Modes* is to show that there is something more valuable than 'holiday excursions' of practice. Oakeshott does not privilege practice, but degrades it. And yet, in this attempt he unavoidably steps into a minefield. For by describing practice as an abstract mode he must assert its identity, suppress his suspicions about it, and provide an apology for its character.

There is, however, an additional reason why one may wish to interpret practical experience as a privileged mode. It is the inclusion into practice of those activities which are usually perceived as being a part of contemplative, and not active life. I already referred to the important role which is assigned to religion. Oakeshott also includes the artist and the mystic under the category of the practical man. As he does not elaborate much on this point, it is difficult to describe the role of the artist and the mystic in this context. Yet this makes Oakeshott's view of practice more ambiguous, because mentioning the artist may indicate that Oakeshott assigned a higher value to practical experience than to scientific and historical experience.

In subsequent writings Oakeshott removes this ambiguity, and makes his position more clear. In 'The Voice of Poetry in the Conver-

---

[22] EM, p. 311.
[23] EM, p. 320.

sation of Mankind' described by Oakeshott as 'a belated retraction of a foolish sentence in *Experience and Its Modes*',[24] he removes poetic experience outside of the realm of practice. Oakeshott purges the language of practice of anything reminiscent of contemplation or detachment. Practical imagining is presented as subject to two postulates. Similar to *Experience and Its Modes* it is described both in terms of the world of will and the world of morals. Yet Oakeshott's description of both worlds and of their relationship is different from that given in the former book. Here the constituents of the world *sub specie voluntatis* are 'images of pleasure and pain', which can also be called the images of desire and aversion.[25] This world is described as consisting of egoistic solitary selves pursuing their desires. The other world, that *sub specie moris* is composed of 'images of approval and disapproval'.[26] This world is concerned with the relations between different selves engaged in practical activities.

This description certainly presents practice as a less attractive voice. While in *Experience and Its Modes* practical experience postulated at least the attempt to reconcile the discrepancy of fact and value, no such qualified reconciliation is suggested here. All activity, though conditioned by morals, is directed to the fulfilment of desires. The description of the world of will is stated in Hobbesian or utilitarian terms. The moral world is presented in terms of the language of approval and disapproval, similar to the 'emotivist' approach developed by logical positivists since Ayer.[27] Practice is the main and most dangerous adversary of those voices which Oakeshott attempts to defend — mainly history and poetry. And in an unpublished essay, 'Work and Play', written apparently at the same period, Oakeshott is even more explicit in his distinction between 'practice' (work) and other voices (play) which are in some sense higher activities.[28]

Another change is that the term 'value' disappears from Oakeshott's vocabulary, and the world of value is called here the world of morals. Therefore, it cannot be argued here that the practical voice is a higher one by virtue of containing the world of value. One can suggest that value is not the exclusive dominion of the world of practice, and that it is possible to speak about non-practical voices as valuable in a certain non-moral sense. Even if Oakeshott

---

[24] RIP, p. xi.
[25] RIP, p. 498.
[26] RIP, p. 501.
[27] See Alfred Jules Ayer, *Language, Truth and Logic* (London: Victor Gollancz, 1967).
[28] WP.

never uses the term 'value' with respect to abstract voices, perhaps because of its ambiguity, his theory no longer precludes interpreting these voices as possessing a value.

Thus, Oakeshott makes his attitude to practice less ambiguous. But there still remains a difficulty inherent in seeing practice as merely another abstract voice. Though in 'Work and Play' Oakeshott puts the practical activity below others, the difference between them in this respect is not yet articulated. Practice remains one of the abstract languages, notwithstanding the great differences between it and other voices.

Only in *On Human Conduct* does Oakeshott radically transform his view in such a way that allows a reinterpretation of the role of practice so that it will fit into his general philosophy. The central change is that Oakeshott completely removes practical experience out of the dimension of abstract worlds. Beyond the distinction between different modes, he postulates a more basic distinction between levels of 'understanding' and 'doing'.[29]

What were previously regarded as modes of experience become theorems *within* the level of understanding. Theorems of different kinds are constructed by a theorist in his attempt to elucidate reality. Historical and scientific understandings are theorems of such sort. The sphere of understanding itself is not a coherent whole. It includes two 'orders of inquiry' completely irrelevant to each other.

There is no place for 'practical experience' on this level. What was previously a 'practical' mode is transferred to the level of 'doing'. 'Doing' relates specifically to human conduct understood as a relation *inter homines*. There are two aspects of human conduct, which are present in every action but are theoretically distinct. Firstly, an action is a performance designed to evoke a certain response from other agents, and it can be analysed in terms of its purpose. Secondly, it can be seen in the context of conditions to which it 'subscribes'. These conditions are considerations which an agent must take into account while performing a certain action, although they themselves do not specify agents' substantive choices of goals and actions. These procedural conditions are called 'practices'. There is a multiplicity of practices in every society, and one performance may be conditioned by several practices — such as the language in which it is uttered, the rules of the game etc. Practices may be articulated in specific rules, but most are implicit, and even those which are explicitly formulated, are usually richer than their rules. The most general practice is called a 'moral practice'. A morality is 'the *ars artium* of

---

[29] HC, p. 33.

conduct; the practice of all practices; the practice of agency without further specification.'[30] In other words, it is a practice to which all performances and all other practices ought to subscribe. Unlike most other practices, morality has no extrinsic purpose. Its rules are not directed to some substantive purpose, and it is subscribed to irrespective of any possible result. Yet it shares the essential characteristics of all practices. Like others, it does not command, does not issue orders to do *this* rather than *that*, but qualifies performances of agents, each pursuing his own choices.

One can immediately see the change in the vocabulary and the structure here. The category of 'conduct' generally corresponds to what was previously regarded as 'practical'. Yet conduct *inter homines* is seen differently from the early notion of practice because it contains not one 'practical experience' but a multiplicity of practices. 'Practice' therefore dissolves into 'practices'.

Thus, Oakeshott operates on two different levels. One level is that of understanding with its multiplicity of theoretical undertakings; the other (bottom) level is that of conduct with its multiplicities of practices and selves. The sphere of 'doing' or 'conduct' is now distinct from the sphere of 'understanding' and no longer occupies the place of an abstract mode alongside others. Homogeneous abstractions are left on the level of theoretical (but not philosophical) understanding. 'Conduct' is no longer seen as such a homogeneous abstraction. It is analogous not to modes of experience but to the level of understanding as a whole. There is no homogeneity in the relationship of different coherent ways of theorising on the level of understanding and, likewise, there is no homogeneity in the sphere of human conduct.

Even religion is no longer seen as supplying the necessary integrity to conduct. It is described as 'a reconciliation to the unavoidable dissonances of a human condition',[31] or 'a reconciliation to nothingness.'[32] Its best achievement is in 'a graceful acceptance of the *rerum mortalia*', its dignity is in 'the intrepidity of its acknowledgement of this human condition'.[33] Thus, no longer the consummation of practical life, religion in this more restrained account plays the role of consolation. It merely reconciles us to the dissonances of life, but does not overcome them.

The joyfulness present in *Experience and Its Modes* disappears. There practical experience was an intimation of eternal youthful-

---
[30] HC, p. 60.
[31] HC, p. 81.
[32] HC, p. 84.
[33] HC, p. 86.

ness, the joy of life, an attempt to live fully and without reservations. The concrete reality had to supersede the world of practical experience, but could never take its place: 'The splendours of the firmament of time / May be *eclipsed*, but are *extinguished* not.'[34]

In *On Human Conduct*, however, Oakeshott uses the same verse in order to say the opposite. Suggesting that the attempt to achieve immortality by the devotion to a great purpose is nothing but an illusion, he speaks about 'the iniquity of oblivion *eclipsed* by posthumous glory. But what is thus concealed in the illusion of affairs is not thereby *extinguished*.'[35] Previously it was life which could by eclipsed, but could not be extinguished. Now, it is the fact of the illusion in practical affairs which is eclipsed by devotion, but not extinguished. Oakeshott seems no longer to believe in the possibility of the full integration of practical experience.

III

The character of the development of Oakeshott's philosophy of practice can be, therefore, summarised in this way. In the beginning, Oakeshott approached practice as a mode of experience. Yet this assumption created more problems than it solved. The mode of practice could not be seen as homogeneous in itself. This destroyed the symmetry of Oakeshott's philosophy of experience and even threatened to collapse the entire framework of his thought.

Later, Oakeshott transformed his notion of practice. He replaced it with the category of conduct which was supposed to be not a coherent whole but a sphere containing a multiplicity of abstract identities. We will see what these identities are in the next part of this section. Beforehand, however, it is necessary to deal with the question of whether the description of morality in *On Human Conduct* is able to bestow homogeneity upon the level of conduct. In order to see this, we should analyse the development of Oakeshott's view of morality more closely.

Oakeshott is often labelled as a traditionalist and is sometimes perceived as a typical conservative moralist. This perception, however, should be located in its proper place. Oakeshott used to call himself an 'Edwardian', and this reference to the years of his early life certainly indicates his distrust of many changes in British society since then. However, his 'Edwardian' identity can also be seen in the context of its relation to the previous Victorian age. Despite the great continuity in the moral attitudes of both periods, the self-under-

[34] EM, p. 321. Italics mine — E.P.
[35] HC, p. 84. Italics mine — E.P.

standing of the intellectuals of the Edwardian era was partly formed in terms of a reaction to the concerns of preceding generations. As Stefan Collini argues, Victorian intellectual life was characterised by the cultural domination of a certain type of intellectual, whom he calls the 'public moralist', and whose main features were an obsessive emphasis on the primacy of the ethical and a concern with the training of will and the building of character. This was combined with an emphasis on altruism, often expressed in religious and quasi-religious rhetoric, leading often to a preoccupation with questions of social responsibility.[36]

To some extent Oakeshott is an heir to this intellectual atmosphere, especially in his emphasis on the idea of 'character', of which the main characteristic is courage, the ability not to be 'unnerved', which, he thought, was an essential element of 'Englishness'.[37] Yet despite the continuity, Oakeshott's thought represents a serious departure from that sort of ethical reasoning. Moreover, it is that type of public moralist who is an implicit target of many of his criticisms.

Of the many British writers of the interwar period Oakeshott seems to be one of the most radical critics of the pre-eminence of the ethical. His attitude towards the intellectual figures of the Victorian period is complex. He may admire some of them, who, like Arnold and Mill, were influenced by European romanticism and humanism, and directed their arrows against what they saw as the middle class philistinism of their own society. Yet he is always suspicious of their role as 'moralists', their perfectionism, which is prone to collapse into preachery. He esteems greatly the figure of F.W. Maitland, yet, as Collini argues, Maitland's writings do not fit into the pattern of the public moralist, representing a further stage of academic specialisation.[38] And this is, perhaps, the reason for Oakeshott's praise of Maitland who is quoted as an exemplar of the historian undisturbed by practical considerations.[39]

By contrast, in an obituary of Lord Acton, Oakeshott explains the latter's failure to produce any substantial body of historical writings, or to become a successful politician, as 'the outcome of his refusal to admit the imperfect, to allow anything to come between

---

[36] See Stefan Collini, *Public Moralists: Political Thought and Intellectual Life in Britain 1850-1930* (Oxford: Clarendon Press, 1991), pp. 91-118.
[37] See Luke O'Sullivan, *Oakeshott on History* (Thorverton: Imprint Academic, 2003), pp. 141-149; Sullivan, *Intimations Pursued*, p. 204n.
[38] Collini, *Public Moralists*, p. 303.
[39] 'The Activity of Being a Historian,' RIP, pp. 173-174.

him and his Ideal'.[40] His fault lay in the constant search for perfection, and this aspiration towards the ideal paralysed the will instead of giving it the necessary energy.

Oakeshott's ethical sentiment is closer to the writers of the Edwardian period such as G.E. Moore. He was familiar with Moore's treatise on ethics,[41] and even used one of Moore's arguments to show the confusion implied in Mill's advocacy of utilitarianism.[42] Although there is a great distance between the philosophical approaches of the two, Oakeshott's stress on the 'poetic' element found in aesthetic contemplation and on love and friendship in human relationships is reminiscent of Moore's attempt to redirect ethical sentiment away from social ethical ideals by defining personal relationships and the enjoyment of beautiful objects as the only goods in themselves.[43]

This does not mean that Oakeshott was indifferent to ethical questions. Not unlike other 'Edwardians', he remained preoccupied with the questions of morality and religion. His disengagement was never a full rebellion, and his criticism of the moral attitudes of the Victorian writers should not be exaggerated. He never slipped into moral nihilism, and his attitude to Nietzsche remained ambivalent.

Yet Oakeshott never fully trusted the ethics of moral responsibility, being suspicious of its enmity to spontaneity, adventure and an aesthetic enjoyment. He disliked Kant's moral theory because of its emphasis on the idea of duty, and chose to adhere to the neo-Hegelian ethical theory of Bradley which showed the way out of the moral imperative by asserting the self-contradicting character of morality and by presenting religion as a distinct experience, 'a completion' of morality.[44]

It seems, however, that in his early writings Oakeshott himself is still uncertain about his own position. Thus, in *Experience and Its Modes* morality is, in some sense, central to practical experience. For every action is seen as reconciling a specific 'is' with a specific 'ought to be'. Such reconciliation is aimed at bringing about a more coherent world and, therefore, can be seen as an obligation. Though morality as a world is never achieved, what seems to be implied in Oakeshott's argument is that every action is somehow done under the category of duty.

---

[40] LA.
[41] George Edward Moore, *Principia Ethica* (Cambridge: Cambridge University Press, 1971). See ERPPR.
[42] EM, pp. 275-276. The confusion in question is between what is 'desirable' and what people 'desire'.
[43] Moore, *Principia Ethica*, pp. 188-189.
[44] 'Religion and the Moral Life,' RPML, pp. 39-45.

Later, in his middle period, Oakeshott attempts to modify and clarify his views. The argument is presented in the essay 'The Tower of Babel' (1948), in which Oakeshott discusses the character of morality prevalent in modern Western civilisation. Having become, together with 'Rationalism in Politics', one of the best known of Oakeshott's essays, it bestowed on him the reputation of a conservative critic of modernity. Both essays, of course, invite such an interpretation being written in a more pessimistic mood than the rest of his writings. However, their apparent traditionalism is likely to be exaggerated. And leaving the discussion of 'Rationalism in Politics' to the next section, I want here to draw attention to the shortcomings of this interpretation of 'The Tower of Babel'.

Modern morality, according to Oakeshott, is a mixture of two ideal types: the morality of habit, and the morality of reflection. In the morality of habit or custom, conduct does not involve reflection and does not spring from the consciousness of possible alternatives. It is the conduct which has become habitual. But it is nevertheless 'moral', since every action tacitly implies an alternative. This morality is learned, similar to one's native language, not by remembering explicitly formulated rules, but by living with people who are used to behaving in the same way. This learning is not compulsory, but inevitable. Nothing in this form of morality is fixed. Because it is not formulated in rules, it is susceptible to the nuances of a particular situation. Like language, it is in the process of constant change. Being very volatile, it presupposes a significant freedom of individual performance. The major defect of this form of morality is that 'it does not amount to moral self-criticism'.[45] Therefore, it may degenerate into superstition and has little power to recover from a crisis.

The second form of morality is the reflective application of a moral criterion. This form presupposes the establishment of a relational system of the desirable ends of conduct, and the confidence of those who practice it in their ability to defend these ends and translate them in specific actions. To learn this morality means to know how to detect these rules or ideals, how to manage them as a coherent system, and how to apply them to specific situations.

This form of morality provides those who practice it with a great confidence in their moral maxims and with the understanding of what they are doing and why. It is well guarded against the danger of the degeneration into superstition which is characteristic of the morality of habit. Yet it has dangers of its own, such as the creation of an uncertainty about how to act. Because every specific situation is

---
[45] RIP, p. 471.

ambiguous, the art of applying ideals and rules becomes very difficult.

Further, Oakeshott distinguishes between the two most common varieties of the morality of reflection: the self-conscious pursuit of moral ideals and the reflective observance of moral rules.[46] He argues that the morality of ideals is the less satisfactory of the two. The morality of rules is not necessarily perfectionist, since 'the rule is not represented as perfection', constituting rather 'a mediation, a cushion, between the behaviour it demands on each occasion and the complete moral response to the situation'.[47] In contrast, the morality of ideals cannot escape from the vision of perfection, and Oakeshott is very suspicious of claimants to moral perfectionism.

The morality of habit and the morality of reflection are just extremes which are always mixed in an actual morality. However, this mixture may be of two types, depending on which of the two forms predominates. Oakeshott advocates the type in which the predominant form is the morality of habit. Those who practice it will enjoy confidence in acting, whereas a certain amount of self-criticism will save their morality from degenerating into a superstition and grant it confidence in its moral standards.

The morality of our civilisation is, however, characterised by the mixture in which the morality of ideals is the dominant one. Oakeshott relates the emergence of this condition to the first four centuries of the Christian era, interpreting Nietzsche's critique of modern Christianity as an attack on 'a morality of ideals which had never succeeded in becoming a morality of habit and behaviour'.[48] This dominance of the morality of ideals in our civilisation seems to be irreversible at the moment. Oakeshott claims that his aim is only to reject the illusion that it is a beneficial development, by speaking against 'the self-deception which reconciles us to our misfortune'.[49]

At first glance, this view seems to be a defence of traditionalist adherence to social customs, yet one should not be misled by the terminology used here. The typical conservative defence of the morality of custom would base itself on the assertion that such a morality preserves the *mores* of a society, saving it from moral nihilism. However, this is not Oakeshott's claim. He advocates the dominance of the morality of habit and custom not because he thinks it to be a safeguard against the collapse of values, but because he sees in it an alternative to moral perfectionism. He emphasises not its alleged

---

[46] RIP, p. 472.
[47] RIP, p. 475.
[48] RIP, p. 486.
[49] RIP, p. 487.

rigorous adherence to the values of the past, but its flexibility. For him, morality of habit has 'poetical qualities' of spontaneity, while the main defect of the morality of reflection is 'its denial of the poetic character of human activity'.[50] The morality of reflection imposes on practice 'an inappropriate didactic form'.[51] And, as Oakeshott once remarked earlier, 'law is the enemy of the moral life; casuistry the grave of moral sensibility.'[52]

The morality of habit leaves room for inventiveness, and therefore a deviation from it may spring 'from a sensitiveness to the tradition itself'.[53] The eccentric who explores the opportunities provided by this morality in an uncommon way is of value to society. And though eccentricity remains an activity of the individual and is not permitted to disrupt the communal life, its influence may be powerful, though oblique. The eccentric 'is admired but not copied, reverenced but not followed, welcomed but ostracised.'[54]

In contrast, the morality of ideals is very rigid. It leads to the clash of different abstract ideals, often ending up either in disillusion or in the choice of one ideal at the expense of others. The society selects a few ideals that 'are turned in an authoritative canon which is then made a guide to legislation or even a ground for the violent persecution of eccentricity'.[55] And when one form of eccentricity becomes authoritative, others are suppressed. Thus, whilst the morality of habit is tolerant of various deviations, the morality of ideals is inherently oppressive, since it does not allow any expression of eccentricity which would not suit its declared ends.

'The Tower of Babel' is certainly a critique of our form of morality, but what is attacked here is not its nihilism, but its rigidity, of which nihilism is only a consequence. Oakeshott does not mourn so-called 'Victorian' values. If anything, this essay is a repudiation of nineteenth-century moral ideals. For, while Oakeshott regards the ideal of the gentleman as a more or less successful experiment, he mentions the character of a gentleman as belonging not only to the class of reflective morality, but also to its most dangerous form: the morality of ideals.[56] The two most important claims of this essay are that reflective morality destroyed the poetic character of life and that the return to the morality of habit is hardly possible.

---

[50] RIP, p. 479.
[51] Ibid.
[52] EM, p. 301.
[53] RIP, p. 472.
[54] Ibid.
[55] RIP, p. 481.
[56] RIP, p. 474.

This view is, however, seriously modified in subsequent writings. While Oakeshott continues to give priority to the morality of habit, he abandons his pessimism, showing instead that Western morality does allow the expression of spontaneity. As we have seen, in *Experience and Its Modes* the function of morality was unclear, and its relation to the world of value remained unelaborated. Though Oakeshott referred to a specific attempt to reconcile 'is' and 'ought' as implying the idea of duty, he abstained from presenting a detailed account of morality, rather seeing in religion the way to achieve the integrated life. In his later book, *On Human Conduct*, the emphasis is reversed. Moral practice, as the practice of all practices, receives the full theoretical elaboration, while the role of religion is limited to reconciliation.

Yet, in order to place morality at the centre of human conduct without abandoning the idea of spontaneity, Oakeshott radically reinterprets his view of morality. In his new approach, morality is understood not through the notion of constraint, but through that of emancipation. In *Experience and Its Modes* 'ought' was omnipresent and, when grasped in reference to a particular situation, implied an obligation. In 'The Tower of Babel' morality was split into two kinds: the one of the rigorous norms and ideals and the other of the spontaneity of habit. In contrast, in *On Human Conduct*, there is no split between two extremes of morality. Every morality is seen as based on habit, and in every morality the auxiliary element of reflection is present. Morality is compared to language, which is never merely a system of grammar, but the tradition of utterances, from which some rules can be abridged. Though capable of being formulated in explicit rules, morality is more than these rules. It allows 'almost endless opportunity for individual style'.[57] It is 'not a device for controlling or suppressing biological urges',[58] but a vernacular from which no one can escape. A human being 'comes to consciousness in a world illuminated by a moral practice and as a relatively helpless subject of it'.[59] And being, thus, inevitable, morality cannot constrain, since our habits become a part of ourselves. Every conduct is always subject to some conditions. 'There is no agency which is not the acknowledgement of a moral practice, and no moral conduct which is not an exercise of agency.'[60] Thus, morality is a general postulate of human conduct, being no longer a collection of moral maxims. This implies that it is senseless to speak of a certain society as

---

[57] HC, p. 62.
[58] Ibid.
[59] HC, p. 63.
[60] Ibid.

'immoral'. If a certain moral maxim is grasped as something which requires a constant conscious effort in performing, this means that it is already not a part of a habitual moral language of a society. For

> if it is without resources to respond to the interrogations of circumstances it is already moribund, and it is only in books (and then only in the worst sort) that moral conduct appears as an incessant lurching from perplexity to perplexity and a contorted endeavour to elicit actions from conditional prescription.[61]

Moreover, Oakeshott removes any ambiguities capable of being interpreted in a teleological light. In *Experience and Its Modes* the world of value, though never reduced to the world of practical life, still may be seen as directing our choices, for the world of practical experience is always an alteration of 'is' to what is 'ought' to be. This picture becomes more complex in 'The Tower of Babel'. The morality of ideals is not the only possible type of the reflective morality, being distinguished from a less dangerous form: the morality of rules. Finally, in *On Human Conduct* the reflective element of morality is always understood as a morality of rules, and it is only a confused reasoning which attempts to understand it in terms of ideals. Thus, while in the earlier essay the morality of habit stood against both forms of the morality of reflection, in *On Human Conduct* every morality is always analysed as a mixture in which the morality of habits predominates, but the reflective morality (understood in terms of rules and not ideals) also plays its role.

To understand morality in terms of practices means here to see it as merely establishing conditions and never determining goals of conduct. The expressions such as 'good life' are acceptable only in so far as they do not indicate some substantive condition of things. A life can be seen as 'good' but 'goodness' here does not relate to the substantive aspect of actions. It may be present in every action, but actions must always be directed to some particular outcome.

> 'Human excellence' or 'the human good' is not a substantive purpose to be achieved ... it is not a purpose which an agent might choose to pursue in preference to the satisfaction of some other want... like joining an expedition to climb Mount Everest or agreeing with another to settle in Katmandu.[62]

Therefore moral practice cannot imply a purpose external to itself.

Morality, then, is only one of the aspects of human conduct. It refers to the conditions taken into account in an action performed, but not to the purpose of conduct. As such, it cannot be seen as pro-

---

[61] HC, p. 64.
[62] HC, p. 61.

viding society with a fully homogeneous character. For societies consist of human agents who act not only in the consideration of their practices, but also in order to achieve some substantive result, and morality cannot account for this aspect of human conduct.

The sphere of conduct, therefore, is no more homogeneous or coherent than 'practical experience' in *Experience and Its Modes*. Although morality is discussed at length in *On Human Conduct*, it is not regarded as the ultimate completion of the social life. Moreover, it cannot be even described by teleological words such as 'completion' or 'aim'. Morality is a language of conditions of human conduct indifferent to substantive outcomes.

IV

The sphere of 'doing' is not a mode of experience. It is a separate level, analogous to the level of understanding. The level of understanding includes various homogeneous abstractions. Likewise, the level of doing includes similar abstractions. Those abstractions are independent individuals.

In order to understand this idea, we should explore Oakeshott's notion of the morality of individuality. This notion is related to his reinterpretation of morality in *On Human Conduct*, and it is based on his account of the emergence of our moral values. In the fifties Oakeshott changed his views expressed in 'The Tower of Babel' and attempted to highlight the intimations of freedom and spontaneity contained in the modern moral sensibility. This is the story of the emergence of the characters of the 'individual' and his counterpart — the 'anti-individual'.

Telling this story, however, required Oakeshott to modify significantly many of his previous views. The young Oakeshott, influenced by classical philosophers (especially Aristotle), by Hegel, and by British neo-Hegelians, was critical of philosophical individualism. Thus, in 'A Discussion of Some Matters Preliminary to the Study of Political Philosophy', he rejected methodological individualism with regard to the concept of 'self', claiming that the self cannot be coherently understood as a combination of an individual body and its thoughts, although this view can serve some practical purposes. The self is a thing and therefore must be self-complete and, as no particular human being is self-complete, 'the only true, because the only perfect, self is the universe.'[63] Only the totality of experience can be absolutely self-complete and therefore possess

---

[63] DSM, p. 130.

individuality. Therefore 'a self *is* its society,'[64] 'the self is the State, the State is the self.'[65] There is no real conflict between the state and the individual. 'Individuality means finding our activity within a whole.'[66] It is expressed in finding one's own place within society and 'only through his particular station and the faithful performance of its particular duties, can [man] take hold of this thing called "humanity"'.[67]

Yet, as one might expect, this view is changed already in *Experience and Its Modes*, where essentially different ideas are incorporated into an apparently monistic framework. Here Oakeshott discusses the question of individuality on two levels: the level of philosophical understanding and the level of practical experience. These two levels have different perceptions of individuality. At the philosophical level, Oakeshott still holds the view of the individual as a self-complete thing. To understand individuality merely in terms of what is specific and distant ultimately leads to an abstraction. For any specification is always relative and arbitrary, being just 'a matter of degree and circumstance'.[68] Such individuality cannot maintain itself, for one can always claim that it is not sufficiently distinct or isolated. There is no final point in which the process of isolation must stop. Therefore, real philosophical individuality is nothing other than the whole of experience.

The principle of individuality in practical experience is of a different sort. Practical experience postulates action, and those who act — that is, thinking selves — are each understood as possessing independent volition. In order to act, the self must be contrary to the world and exclusive of it, and be surrounded by a world of other selves. That is, in such a world there is a multiplicity of selves, each understood to be self-determined, or an end in itself. The definition of selves in practical experience can never be philosophical. The self of practice is the one observed by D.H. Lawrence or Kant — the self whose integrity is maintained through its own separateness.[69] Indeed, individuality understood as a single self is nothing more than an abstraction: it is never fully and properly 'real'; but 'to take the self as separate, single, unique, and to take it to be real because it

---

[64] DSM, p. 131.
[65] DSM, p. 133.
[66] DSM, p. 135.
[67] DSM, p. 140.
[68] EM, p. 44.
[69] EM, p. 271.

is separate, single and unique, is an absolute necessity in practical experience'.[70]

This is not to suggest that Oakeshott regarded this practical self as completely satisfactory. According to him, there are moments in which we become aware of the illusion of individuality. On the one hand, love can push us towards self-abnegation in another person, or in something bigger. This is 'the attempt to lose oneself, to find oneself in another, to preserve oneself in abandoning oneself...'[71] On the other hand, we happen to recognise that our self is not a unity, as 'we are aware of a thousand selves within this single self.'[72] Thus, sometimes we recognise that our self is an abstraction, and we are united with a larger individuality, or fragmented into many pieces. Yet this recognition is always limited, for one cannot go too far in either direction without losing the individuality which is necessary for conduct. Therefore, there is a certain uneasiness here, since the most worthy affects such as love are seen as, in some sense, inimical to individuality. This uneasiness is present in most of Oakeshott's writings of his early period up to the fifties, when a different attitude enters his social philosophy, at the centre of which there is the notion of the morality of individuality.

The new view first appears in Oakeshott's reinterpretation of many Western political thinkers as moral philosophers, who were mainly concerned with the character of the individual. The 'individual' as 'a great achievement but one difficult to manage' is, in his opinion, one of the central motives of Hegel's political philosophy.[73] In a series of Harvard lectures Oakeshott refers to such different thinkers as Locke, Burke, Adam Smith, Bentham, Kant, and in part Mill as the proponents of the morality of individuality.[74] And he approaches Hobbes as the earliest theorist of this morality.[75]

In this light *On Human Conduct* may be regarded as Oakeshott's own theoretical contribution to the articulation of the character of the modern individual. Oakeshott is engaged in theorising conduct *inter homines* as a certain abstraction denoting our understanding of the relationship between intelligent human agents pursuing choices of their own. He does not claim that human relationships are essentially of such a character, for he is concerned not with metaphysics but with our understanding. Oakeshott's purpose is rather to show

---

[70] EM, p. 272.
[71] EM, pp. 271-272.
[72] EM, p. 272.
[73] Review of H. Marcuse, *Reason and Revolution*, in *Spectator* 194, 1955, pp. 404-405.
[74] See MPME.
[75] See 'The Moral Life in the Writings of Thomas Hobbes,' RIP, pp. 295-350.

what view of human conduct one must hold in order to understand human relationships as qualitatively distinct from other phenomena by being the relationships between agents who attribute meanings to their own performances. Neither does he claim that human societies must necessarily grasp themselves in the terms of conduct. On the contrary, he seems to imply that the recognition of behaviour as 'conduct' is a cultural achievement, which reaches its highest expression in the moral consciousness of modern Western civilisation, though intimated already in the classical and Christian tradition.[76]

This modern consciousness, then, is characterised by the recognition of human beings as agents, who possess an understanding of themselves as reflective intelligences pursuing choices of their own. Oakeshott is not an essentialist, and individuality does not mean for him an authentic 'self'. The self is mutable and is always an historical outcome, being 'a substantive personality, the outcome of an education, whose resources are collected in a self-understanding'.[77] Yet this does not mean that this 'self' is false, that there are multiple selves in this single self, or that this self is simply subject to the influence of its environment. It is indeed 'composed of actions and utterances which reflect... contingent sentiments, affections, and beliefs',[78] but this composition is not merely an intrusion of the external world, because this particular self has made these particular beliefs its own. Neither is it a 'fragmented' self. Certainly, it expresses itself by pursuing a variety of purposes, being engaged in the activity of 'self-disclosure'. But this does not mean that its activities are completely disconnected. The self does not only disclose itself in actions, but also acquires a character through 'enacting' itself. 'Self-enactment' is actions perceived 'in terms of the motives in which they are performed'.[79] That is, an agent may perform the same action from different motives or from a different mixture of motives, such as jealousy, pride, pity, generosity, or fear. These motives provide the self with the durability of character and 'endow human conduct with a formality in which the contingency is somewhat abated'.[80] And these motives are an integral part of our understanding of conduct.

The self is therefore not merely a collection of miscellaneous actions, but is a more or less homogeneous system of beliefs,

---

[76] HC, p. 235.
[77] HC, p. 236.
[78] HC, p. 237.
[79] HC, p. 70.
[80] HC, p. 74.

expressed in a disposition to act in a certain way. Oakeshott transforms the idea of character prominent in the cultural context of the Victorian and Edwardian ages into one of the major concepts of his thought.[81] And yet his idea of character is devoid of the strong altruistic implications of this term. For one to possess a character does not necessarily mean to possess a specific character. Oakeshott assigns no normative substantive content to this word. For him, the term 'character' is convenient as a way to avoid the danger of essentialism. 'Character' is not a rigid substance; it is being modified continuously. Yet, while modified, it preserves its historical identity. The self is always a character. Though it is not an atom with pre-established qualities, it is a separate identity, existing among other selves and understanding itself as distinct. And so far as one theorises society in the terms of human conduct, one must regard it as composed of unique selves, each pursuing choices of their own. Therefore, the analysis of society must be based on methodological individualism. The social life cannot be understood through artificial theoretical constructions such as 'society', 'collective', or 'humanity'. It must always be perceived as an outcome of the actions of individual selves. The

> so-called 'social inheritance' is an accumulation of human understandings and is composed of the moral and prudential achievements of numberless individuals... It is a collected, not a 'collective' achievement... None but an individual initiate can either use it or educate others in its use.[82]

'Self' is, therefore, an abstraction, but it is the abstraction which has acquired separateness and individuality. Its role in Oakeshott's social philosophy is analogous to the role played by modes in his philosophy of experience. Similarly to modes, the self is an abstract product of our understanding rather than the whole of reality. At the same time, it creates a homogeneous world and becomes valuable by virtue of possessing an identity. It is seen as an end in itself, and therefore worth being defended. Oakeshott approves individuality not because it is perfect, but because it is a beautiful abstraction.

Moreover, Oakeshott argues that this perception of human agency is well embedded in the consciousness of modern civilisation, constituting 'the morality of individuality'. The story of the emergence of this morality, which is strongly influenced by

---

[81] See O'Sullivan, *Oakeshott on History*, pp. 141-149.
[82] HC, pp. 86-87.

Burckhardt,[83] first appears in Oakeshott's essay 'The Masses in Representative Democracy' (1957)[84] and its main ideas are later incorporated in *On Human Conduct*.[85] According to the story Oakeshott tells, this morality appeared as an outcome of the long process of modification of the medieval European morality of communal ties. In that old morality people were mainly regarded in respect of their status and family affiliation. Their respective positions in the social order were the central component of their identity. From the twelfth century onwards, however, this morality started to be gradually dissolved due to contingent historical circumstances as old ties were often destroyed, and new opportunities arose for individuals to attempt making choices of their own not determined by birth or family affiliation. This gradually led to the emergence of the character of a person who enjoyed making choices for himself. Oakeshott suggests that this type of personality established itself unambiguously towards the age of the High Renaissance.

This disposition was not merely about making choices in order to achieve certain outcomes, for even those who are devoid of any awareness of their individuality may like substantive profits resulting from the engagement in making choices. The distinctive feature of this disposition was that it valued not only the satisfactions achieved, but also the self-determination present in an adventure of making choices, thereby preferring journey to destination.[86]

Moreover, this disposition did not just remain at the level of personal preference. As this new character acquired confidence in himself, he transformed his disposition into a moral quality, thereby making a virtue from the sentiment. It meant that 'individuality' came to be regarded as a quality to be sought and approved of in every human agent. The morality of individuality, then, emerged when the existence of the individualistic disposition became a matter of moral judgement and, when the demands were raised to create such conditions which would favour the full enjoyment of individuality, now regarded as a virtue. For it is in such an approval, 'not merely on one's own account but in respect of others also — that the impulse towards individuality becomes a moral disposition'.[87]

Thus, Oakeshott's understanding of the meaning of 'morality' and 'individuality' is very peculiar. Oakeshott is very apprehensive

---

[83] Jakob Burckhardt, *The Civilization of the Renaissance in Italy*, trans. S.G.C. Middlemore (London: Phaidon, 1995).
[84] RIP, pp. 363-383.
[85] HC, pp. 234-242, 274-279.
[86] HC, p. 236. This claim is not made in 'The Masses in Representative Democracy'.
[87] MPME, p. 21.

about the old-style moralism associated with altruism and social devotion, and he presents morality as a language, and not as a system of obligations. Morality is characterised not by the system of rules, but by the mutual recognition of the common tongue. At the same time, the emphasis on individuality does not imply a mere selfishness. For what distinguishes the individual is his disposition to make choices for himself, and not the quest for self-gratification.

And this understanding of 'morality' and 'individuality' lets Oakeshott avoid the clash between the two. On the one hand, morality, being one's own way of life, cannot be external to individuality. On the other hand, the individual who ascribes virtue to autonomy is the one who is inclined to recognise individuality in others as well as in himself. Individuality and morality are therefore fully compatible.

This celebration of individualism as compatible with morality and not necessarily leading to selfishness or nihilism, was common to many other liberal authors of the Cold War period, often implying a critique of the projects of social redemption associated with the totalitarian regimes.[88] Yet it is Oakeshott who seems to have provided this view with its most elegant theoretical foundations. For him, the adoption of the individualistic perspective is necessarily implied in theorising human conduct. So long as human conduct is understood in the terms of relationships between intelligent agents, the notion of individuality is postulated in it. It is theoretically necessary, and not contingent. What is, however, contingent, is the emergence of the notion of human conduct in the first place, when certain individuals began to see themselves as intelligent beings pursuing choices of their own, and acquire 'a historic disposition to transform this unsought "freedom" of conduct from a postulate into an experience'.[89]

The 'individual' is however, not the only character present on the scene of modern European history. For whereas some people responded favourably to the invitation to make choices for themselves and developed the disposition for personal autonomy which they transformed into the moral attitude, there were some for whom the dissolution of the old morality of communal ties was a loss, and who were not capable or did not wish to make choices for themselves. This character was the 'individual *manqué*', who could not make choices and needed direction from someone else to make choices for him. He sought such direction from leaders and

[88] See, for example, Karl Popper, *The Open Society and Its Enemies* (London: Routledge, 1995), pp. 100-101.
[89] HC, p. 236.

demanded the provision of substantive goods from the government. And some such people also felt a strong resentment against those who knew better how to respond to the new condition. Driven by jealousy, and suffering from the radical guilt of their own inadequacy, they established themselves as an opposite character — that of 'anti-individual'. This character expressed itself in the revulsion from any distinctions and differences, and sought to remedy the predicament of individuality by creating a social solidarity in which no differences would be tolerated, 'a therapeutic corporation devoted to remedying the so-called self-alienation'.[90]

Yet the 'anti-individual' is no less a modern character than the 'individual'. Although he emerged partly as a response to the nostalgia for old certainties, he came to possess a distinctively modern consciousness, at the centre of which is the recognition of the human being understood as a reflective agency making choices of its own. The difference between the 'anti-individual' and the 'individual' is not that they have different understandings of the character of human agents, but that the 'anti-individual' resents what the 'individual' enjoys. Therefore, the solution of the 'anti-individual' is not, as it sometimes seems, the return to the warmth of organic communities with their complex differentiation of roles, but an atomistic solidarity devoid of any difference.

Now, Oakeshott's description of the two characters is inherently biased towards the individual. The modern condition may provoke two different responses: acceptance or rejection. But the appreciation of human conduct is only truly possible when the standpoint of individuality is adopted. 'Anti-individuality' is a mere rejection, or protest, which carries nothing positive in itself. Unsurprisingly, the 'individual *manqué*' is described as the one who has 'feelings rather than thoughts, impulses rather than opinions, inabilities rather than passions'.[91] Therefore he cannot create an alternative morality. Although in an earlier essay Oakeshott described an 'anti-individual' as capable of inventing a morality of his own,[92] in *On Human Conduct* he omits any mention of this. As he claims, the disposition to cultivate freedom inherent in agency 'has remained the strongest strand in the moral convictions of the inhabitants of modern Europe'.[93] The 'anti-individual' is described as being a character, but one who is hardly capable of competing on the moral field. Thus, modern European history witnessed two competing characters, but

[90] HC, pp. 278-279.
[91] HC, p. 277.
[92] RIP, pp. 374-376.
[93] HC, p. 242.

it displayed only one dominant morality. And this makes the anti-individual a derivative character, a mere negation of individuality.

V

Oakeshott's main ethical ideas, therefore, developed during a long period of time and found their most refined expression in *On Human Conduct*. In his mature philosophy Oakeshott separates the bottom level of the reflective consciousness of doing from the middle level of theoretical understanding. The level of doing is not a homogeneous abstraction. Therefore it should be compared not to a particular mode of understanding, but to the level of understanding as a whole. The level of understanding is not homogeneous but consists of abstract modes each possessing an identity of its own. Analogously, the level of doing is not a homogeneous whole represented by practical experience or society in general, but is composed of the multiplicity of abstract identities, namely distinct individuals, or selves.

The level of conduct can, therefore, be understood as composed of a variety of homogeneous modes which have no external purposes but are the ends in themselves. These modes are human agents. The self is merely an abstraction but it is valuable as such an abstraction, and the recognition of individuality is well embedded in the moral consciousness of modern civilisation.

We can see, then, that individuals on the level of doing possess at least two features of modes on the level of understanding. They are homogeneous and purposeless individuals. But what about the third characteristic? Modes of experience are irrelevant to each other. And what is the relationship between selves in the world of conduct? What is the appropriate understanding of a society of such individuals? What form of society is conducive to full self-determination? These are the questions which will be discussed in the last section of this chapter. Yet before discussing the socio-political theory articulated in *On Human Conduct*, it is important to focus on the development of Oakeshott's views from another aspect. Here I presented the evolution of his thought in the realm of ethics and morality in general. In the next section I want to discuss the origins of Oakeshott's specifically political thought. After this we will be in a better position to analyse the central argument of *On Human Conduct*.

LIBERALISM

I

Oakeshott taught the history of political thought at Cambridge University and the LSE, published numerous essays and reviews on politics during his long career, and his reputation as a political thinker was well established before the publication of *On Human Conduct*. However it was in this work that Oakeshott, for the first time, offered a systematic elaboration of his political philosophy, undertaking, as he said, the task of putting his thoughts together about the themes he had been exploring as long as he could remember.[94]

Yet some discussion about Oakeshott's early political writings may be worthwhile. For, even if they do not offer us a coherent philosophical view of politics, they certainly reveal the questions with which Oakeshott was preoccupied early on, and this may shed light on some ideas expressed in his later book and on the vision which underlies them.

This leads us to the question of the connection between Oakeshott's writings of the middle and the late period. Whilst *Rationalism In Politics* earned him the reputation of a political conservative,[95] *On Human Conduct* was perceived as a piece of liberal theory.[96] It was, indeed, sometimes claimed that there were two Oakeshotts: the liberal Oakeshott of *On Human Conduct* and the conservative Oakeshott of *Rationalism in Politics*.[97]

---

[94] HC, p. vii.

[95] On Oakeshott as a conservative see Perry Anderson, 'The Intransigent Right at the End of the Century,' *London Review of Books* 14, September 24, 1992, pp. 7-11; Russell Kirk, *The Conservative Mind* (London: Faber and Faber, 1954), pp. 413-414; Kirk F. Koerner, *Liberalism and its Critics* (London: Croom Helm, 1985), pp. 270-308; Hanna F. Pitkin, 'The Roots of Conservatism: Michael Oakeshott and the Denial of Politics,' *Dissent* 20, 1973, pp. 496-525; Anthony Quinton, *The Politics of Imperfection: The Religious and Secular Traditions of Conservative Thought in England from Hooker to Oakeshott* (London: Faber and Faber, 1978), pp. 90-96.

[96] On Oakeshott as a liberal see Corey Abel, *Michael Oakeshott's Liberalism: The Epistemology of Experience and the Morality of Individualism* (PhD diss., Chicago University, 1995); W. John Coats Jr., 'Michael Oakeshott as Liberal Theorist,' *Canadian Journal of Political Science* 18(4), 1985, pp. 773-787; Paul Franco, 'Michael Oakeshott as Liberal Theorist,' *Political Theory* 18(3), 1990, pp. 411-436; *The Political Philosophy of Michael Oakeshott* (New Haven: Yale University Press, 1990); John Gray, *Post-liberalism: Studies in Political Thought* (New York: Routledge, 1993), pp. 40-46; Jacob Segal, 'A Storm from Paradise: Liberalism and the Problem of Time,' *Critical Review* 8(1), 1994, pp. 23-48; Michael Williams, 'Liberalism and Two Conceptions of the State,' in D. MacLean & C. Mills (eds.), *Liberalism Reconsidered* (Totowa, NJ: Rowman & Allanheld, 1983), pp. 117-129.

[97] See, for example, Charles Covell, *The Redefinition of Conservatism: Politics and Doctrine* (London: Macmillan, 1986), p. 136; Anthony Farr, *Sartre's Radicalism*

This study offers a different assessment, rejecting the view that there is a gap between Oakeshott's middle and late periods. On the contrary, Oakeshott's thought as a whole should be understood as a sort of liberalism, and all the ideas and sentiments that are given a full theoretical elaboration in *On Human Conduct* are already present or intimated in his writings of the forties and fifties. *On Human Conduct* presents a sophisticated theoretical framework for the liberal vision that Oakeshott already espoused in his middle period.

However, this characterisation of Oakeshott as a liberal thinker, while being shared by many commentators, is not sufficient in itself. It leaves the precise character of his liberalism unclear. Thus, according to Coats, the term 'liberal' in the history of political thought may be regarded as standing for 'a view of the state as subordinate to, and arising from, the freedom of individual conscience — or sometimes individual appetite'.[98] It is true that a view like this is present in Oakeshott's thought. But it is too wide, and it lacks an historical specification which would place Oakeshott's ideas within a more specific tradition. And my aim here is to undertake such a specification.

This section will, therefore, argue that the development of Oakeshott's political thought prior to *On Human Conduct* should not be understood in terms of a tension between *Rationalism in Politics* and *On Human Conduct*, or as an evolution from conservatism to liberalism. Oakeshott's political thought is best understood when it is seen as springing from two traditions of European liberalism, which can be called 'Whig' and 'Romantic' liberalism. These two traditions share many features in common, but they are distinct in several basic points. The section will attempt to show that what is usually perceived as a tension between Oakeshott's conservatism and liberalism is just the reflection of the shift of an emphasis in his writings from the 'Whiggish' to 'Romantic' element of his liberalism.

II

In what sense is Oakeshott a liberal writer? He himself was not well disposed towards the term 'liberal'. He used it infrequently and often in the negative sense, especially in his early writings. For example, he criticised liberalism for its association with a 'crude and

---

and *Oakeshott's Conservatism: The Duplicity of Freedom* (London: Macmillan, 1998), pp. 241-255.
[98] Coats, 'Michael Oakeshott as Liberal Theorist,' p. 773.

negative individualism',[99] or for being the most complete expression of rationalism and scientism.[100]

There are, however, signs of a more complex attitude towards liberalism. Usually Oakeshott is careful to mention that he is critical not of liberalism as such, but of what it came to be perceived as. Liberalism suffers from an 'ignorance of who its true friends are', from its fascination with the idea of 'progress',[101] and its narrow identification with the programme of a certain party.[102]

Towards the end of his life Oakeshott was ready to admit the liberal character of his philosophy. Thus, he considered an article, in which he was identified as a liberal theorist, to be the most correct interpretation of his position.[103] And he also became dissatisfied with the term 'conservatism', claiming that this word had been overtaken by corruption and ambiguity. As he pointed out, 'Stalinists in Russia are now commonly called "conservatives".'[104]

A hint of Oakeshott's basic view of liberalism can be found in his insistence that the concept of representative democracy as a whole has to be understood as a liberal doctrine.[105] He is unhappy that in the English, and perhaps American political context, liberalism came to signify a particular political creed, which was quite different from the original character of European liberalism. Indeed, the British Liberal party from its outset included a radical wing, associated with philosophical utilitarians, and the non-conformist movement. These had little in common with European sceptical liberals, and were certainly disliked by Oakeshott. When he scorns liberalism he usually refers to its affiliation with radical movements, and later with collectivism.

But the term 'liberal' was not originally English. It was born in continental Europe in a particular historical context. In order to understand Oakeshott's philosophy, we should see his liberalism not in any narrow party sense, but in the wider historical context of European liberalism. And if affinities between Oakeshott and some other English liberals are found, it is only when these liberals themselves follow the original tradition of European liberalism.

I am concerned here with two specific trends within continental European liberalism, the influences of which are most prominent in

[99] SPD, p. xvii.
[100] 'Scientific Politics,' RPML, p. 100.
[101] 'The Political Economy of Freedom,' RIP, p. 385.
[102] SPD, p. xviii.
[103] Gray, *Post-liberalism*, p. 40; O'Sullivan, *Oakeshott on History*, pp. 3–4.
[104] Review of R. Scruton (ed.), *Conservative Thoughts: Essays from The Salisbury Review*, in *Spectator* 261, 1988, p. 60.
[105] SPD, p. xviii.

Oakeshott's thought. These trends can be called 'Whig' and 'Romantic' liberalism. This distinction is partly recognised by Oakeshott himself in his treatment of individualism. In his essay on John Locke (1932) he distinguishes between two kinds of individualism. The first traces its legacy to Locke who 'served as the filter by means of which Puritanism was drained of its immoderation and its "enthusiasm" and was converted into what the 18th century knew as Whiggism and the 19th as Liberalism'. Locke believed in truth, progress, freedom, compromise, stability, and his main disposition was his moderation. His liberalism 'is more conservative than conservatism itself... liberalism which is sure of its limits, which has a horror of extremes, which lays its paralysing hand of respectability upon whatever is dangerous or revolutionary.'[106] The other is a radical, Epicurean individualism, which might rescue liberalism from its respectability, and 'at one time it seemed that liberalism, under the stimulus of the romantic movement, might be transformed into something less boring and upholstered.'[107] Yet, although in this essay Oakeshott is very critical of the former, both trends can be found in his thought.

Oakeshott attributes Whig liberalism to Locke, and in a certain sense this is true. Of course, the historical Locke was not a liberal.[108] But his thought contributed to the emergence of modern European liberalism. The important point to notice is that Whig liberalism is predominantly a continental European phenomenon. Liberalism in its specifically historical sense is the political ideology that developed in the course of the nineteenth century in major European countries, like France, Prussia, Spain and Italy. Its explicit major principle was the idea of freedom. 'Putting liberty first',[109] constitutes the political identity of European liberals. But liberty is understood by these thinkers not so much as an abstract ideal, but as the actual practice of two societies which are perceived as 'free': Britain and the United States. The explicit purpose of European liberalism was to implant new political institutions which would be similar to English or American ones. In other words, European liberalism advocated reform towards what was perceived as the successful Whig political settlement.

[106] JL, p. 73.
[107] Ibid.
[108] See John Dunn, *The Political Thought of John Locke* (Cambridge: Cambridge University Press, 1969); *Locke* (Oxford: Oxford University Press, 1982); James Tully, *An Approach to Political Philosophy: Locke in Context* (Cambridge: Cambridge University Press, 1993).
[109] George Armstrong Kelly, *The Human Comedy: Constant, Tocqueville and French Liberalism* (Cambridge: Cambridge University Press, 1992), p. 1.

English Whiggism of the eighteen century was not liberalism itself, for it lacked the self-awareness of having liberty as its major political principle. English political observers of the eighteenth century would not usually emphasise liberty as the sole and most important feature of the Whig political establishment.[110] Liberalism emerged when what came to be perceived as Anglo-Saxon political practice was elaborated into a set of ideas about freedom.

This liberalism appeared only in the aftermath of the French revolution, although its intellectual foundations can be found in the thought of eighteenth century Anglophiles such as Montesquieu. It was a response to the lesson of the French revolution that political radicalism was not always a friend of the party of liberty. For a European liberal, Britain, and in some senses America, were the exemplars of how liberty could be achieved without the horrors of revolution, and how a system of laws and a political tradition could contribute to the stability of a free society. The main concern of this liberalism was how to turn freedom into a living tradition.[111] Therefore, a genuinely liberal party simply could not appear in Britain and America, for Whig liberalism saw Britain and America as liberal *societies*, which liberal *parties* in Europe took as their model.[112]

This is why continental European liberalism was so intimately connected with the question of Anglo-Saxon political development. It was a Frenchman who described the English constitution as the constitution of liberty.[113] And when, for example, the German liberal thinker Robert von Mohl described his views in the 1820s as those of 'an English Whig, a member of the French left-centre, and an Ameri-

---

[110] Reed Browning, *Political and Constitutional Ideas of the Court Whigs* (Baton Rouge: Louisiana State University Press, 1982), pp. 201-206; J.G.A. Pocock, 'Introduction,' in E. Burke, *Reflections on the Revolution in France* (Indianapolis: Hackett, 1987), pp. xviii-xxii.

[111] As Guido de Ruggiero noticed, the French liberalism of the nineteenth century tended to reproduce the traditionalism of the English liberalism of the eighteenth century. But it would be more correct to say that it is precisely this combination of the ideal of freedom with the emphasis on tradition which gives birth to European liberalism. See G. de Ruggiero, *The History of European Liberalism*, trans. R.G. Collingwood (London: Oxford University Press, 1927), p. 13.

[112] For America understood as a liberal society, see Hartz's notion of 'Grand Liberalism' and Shils' analysis of different strains within this liberalism. Louis Hartz, *The Liberal Tradition in America* (New York: Harcourt, Brace & World, 1955); Edward Shils, 'The Antinomies of Liberalism,' in *The Virtue of Civility* (Indianapolis: Liberty Fund, 1997), pp. 123-187.

[113] See Charles de Secondat, baron de Montesquieu, *The Spirit of the Laws*, trans. T. Nugent (New York: Hafner, 1949), ch. XI.

can Federalist',[114] he simply underlined the fact that the identity of European liberals of the time had been based on a reference to Anglo-Saxon political experience.

The programme of European liberalism often referred to existing British (or American) political institutions. Its central preoccupation was not with the free market as such, but with constitutionalism, balance of powers, rule of law, and basic civil and political liberties. A preferred regime for such a liberal would be based on constitutional monarchy, cabinet government and a respect for basic civil freedoms.[115] Liberalism was suspicious of Jacobinism, and was moderately conservative with regard to religion and morals. Instead of pursuing a secular agenda, it tried to reconcile religion with the free political order, and it usually found Protestantism to be more conducive to freedom than Catholicism. European liberals differed amongst themselves as to the degree of respect they showed towards religion, but they rarely went to the extremes of evangelical zeal, or of radical anti-clericalism.[116] They also tended to emphasise the importance of a strong morality as the ground of political freedom.[117]

Whig liberalism tended to recede where its programme had been implemented and society had become more liberal. This may explain the disappearance of liberal parties in twentieth century Western Europe.[118] As a political philosophy, however, Whig liberalism was not confined to the nineteenth century. Its advocates are likely to gain prominence whenever a liberal society is challenged from within or from without, and in such circumstances this liberalism acquires the character of the defence of the general political settlement of the liberal society. Cold War liberalism is one such example.

Oakeshott's liberalism should be understood as a part of this tradition. His favourite political thinkers, such as Montesquieu, Hegel, and Tocqueville, are directly associated with the variations of Whig

---

[114] Erich Angermann, *Robert von Mohl 1799-1875: Leben and Werk eines altliberalen Staatsgelehrten* (Neuwied: Hermann Luchterhand, 1962), p. 28. The French left of centre was at that period associated not with the anti-religious radicals of the Third Republic, but with liberals such as Constant or Guizot.

[115] See de Ruggiero, *The History of European Liberalism*, pp. 158-176; Dieter Langewiesche, *Liberalism in Germany*, trans. Ch. Banerji (London: Macmillan Press, 2000), pp. 1-16.

[116] See Kelly, *The Human Comedy*, pp. 93-114. Most of the French liberal Anglophiles such as Constant, Guizot and Madame de Staël, were Protestants.

[117] For example, see on Mme de Staël's views in Kelly, *The Human Comedy*, p. 99.

[118] Gordon Smith, 'Between Left and Right: The Ambivalence of European Liberalism,' in E.J. Kirchner (ed.), *Liberal Parties in Western Europe* (Cambridge: Cambridge University Press, 1988), p. 18.

liberalism. And what brings Oakeshott closer to Whig liberals is the importance that he attaches to British political experience, seen under the category of freedom. His thought cannot be reduced to British party politics, for what is important to him is the political consensus in his society. And if in the twentieth century this consensus is threatened, he attributes the responsibility for that to the collectivist policies of all parties.[119]

This position is most explicitly stated in the essay 'The Political Economy of Freedom' (1949), written as a review of H.C. Simons' *Economic Policy for a Free Society*. Mentioning that Simons is an American Oakeshott describes him as 'a libertarian, not because he begins with an abstract definition of liberty, but because he has actually enjoyed a way of living (and seen others enjoy it) which those who have enjoyed it are accustomed... to call a free way of living, and because he has found it to be good.'[120]

This 'libertarian' view is outlined here in terms akin to those of moderate liberal constitutionalism.[121] Freedom, for Oakeshott, is a peculiarly British experience, which is merely an abstraction for 'a Russian or a Turk'.[122] British freedom finds its expression not in any specific feature of its constitution, like private property, freedom of speech or parliamentary government but in the principle underlying all those liberties — 'the absence from our society of overwhelming concentrations of power'.[123] This distribution of power is found in 'a diffusion of authority between past, present and future',[124] in the dispersal of power among the multitude of interests in society and in the constitution, which limits government power. The method of government in such a society is the rule of law which removes from the citizens 'the fear of the power of our own government'.[125] It protects many species of freedom, among which the freedom of association and the freedom of private ownership are seen as especially important.

There are two enemies of this freedom. The first is collectivism, the attempt to build a planned society, 'the mobilisation of a society for

---

[119] CBP.
[120] RIP, p. 387.
[121] Oakeshott uses the term 'libertarian' only as a substitute for the word 'liberal' which he dislikes. It should not be confused with various contemporary libertarian doctrines.
[122] RIP, p. 387.
[123] RIP, p. 388.
[124] *Ibid.*
[125] RIP, p. 391.

unitary action'.[126] The other and perhaps the more dangerous of the two for Britain, is syndicalism, by which Oakeshott means the power of monopolies. Among them, trade unions are the strongest and most dangerous monopolies, for they, more than others, are able to impose their particular interests on the whole society.[127]

This view contains all the major assumptions of Whig liberalism. It is a reflection on the peculiar character of British and American societies through the concept of freedom. The emphasis on the importance of the continuity between past, present and future is combined with the 'libertarian' sentiment. Its discussion of economic policy is derivative of the implications that this policy is likely to have on the general experience of freedom in society. Its main concern is with the typically Whig problem of preventing the concentration of social power. It is suspicious of factionalism, thus reminding us of such Whig thinkers as Madison. Oakeshott himself names Tocqueville, Burckhardt and Acton as writers belonging to this tradition. His views are also similar to those of Cold War liberals, such as Hayek, Popper and Berlin who combine their adherence to freedom with the Anglo-Saxon socio-political model and thus follow the tradition of Whig liberalism.[128]

The peculiarity of Oakeshott's position is that usually the most outspoken thinkers of Whig liberalism came from the continental European political tradition. Hayek, Popper and Berlin were all continental Anglophiles. Unlike them, Oakeshott is an English thinker, and nevertheless his liberalism is European, and not specifically English. Oakeshott's English patriotism is, therefore, not accompanied by an intellectual parochialism. His intellectual perspective is not narrowly partisan. His liberalism is an exercise in self-awareness, an ability to see his own society from without as well as from within. Yet this double perspective enables him to adopt a more traditionalist rhetoric than the one characteristic of continental liberals. The rhetoric of European liberals was usually progressive and reformist, for their political ideal was external to their society. For Oakeshott, however, the same freedom is inherent in the tradition of

---

[126] RIP, p. 400.
[127] Cf. F.A. Hayek, *The Road to Serfdom* (London: George Routledge & Sons, 1944), pp 144-149. This point will be later elaborated by Mancur Olson, *The Logic of Collective Action: Public Goods and the Theory of Groups* (Cambridge, Mass: Harvard University Press, 1965).
[128] See Noël O'Sullivan, 'Visions of Freedom: The Response to Totalitarianism,' in J. Hayward, B. Barry & A. Brown (eds.), *The British Study of Politics in the Twentieth Century* (Oxford: Oxford University Press, 1999), pp. 63-88.

his own society, and where the reform is required, its purpose is the restoration of what this society has lost or is in danger of losing.[129]

There is, however, another, more radical sentiment present in Oakeshott's writings alongside Whig liberalism, which can be called 'Romantic liberalism'. Although the Romantic element never came to dominate European liberalism, Romanticism did leave its mark on liberal thought. The Romantic movement is usually perceived as an adversary of liberalism. Indeed, its rejection of the petit-bourgeois values, fascination with heroism, flirtation with the glorious past, aversion to routine, and hence its rejection of the principle of legality, are all contrary to liberal consciousness. However, as Nancy Rosenblum has shown, there are some elements which are common to both Romanticism and liberalism. This makes possible the construction of a coherent Romantic liberal worldview.[130]

This is especially true of proto-Romantic thinkers such as Herder and the young von Humboldt, or Romantic writers of an early generation such as Constant. They often combined an adherence to the idea of radical individuality with the cultural universalistic premises of the Enlightenment. They cherished the idea of diversity, originality and spontaneity, stressing the ideal of human self-development achieved through the free and harmonious exercise of individual capacities. Nevertheless, they did not follow more radical Romantics in confining this ideal to heroic individuals who rebelled against society. Instead, they perceived this individual self-development as a social ideal, which should be applied universally. The main question was how to avoid the clash between such spontaneous individuals.

Thus, von Humboldt recognised that the return to the ancient ideal, in which the reconciliation of spontaneity and sociality had been performed through public activity and heroic warfare, was no longer possible. In modern conditions the only way to ensure the development of individuality was through the enlargement of the private sphere to the maximal extent so that an individual would be able to exercise freely his capacities without hindering the similar development of others. This is achieved by minimalist government, the only task of which is to maintain the security of its citizens by means of law.[131]

---

[129] RIP, pp. 402-403.
[130] Nancy Rosenblum, *Another Liberalism: Romanticism and the Reconstruction of Liberal Thought* (Cambridge, Mass: Harvard University Press, 1987).
[131] Wilhelm von Humboldt, *The Limits of State Action*, trans. J.W. Burrow (Indianapolis: Liberty Fund, 1993).

Oakeshott was strongly influenced by this view,[132] although he often relates it to a more ancient tradition of Epicureanism. This is the perception of human beings as enjoying their freedom and developing their own capacities. This freedom is seen as inherent in human beings and valuable in itself. Oakeshott argues against the claim that freedom of speech, for example, should be based on utilitarian arguments. We cherish this right, he says, 'because we have become a people with a variety of opinions about all sorts of matters and we do not see why we should not utter them'.[133]

This view is most explicitly presented in 'On Being Conservative' (1956). Oakeshott begins with the analysis of what it means to have a conservative disposition in general. According to him, the conservative disposition is centred upon 'a propensity to use and enjoy what is available'.[134] It is attached to the present by virtue of its familiarity. It is conservative because it enjoys what the present offers rather than what the future promises. There are some activities which are inherently conservative, and they are those in which the enjoyment of the activity itself is sought, and not the outcome. These are friendship, conversation and patriotism. Others, such as fishing, can become conservative when pursued for their own sake.

But even activities which are not engaged in for their own sake entail a conservative element. In most activities there is a distinction 'between the project undertaken and the means employed, between the enterprise and the tools used for its achievement'.[135] The disposition towards tools is likely to be more conservative than the disposition towards projects, because, in order to use tools well, one needs to become familiar with them and this familiarity can be achieved only if the tools remain relatively unchanged. Sometimes there is a need to improve tools or to adapt them to new circumstances, yet tools will become useless if they are subject to continuous innovation.

General rules of conduct and, more specifically, civil rules can be regarded as such tools. Therefore, it is important that these rules are not being constantly changed. This attitude to rules is the essence of the conservative disposition in politics. But it is not necessarily connected to conservative conduct in other realms. Being conservative in politics can go together with being radical about everything else. Moreover, the conservative disposition in politics is even more

---
[132] *Ibid.*, pp. 16-21. In *On Human Conduct* Oakeshott employs Humboldt's vocabulary, such as 'human agency', 'spontaneity' or 'satisfaction of wants'.
[133] 'The Customer is Never Wrong,' RPML, p. 116.
[134] RIP, p. 408.
[135] RIP, p. 418.

appropriate for a society of passionate people. It starts with the acceptance 'of the current condition of human circumstances' which is 'the propensity to make our own choices and to find happiness in doing so'.[136] The government must regard citizens as adults who 'do not consider themselves under any obligation to justify their preference for making their own choices'.[137] And the task of the government is merely to rule, that is, to enforce general rules of procedure upon all subjects, in order to prevent some collisions arising from the pursuit of the variety of beliefs and activities; in other words its function is to maintain peace. The tools employed in this task are general laws, which are not concerned with moral right or wrong but only with activities 'in respect of their propensity to collide with one another'.[138] And this is a liberal doctrine. By limiting the sphere of law only to actions which are likely to lead to a 'collision', Oakeshott simply repeats the thesis of Mill's *On Liberty*, the essay which was strongly indebted to the young von Humboldt. He accentuates the values of privacy and individual choice and advocates the style of government which is most favourable to the conduct of affairs by independent individuals.

III

Whig and Romantic liberalism are not, of course, two opposite strains of thought, for their political sentiments are very similar. Both emphasise individuality, advocate the principle of freedom and support the idea of government by means of the rule of law. The elements of both views are often mixed in writings of many liberal authors.

However, there are implicit differences between these two kinds of liberalism. One of the most important is the different perspective they take towards the state and its relation to the individual, society and government. Whig liberalism recognises the distinct character of modern government and modern individuality. Yet it is often suspicious of their impact on freedom. Its nightmare is the tyranny of the all-powerful state over isolated individuals. Therefore it tends to emphasise the importance of society as a safeguard against this threat. It asserts the importance of the intermediate social structures and of the communal ties among individuals, and it sees the rule of law as the means of the distribution of power within the society. It objects to the complete break with the pre-modern polity, and tries

---

[136] RIP, p. 426.
[137] RIP, p. 427.
[138] RIP, p. 430.

to maintain continuity, whereby the sovereignty of the state and radical individuality are tempered by society. Thus, society as a whole, however complex and diverse, often becomes the basic unit of this approach.[139]

By contrast, Romantic liberals embrace individuality wholeheartedly. They recognise that the threat to individual freedom is twofold, coming from society as well as from government. Therefore, they are more sympathetic to the destruction of intermediate structures by the modern state, seeing in this the emancipation of the modern individual from various social constraints. The rule of law is understood to play an enabling rather than a preventive role. It is a mechanism, not for the dispersal of power, but rather for the creation of opportunities for free development. Whereas Whig liberals emphasise society as a whole, being concerned with the constitutional distribution of powers in such a society, Romantic liberals suggest that what is important in modern society is not a constitution, but the character of government activity. They tend to see the state not as a social unit but as a system of government which rules the multitude of independent individuals.

These two different perspectives on the character of the state can be found in Oakeshott's thought, and they replace holistic Idealism found in his earliest writings. In 'A Discussion of Some Matters Preliminary to the Study of Political Philosophy' Oakeshott described political life in the widest possible terms as life in society, in which 'we become subject to those sweet and profitable laws of conduct which bring with them such conditions of life as will answer to our real needs and desires'.[140] In other words, political life is understood in terms of the will 'to live a good life'.[141] It is a mistake to seek the good life 'in government rather than in friendship, in law rather than in moral sensibility, in ownership and rule rather than in religion and culture'.[142] For society is a moral relationship. It is 'a union of minds, and its solidarity... is a solidarity of feeling, opinion and belief.'[143]

The ultimate society is the state, the purpose of which is the good life. The state is a 'cultural unit'[144] and 'culture' is the end 'a state sets

---

[139] Alexis de Tocqueville, *Democracy in America*, trans. G. Lawrence (London: Fontana, 1994); G.W.F. Hegel, *Elements of the Philosophy of Right*, trans. H.B. Nisbet (Cambridge: Cambridge University Press, 1991).
[140] DSM, p. 37.
[141] DSM, p. 39.
[142] *Ibid.*
[143] DSM, p. 64.
[144] DSM, p. 72.

before itself'.[145] This means that the state 'possesses more than a mere unity of action; it must also have some degree of unity of purpose'.[146] Oakeshott speaks about the state as a self-sufficient moral and cultural association and cites Burke, who sees in the state a 'partnership'.[147] The more an association is a real unity with a common tradition, memory and purpose, the more it is a state in the true meaning of the word.

In 'The Authority of the State' (1929) Oakeshott repeated this idea, defining the state as 'the totality in an actual community which satisfies the whole mind of the individuals who comprise it'.[148]

This view of the state is congenial with the views of the British Idealists, for whom the state is 'not only the apparatus of governance', but is also 'inclusive of the whole social organism'.[149] The following discussion of the role that government and law play in society also proceeds along familiar Idealistic lines, where a holistic framework is called upon to shore up liberal political convictions. Although, or because, the state is an association with a clear moral purpose, government should not be equated with the state. In fact, its authority is self-limiting. The purpose of government is to serve the moral end of the society but government 'may not attempt that which it is unable to achieve'.[150] Government is only one of the associations within the state that serve the main purpose of the state. It is just a public service, although indeed 'a public service in scope and power far superior to other associations'.[151]

In the course of time, however, Oakeshott abandoned this explicit holism. His views of society underwent a change similar to the transformation of his philosophy of experience. Having started with the emphasis on totality, Oakeshott ended up with the vindication of plurality. Yet the evolution of his views of social life proceeded more slowly. After the publication of *Experience and Its Modes* he did not come out with uncompromising holistic claims with regard to the state. Nevertheless, up to the early fifties he spoke about politics and society in similar terms, describing politics as a concrete activity, and society as a partnership between past, present and future.[152] He

---

[145] DSM, p. 73.
[146] DSM, p. 75.
[147] DSM, p. 77.
[148] RPML, p. 83.
[149] David Boucher and Andrew Vincent, *British Idealism and Political Theory* (Edinburgh: Edinburgh University Press, 2000), p. 11.
[150] DSM, p. 160.
[151] DSM, p. 173.
[152] 'Political Education,' RIP, p. 56; 'The Political Economy of Freedom,' RIP, p. 388.

tended to see the state neither as a government nor as a multitude of people but as a social whole.

Yet he spoke in a more restrained way, and the emphasis on the centrality of society in his writings of the forties and fifties is reminiscent of classic nineteenth century Whig liberalism, rather than British Idealism. What is characteristic of French liberals and even British Whigs of that time is the change of emphasis in their thought from politics to society in general.[153] These liberals conceived the French revolution as an attempt to impose politics on society, and partly as a reaction to this, they tried to give primacy to society in understanding the historical process, thereby laying down the foundations of classical sociology. Politics was perceived as an important, but limited activity, the main purpose of which was to adjust political institutions to changes in the overall social structure. Social development was conceived through the idea of progress, yet this progress was seen as a gradual continuous development, abrupt changes being regarded as merely superficial events often concealing the true significance of the social process. The politics recommended was usually that of an optimistic, moderate reformism as an alternative to the extremes of the reactionary attempt to abolish the achievements of the Revolution and of the ideological zeal calling for a leap forward. Both extremes were understood to be the expressions of the ignorance of social reality.

Oakeshott's lecture 'Political Education' (1951) can be seen as the twentieth century restatement of this position. Oakeshott, of course, rejects any notion of a teleological direction of social development. As he says, 'in political activity... men sail in a boundless and bottomless sea; there is neither harbour for shelter nor floor for anchorage, neither starting-place nor appointed destination. The enterprise is to keep afloat on an even keel.'[154] This can be seen as a response to those who, like Tocqueville and Chateaubriand, being terrified by the dynamic of social change, described their condition as sailing in the sea, desperately trying to find a shelter in the storm.[155] Tocqueville hoped to find such a shelter in a 'new political science'.[156]

---

[153] See Larry Siedentop, 'Two Liberal Traditions,' in A. Ryan (ed.), *The Idea of Freedom: Essays in Honour of Isaiah Berlin* (Oxford: Oxford University Press, 1979), pp. 153-174; J.W. Burrow, *Whigs and Liberals: Continuity and Change in English Political Thought* (Oxford: Clarendon Press, 1988).

[154] RIP, p. 60.

[155] See Kelly, *The Human Comedy*, p. 27.

[156] *Ibid.*

Oakeshott, being a twentieth century liberal, does not believe in the nineteenth century liberal notion of progress.[157] However, notwithstanding this important departure, his analysis of political activity springs from the ideas of classic liberal sociology. Oakeshott distinguishes between two extremes in the understanding of political activity. One is the view of politics as a purely empirical activity, by which he means politics without policy, understood only as a power game. He perhaps refers to a sort of Namierite approach which focuses exclusively on interests and patronage, ignoring the role of ideas and beliefs in human activity. According to Oakeshott, such politics is impossible. This view of politics ignores the fact that human activity is not the function of a series of desires, but 'concrete activity', which probably means for Oakeshott that it always involves a system of beliefs.

The other view is that of politics as an ideological activity, springing from the attempt to implement some general principles. But this view is also misguided. Politics as an ideological project is an illusion, and the emphasis on some abstract principles only prevents us from grasping political changes in terms of the character of a society as a whole. Thus, the Russian and French Revolutions should not be understood in terms of their alleged ideological purposes, but as modifications of the entire circumstances of Russian and French society.[158]

In response to these two extremes Oakeshott recommends the view of politics as an activity which springs 'neither from instant desires, nor from general principles, but rather from the existing traditions of behaviour themselves'.[159] This view perceives politics as a pursuit of intimations of the tradition of a given society. Instead of seeing politics either in terms of a power game, or as an ideological project, Oakeshott seems to suggest that it should be perceived as a function of the *moeurs* of a society, of the habits and the character of its citizens, and of their own understanding of themselves. These *moeurs* are the context which puts limits on political activity, though without determining its particular directions. This kind of inquiry was undertaken in the past by thinkers such as Montesquieu and Tocqueville.[160] The difference, however, is that French liberals hoped that this 'new political science' would show the way to safety in the age of permanent change. Oakeshott cherishes no such illusions. The study of politics will never become a substitute for politi-

[157] Segal, 'A Storm from Paradise.'
[158] RIP, p. 59n.
[159] RIP, p. 56.
[160] Montesquieu, *The Spirit of the Laws*; Tocqueville, *Democracy in America*.

cal judgement, and 'political philosophy cannot be expected to increase our ability to be successful in political activity.'[161]

There is, however, a different perspective in Oakeshott's writings in which the central units of analysis are independent individuals and the government which regulates their actions. Individuals are indeed products of a certain tradition of behaviour and they act within various social associations and networks. But the emphasis here is different because of the strict distinction between society and government. Voluntary associations are perceived neither as composing the society as a whole, nor as playing the role of intermediate structures. They are just the outcome of the choices of citizens who see themselves as independent actors. The society is not perceived as an integrated whole, and the term 'sovereignty' is confined to the authority of the ruler.

This view is fully elaborated in *On Human Conduct*, yet its elements can be found in Oakeshott's earlier writings. The philosophical authority for this perspective is Hobbes, in whose thought Oakeshott had been interested since the thirties.[162] Oakeshott saw Hobbes as a moralist whose starting point had been 'unique *human individuality*',[163] and who had offered the most profound philosophical exploration of the morality of individuality. Moreover, Oakeshott drew a direct line between the dominant element of Hobbes' thought and 'the romantic doctrine of personality with its assertion of the primacy of will'.[164] Under his influence, Oakeshott became more and more concerned with the questions of individuality and of the legal order of the state, shifting the focus of his attention to the character of the office of modern government.

Oakeshott came to see the modern state as combining two possible attitudes towards government activity. In 1939 he argued that modern politics was the scene of the struggle between two kinds of doctrines, whose 'fundamental cleavage' lay

> between those which hand over to the arbitrary will of a society's self-appointed leaders the planning of its entire life, and those which not only refuse to hand over the destiny of a society to any set of officials but

---

[161] RIP, p. 65.
[162] On Oakeshott as a commentator of Hobbes' philosophy see Bruce P. Frohnen, 'Oakeshott's Hobbesian Myth: Pride, Character and the Limits of Reason,' *Western Political Quarterly* 43(4), 1990, pp. 789-809; Ian Tregenza, 'The Life of Hobbes in the Writings of Michael Oakeshott,' *History of Political Thought* 18(3), 1997, pp. 531-557; David Runciman, *Pluralism and the Personality of the State* (Cambridge: Cambridge University Press, 1997) pp. 15-16.
[163] 'The Moral Life in the Writings of Thomas Hobbes,' HCA, p. 84.
[164] 'Introduction to *Leviathan*,' HCA, p. 65.

also consider the whole notion of planning the destiny of a society to be both stupid and immoral.[165]

Ten years later he favourably noticed the view, later to be explored in *On Human Conduct*, which distinguished between political conduct that is based on general laws, and one based on the pursuit of an ideal.[166] And he was unambiguous in his criticism of factional 'pluralism', seeing 'syndicalism' as the main threat to English liberties.[167]

Gradually, a perspective emerges in which the state is the scene of the relationship between free individuals and the government by means of law. This perspective is central to *On Human Conduct*, but it is already unambiguously stated in 'On Being Conservative'. Moreover, the conceptual vocabulary of *On Human Conduct* seems to have been in part formed in the fifties. Oakeshott speaks about the distinction between 'ruling' and 'management', or between 'individual' and 'individual *manqué*'.[168] Thus, by the time he arrives at his main ideas about the character of the individual in the modern age, Oakeshott also shifts the emphasis from the holist view of society to one which would be more coherent with this assertion of radical individuality.

IV

Oakeshott is therefore a liberal writer, and the tensions found in his writings are those within liberalism itself between its Whig and Romantic elements. Our discussion, however, will not be complete without dealing with the question of Oakeshott's alleged conservatism. It is true that Oakeshott can partly be regarded as a conservative when this term is called upon to indicate a certain tendency within liberalism. For Whig liberalism is also known as 'conservative liberalism'.

Yet Oakeshott also earned the reputation as being a representative of a more distinct 'conservative' tradition, allegedly exemplified by Hooker and Burke. This conservatism is perceived as being opposed to modernity, liberalism, the Enlightenment and rationality. Some

---

[165] SPD, p. xxii n.
[166] Review of G.C. Field, *Principles and Ideals in Politics*, in *Cambridge Journal* 2(7), 1949, p. 446.
[167] RIP, p. 401. For 'pluralist' theories of the state see Runciman, *Pluralism and the Personality of the State*. These should not, of course, be confused with the plurality advocated by Oakeshott.
[168] Review of K.C. Wheare, *Government by Committee*, in *Spectator* 194, 1955, p. 129. Cf. HC, pp. 141-147. 'The Masses in Representative Democracy.' Cf. HC, pp. 234-242, 274-279.

writers even put him together with outspoken critics of modernity such as Carl Schmitt.[169]

The reputation of Oakeshott as a conservative in this sense seems to be solely based on his essay 'Rationalism in Politics' (1947), which is, perhaps, Oakeshott's most famous piece of writing, being included in many anthologies of conservative thought. This essay is, indeed, significantly different from most of Oakeshott's writings. 'The Tower of Babel' and 'On Being Conservative' cannot be regarded as conservative essays. And even in his most polemical pieces of the late forties, Oakeshott sounds more like a libertarian than a conservative traditionalist.[170]

'Rationalism in Politics', by contrast, does appear genuinely conservative. Here Oakeshott describes the character of the Rationalist, who, as he claims, came to dominate modern European life in general and its political arena in particular. The Rationalist is characterised by his disposition to stand for independence of mind on all occasions. He believes in the authority of reason, and his aspiration is to free the mind of all traditions and prejudices, to purge it before embarking upon critical inquiry, in order to achieve knowledge, unhindered by superstition.

This attitude is grounded upon a certain theory of knowledge. According to Oakeshott, every practical activity involves knowledge, and it is always of two sorts: 'technical' and 'practical'. Technical knowledge is that which can be formulated by explicit rules, deliberately learned, and put into practice. Practical knowledge, by contrast, is not reflective and cannot be explicitly formulated. This is the knowledge of how to do something, and it can be learned only by actually doing it. The fallacy of the Rationalist is that he does not recognise this second sort of knowledge, and believes that all knowledge can be reduced to 'technique'. For him, learning any activity is merely learning a set of defined rules. Therefore, 'his knowledge will never be more than half-knowledge, and consequently he will never be more than half-right.'[171] According to Oakeshott, this intellectual fashion acquired significance in post-Renaissance Europe, due especially to the vulgar interpretation of the philosophies of Bacon and Descartes, whose aim was to find a new infallible method of gaining knowledge of the world.

In politics Rationalism has become the prevalent style. It expresses itself in the 'problem-solving' approach. Rationalistic politics is the politics of the 'felt need'. The Rationalist sees society as

[169] Anderson, 'The Intransigent Right at the End of the Century.'
[170] These are CBP, 'The Political Economy of Freedom,' 'The B.B.C.'
[171] RIP, p. 36.

composed of problems, and he believes in the existence of the best administrative solution for every problem, although he is sometimes aware of his own inability to find this solution. For the Rationalist, politics turns into an engagement in permanent actions in order to 'improve' society by means of a defined set of rules, i.e. ideology or doctrine. Every tradition which does not fit his doctrine is rejected as a superstition. He wants to purge society of any tradition which cannot be rationally justified.

The reason for the victory of Rationalism in politics was, that the old classes, traditionally educated in the art of politics, had been replaced by new players who had not possessed practical political knowledge and whose only way of learning how to participate in political affairs had been by acquiring some sort of doctrine. Among such new players, there were a new ruler (like Machiavelli's prince), a new class (like Marx's proletariat), a new society (like the American colonies), and perhaps a new sex, each of whom exemplified the new style of Rationalistic politics.

Today, almost every political project is the expression of this Rationalism. Even the resistance to Rationalism must now be dressed in Rationalistic clothes, and this is 'the main significance of Hayek's *Road to Serfdom* — not the cogency of his doctrine, but the fact that it is a doctrine. A plan to resist all planning may be better than its opposite, but it belongs to the same style of politics.'[172] This is pernicious since Rationalism, involving a serious error with regard to human knowledge and activity, will always lead to the corruption of politics. The Rationalist will never achieve what he intends to achieve but, in his attempts to repair the shortcomings of his own actions, he will not be able to escape his Rationalistic approach and this will just deepen the problem.

This view certainly sounds like an exposition of what a conservative doctrine might look like. Oakeshott traces the origins of the evils of the modern style of politics to post-Renaissance Europe, and seems to be sympathetic to the pre-modern way of political conduct. The attribution of the ills of Rationalism to the rise of new political classes sounds extremely anti-egalitarian. Oakeshott is equally critical of socialist and liberal ideologies. And he obviously prefers pragmatic traditionalism to the individualism and self-reliance of the Rationalist.

Yet this polemic should not be taken out of proportion both with regard to the content of the essay, and to its place in Oakeshott's thought in general. The style of the essay is very polemical, but we

---

[172] RIP, p. 26.

must not be misled into taking it as a criticism of specific policies. Oakeshott offers here a sort of *longue durée* historical sketch, in which what is attempted is the critique of the overall tendency in the style of modern politics. And when the entire modern condition is criticised, no specific remedy can be suggested. Oakeshott's critique does not imply any particular political programme. Moreover, the criticism of modern rationalism does not entirely belong to conservative thought. In fact, 'Rationalism in Politics' was written just after the publication of Horkheimer's and Adorno's *Dialectic of Enlightenment*, which contained a similar critique of rationalism, the spirit of which it found in the legacy of Francis Bacon.[173]

Thus, mentioning 'a Declaration of the Rights of Man' or 'Votes for Women' among the examples of Rationalistic politics does not necessarily mean that Oakeshott rejects outright the political experience of American society often understood to be based on the idea of human rights and universal suffrage. We have already seen that Oakeshott regards Hayek's book as an example of Rationalism, yet we can hardly conclude from this that he rejects Hayek's political ideas.

Furthermore, Oakeshott's critique must not be confused with the rejection of rationality. He did not object to technical knowledge so long as its importance was not exaggerated at the expense of practical knowledge. He himself distinguished between 'rationality' and 'rationalism' — seeing the latter as the perversion of the former. In 'Scientific Politics' (1947) he criticised Hans Morgenthau for making himself 'appear the advocate of irrationality'.[174] The suggestion that there was a past golden age of true and successful politics which preceded the rationalist age seem to Oakeshott to come 'pretty close to the higher nonsense'.[175] As he said in a letter to Karl Popper, 'Rationalism in my sense is, among other things, thoroughly *un*reasonable.'[176]

The genuinely conservative element of 'Rationalism in Politics' is found neither in its mentioning of specific policies, nor in its alleged rejection of rational inquiry, but in its critique of post-Renaissance European history. Modern Western liberty is the outcome of post-Renaissance European historical development, and, therefore, the rejection of this development sounds strongly illiberal. Yet the sentiment expressed in 'Rationalism in Politics' is not characteristic

---

[173] Theodor W. Adorno and Max Horkheimer, *Dialectic of Enlightenment*, trans. J. Cumming (London: Verso, 1979), pp 3-5.
[174] RPML, p. 100.
[175] RPML, p. 107.
[176] Letter to K. Popper, January 28, 1948, Hoover Institute Archives.

of Oakeshott's thought in general. Only a few years later Oakeshott suggests that modern political experience is composed of two opposite views of the character of government activity. One regards ruling as 'a first order activity', implying the ideological politics of a sort criticised in 'Rationalism in Politics', and the other sees it as 'a second order activity', in which the government is recognised as a custodian of general rules of conduct.[177] Oakeshott stresses that the purpose of his paper is to show that the second view plays a no less important role in modern European political experience than the first one.

Finally, in 'The Masses in Representative Democracy' (1957) a completely different picture emerges. European politics is seen as being a scene of two opposite characters: one is the 'individual' and the other is the 'individual manqué' who sometimes turns into the 'anti-individual'. While in 'Rationalism in Politics' the Rationalist is regarded as a dominant type, here the 'individual' is the superior character and the 'anti-individual' is just a shadow. The 'anti-individual' is unable to present a victorious alternative to the 'individual', for the anti-individual 'has imposed himself emphatically only where the relics of a morality of communal ties survived to make plausible his moral and political impulses'.[178] Oakeshott seems to suggest that totalitarianism is not an essentially modern phenomenon and that it becomes a plausible alternative only in the societies which are half modern, in which a morality of individuality has already appeared but a morality of communal ties still exists. Only such half-developed societies are inclined to chose the alternative suggested by the 'anti-individual'.

Thus, ten years after the publication of 'Rationalism in Politics', Oakeshott offers a completely different interpretation of modern European history, associating it not with the arrogant Rationalist, but with the confident individualist. The alarmism of 'Rationalism in Politics' is genuine, but transitory in Oakeshott's thinking. One should not be tempted to make a superficial interpretation of Oakeshott's entire thought simply in the light of 'Rationalism in Politics' just because this is the most popular of his essays.

Furthermore, 'Rationalism in Politics' cannot be reduced exclusively to the analysis of politics. We have already seen that it is partly a philosophical essay, which offers a certain theory of knowledge. Even more importantly, at the end of the essay, we learn that its major concern is not politics. Although Oakeshott is critical of the

---
[177] IC.
[178] RIP, p. 382.

great influence of Rationalism on modern politics, he qualifies himself by saying that in this field Rationalism is never the sole disposition as 'there have always been men of genuine political education'.[179] What he is really worried about is that the embracing of the Rationalist idiom in politics will lead to its intrusion into other aspects of social life and, especially, into education. The primary object of the Rationalist attacks in the field of education are universities. However, the loss here 'may not be irreparable'.[180] Universities have enough power to defend themselves, if they are prepared to use it. The situation is more grave in the field of moral education in which the Rationalist has already won by turning our morality into the morality of the self-conscious pursuit of moral ideals.

It follows, then, that this essay which appears first as a critique of politics turns out to be mostly concerned with the condition of modern education. Oakeshott often sounds more pessimistic and traditionalist when it comes to the question of education rather than politics, at least at first glance. Why this is so will be discussed in the last chapter. What is important here is that, even granted the conservative character of this specific essay, one can notice that its pessimism does not necessarily relate to politics.

V

Thus, in his writings on politics prior to *On Human Conduct* Oakeshott reveals a strong liberal sentiment, promoting the ideas of freedom, individuality and the rule of law. This sentiment is composed of two different strains: a more conservative society-oriented Whig liberalism, and a more radically individualistic Romantic liberalism. They coexist in Oakeshott's writings in all periods, yet Romantic liberalism gains pre-eminence from the middle fifties onward.

Oakeshott's kind of liberalism had predecessors in English political thought. The Whig and Romantic elements are clearly present, for example, in the writings of J.S. Mill. Yet it is important to understand that Oakeshott, like Mill himself a hundred years earlier, is indebted to the continental Anglophile liberal political tradition. Interestingly, this is noticed by Ian Buruma who speaks about the Anglophile writings of the Russian nineteenth century émigré Alexander Herzen, arguing that this Russian Anglophile 'sounds like a classic English Tory philosopher, a Bagehot, an Oakeshott, a Roger

---
[179] RIP, p. 35.
[180] RIP, p. 40.

Scruton before his time'.[181] At least with respect to Oakeshott, Buruma misses the point. It is not Herzen who sounds like Oakeshott. It is Oakeshott who sounds like a European Anglophile.

We have taken, then, a look at Oakeshott's political opinions, however we cannot yet speak about Oakeshott's political philosophy. His miscellaneous writings on politics are not necessarily systematic or original. Oakeshott follows the thought of others, rather than developing a coherent political philosophy of his own. Consequently, this section have dealt more with the context of Oakeshott's opinions than with the analysis of his ideas.

The change comes with *On Human Conduct*, where Oakeshott transforms his opinions into an original philosophical statement. While retaining his liberal vision, Oakeshott expresses it in the language which is consistent with his philosophy of society and fits into his philosophy in general. How this is done is the subject of the next section.

THE CIVIL PHILOSOPHY
I

We have finally arrived at what Oakeshott calls his 'civil philosophy'. In it he completes his philosophy of society by theorising the appropriate terms of a comprehensive association of human beings which would be compatible with the character of such beings as delineated in the philosophy of practice and morality. The terms of such an association are those of 'civility'.

Civil philosophy is, perhaps, the most distinctive part of Oakeshott's thought. This does not mean that there is no element of originality in the rest of his philosophy, yet, as we have seen, in his philosophy of experience Oakeshott largely employs the available intellectual resources of his time while the originality of his approach lies not in any specific set of ideas but in the juxtaposition of several apparently different or contradictory schools of thought. The originality of his philosophy of society, and particularly of his civil philosophy, is of a different kind. Its vocabulary and central postulates are Oakeshott's own. It is, of course, related to the contemporary intellectual context and to some of its dominant questions such as the character of the modern state and of modern freedom. Yet Oakeshott succeeds in radically transforming these questions by moving beyond the conventional conceptual apparatus of modern political thought.

[181] Ian Buruma, *Voltaire's Coconuts, or Anglomania in Europe* (London: Weidenfeld & Nicolson, 1999), p. 122.

As a teacher in the history of political thought, Oakeshott was very familiar with texts in this subject across all periods and this made his own philosophy less confined to any specific trend or influence. Certainly, some more specific links can be found between Oakeshott and other authors, as this study attempted to show in the previous section. Yet the more philosophical his thought becomes, the more distant appears its relationship to a particular context.

Therefore, in order to understand Oakeshott's civil philosophy, it is more important to focus on the analysis of its connection with the rest of his thought. Its significance lies in the degree of coherence that it bestows upon the whole. This section will attempt to highlight various threads of Oakeshott's civil philosophy in order to elucidate its central place in his philosophy of society and, thereby, to connect it with his philosophy of experience. Only then will it be possible to see in what sense Oakeshott's civil philosophy is the reflection of what is claimed here to be the underlying vision of his thought in general: the defence of Western modernity.

The civil philosophy is, certainly, one of the best known parts of Oakeshott's thought. Many commentators have engaged in interesting discussions about its merits or in clarifications of its specific details.[182] Yet the question of its relation to the whole has not been answered satisfactorily and this is the question which I regard to be central for an adequate understanding of his thought.

The task here is, therefore, to determine the place of Oakeshott's civil philosophy in his thought as a whole. This is the sort of analysis which Oakeshott appears to be advocating in respect of the history of political thought. Thus, in his introduction to *Leviathan* he claims that Hobbes' civil philosophy must be understood as a reflection of Hobbes' general philosophy. He argues that the general character of Hobbes' thinking is reflected in every specific object of his attention. Since, for Hobbes, philosophy 'is the world as it appears in the mirror of reason,' his civil philosophy 'is the image of the civil order reflected in that mirror'.[183] The claim of this study is that this state-

---

[182] For example, Benjamin R. Barber, 'Conserving Politics: Michael Oakeshott and Political Theory,' *Government and Opposition* 11, 1979, pp. 446-463; R.N. Berki, 'Oakeshott's Concept of Civil Association: Notes for a Critical Analysis,' *Political Studies* 29(4), 1981, pp. 570-585; Richard E. Flathman, *The Practice of Political Authority* (Chicago: The University of Chicago Press, 1980); John Liddington, 'Oakeshott: Freedom in a Modern European State,' in J. Gray & Z. Pelczynski (eds.), *Conceptions of Liberty in Political Philosophy* (London: The Athlone Press, 1984), pp. 289-320; David R. Mapel, 'Civil Association and the Idea of Contingency,' *Political Theory* 18(3), 1990, pp. 392-410; Bhikhu Parekh, 'Oakeshott's Theory of Civil Association,' *Ethics* 106, 1995, pp. 158-186.
[183] HCA, p. 17.

ment betrays Oakeshott's own criterion of philosophical reflection and that his civil philosophy is an attempt to achieve coherence which would reflect the character of his philosophy in general.

II

Oakeshott's most elaborate and mature presentation of his civil philosophy can be found in the second and the third essay of *On Human Conduct* (1975) and in the writings related to this book. These are the collection of earlier essays *Hobbes on Civil Association* (1975), which includes the revised introduction to *Leviathan*, and the essay 'The Rule of Law' appearing in the volume *On History* (1983). Here I will concentrate on the argument presented in *On Human Conduct*, yet occasional glimpses at the related writings will offer interesting insights into the character of Oakeshott's thinking.

For Oakeshott, theorising the political and social institutions of a society is intimately connected with understanding the basic questions of human intercourse and morality and, therefore, his analysis of the postulates of modern society is related to his understanding of the character of modern human beings. We have seen that Oakeshott claims that the peculiar feature of modern consciousness is the perception of human beings as free agents making choices of their own. The most vibrant members of modern society enjoy this condition yet even those who deplore it do not contest the premise of the individuality of agency. Therefore, one of the central questions of social theory must be what kind of durable social arrangements are compatible with the existence of the modern individual and, more specifically, how his quest for freedom can be reconciled with the necessity of social coexistence.

Oakeshott's exploration of the civil condition in terms of an ideal type and in terms of an imperfect reflection of this type in European history is the attempt to answer this question. He starts with the analysis of the civil condition as an ideal character, which exists nowhere specifically, but which can be used as a device for a better understanding of some central characteristics of modern society. Briefly, his view is this.

We have seen that human conduct, understood as an intercourse between free human agents, can be analytically distinguished into two aspects, each present in every actual performance. One is the substantive aspect in which action is understood as a specific choice to do *this* rather than *that* in order to achieve a particular satisfaction. The other is the formal aspect, in which action is understood as being made under the conditions of a practice or practices. Therefore, action is always a performance designed to achieve a certain substantive outcome under general conditions which do not specify the character of the action involved or the outcome desired.

Similarly, any more or less durable relationship of human agents can be understood in two different ways, or 'modes of association'.[184] One is association in respect of the substantive element of human conduct which is the pursuit of the satisfaction of specific wants; the other is association in respect of the formal character of human conduct, that is, in terms of practices governing these actions. These two modes are not types of actually existing associations, but represent two categorially distinct ideal characters.

An association in respect of the pursuit of wants may take different forms. One is the 'intermittent, transactional association'[185] where agents are bargainers entering into a relationship with each other in order to pursue their own individual wants. A more durable association is, however, an 'enterprise association' where members are joined in the pursuit of some common goal. In order to pursue this goal in contingent and always changing circumstances, the members design a certain procedure of making managerial decisions, appoint those responsible for making such decisions, and may formulate a certain system of rules conducive to the achievement of their common purpose. However, the terms of the association are not its rules but the purpose and its pursuit in contingent circumstances.

It is this last consideration that distinguishes such an association from the categorially different 'moral association' which is an association in terms of its own conditions. Its rules are perceived as not having an extraneous purpose but as being the very terms of the association, irrespective of whatever goals its members may pursue. The civil association is a moral association, the peculiarity of which is that its practice is the system of the deliberately enacted and alterable law.[186]

To put it briefly, the civil association is everything that the enterprise association is not. It is a non-purposive moral association in terms of its conditions, whereas the enterprise association is a purposive instrumental association in terms of the pursuit of substantive satisfactions. The requirements of its law (which Oakeshott calls *lex*) are general rules and not specific commands. They demand not

---

[184] HC, p. 108. Sometimes Oakeshott sounds as if he regards the relationship of affection as another mode of association (p. 123), but he nowhere develops this point.
[185] HC, p. 112.
[186] HC, p. 182.

the performance of specific actions but the subscription to their conditions in any self-chosen action. These rules are equal and general, referring not to particular persons or places, but to a certain kind of relationship. Therefore, no action can escape, in principle, from the jurisdiction of law.

Now, because the rules of *lex* are general and refer to future and unforeseeable situations, the civil association presupposes the process of 'adjudication', and the office of judge, in order to clarify the meaning of *lex* in particular situations where there is uncertainty or dispute. However, the character of this deliberation is strictly limited. Although it is impossible to deduce a particular inference from the general rule, the decision is expected to be contingently related to the invoked rule and be compatible with the overall system of law. Considerations of the legislative intention, or of the subjective opinion of the judge, are excluded. The precedent is invoked only as an analogy which cannot be the ground of the decision in a different situation. The only relevant considerations are whether a particular action falls under the jurisdiction of some rule, whether this rule is valid and whether the action failed to subscribe properly to the conditions of the rule.[187]

Further, the rules of civil association are alterable, which presupposes the existence of an office authorised to deliberately enact and change laws. However, unlike in the enterprise association, this is done not on the grounds of the propensity of laws to promote a certain goal but on the account of the desirability of the conditions of conduct they prescribe, irrespective of the substantive outcomes of the observance of those laws. Also, civil association presupposes the office of rulers whose task is to enforce adequate subscriptions to the rules of the association. Rulers cannot use the office for the satisfaction of their private wants and their only concern is to take care of the continuous general observance of the rules.[188]

Now, civil association is a self-sufficient association and therefore it is the foundation and justification of its own terms. Civil authority and civil obligation are inherent in the association and are irrelevant to any extraneous considerations. The rules are authoritative and the subjects (*cives*) have the obligation to subscribe to them not because these rules are established in accordance with some criterion of desirability, nor because they are either approved or habitually obeyed by subjects or efficiently enforced. They are authoritative because they are valid rules and are acknowledged to be valid rules.

---

[187] HC, pp. 130-138.
[188] HC, pp. 138-147.

Obligation is not renounced in the disapproval of a rule or in the failure or even the refusal to comply. It is terminated only when the authority of rules, not their desirability, is challenged. This acknowledgement of rules in terms of their authority, as distinct from their desirability, Oakeshott calls 'assent'.[189]

This association in terms of the acknowledgement of the authority of general rule postulates 'civil freedom'. *Cives* are inherently free in such an association. Firstly because general rules do not specify particular actions so that everyone is free to pursue any goals in his self-chosen actions so long as the conditions of the association are not violated. Secondly because these conditions are recognised only in terms of their authority, while their desirability can always be contested. This is not true for the enterprise association, in which the members are required to recognise the common purpose of such an association and to approve specific performances which supposedly promote this purpose. This freedom does not belong to the postulates of such an association and it is contingent upon members acknowledging this purpose and these decisions as their own and being capable of extricating themselves from their choice to be associated in case they no longer agree with it.[190]

In contrast, in the civil association, the deliberation about rules in terms of their desirability is separated from the recognition of their authority, which presupposes a distinct activity — that is an engagement in 'politics'. This is the activity of considering the desirability of certain provisions of law and influencing the occupants of the legislative office to enact, alter or keep intact a certain rule.

The difficult question, however, is what kind of deliberation can be considered appropriate in this engagement, for the peculiar character of the civil association excludes many possibilities. Thus, desirability of rules cannot be considered in terms of their utility, because laws are not supposed to have any substantive purpose, and the rules are not devices for reconciling different interests or promoting a common goal. One could then suggest that the relevant consideration might be the correspondence of rules with the moral maxims of a society so that changes of laws would be an outcome of changes in moral sentiments. This link between civil rules and moral precepts is a more plausible consideration because civil association is a moral

---

[189] HC, p. 183. See an interesting interpretation of the notion of 'assent' in W. John Coats Jr., *Oakeshott and Its Contemporaries* (Selinsgrove: Susquehanna University Press, 2000), p. 83. The use of this term also hints at a possible influence of R.M. Hare. See Hare, *The Language of Morals* (Oxford: Clarendon Press, 1952), pp. 13, 18-20.

[190] HC, pp. 157-158.

association and, indeed, Oakeshott characterises the civil association as 'a very imperfect reflection of what are currently believed to be "just" conditions of conduct'.[191] However, he insists that there is no direct link here and that the civil association cannot incorporate moral rules just on account of their being held by associates. He specifically says that the political utterance is one 'about which there is something to be thought and said other than what may be thought and said in terms of fact or moral conviction'.[192] Oakeshott is extremely careful not to give the impression that the civil association is an association which enforces a particular morality.

There is a third possibility which is that the desirability of civil rules can be considered in terms of what the American theorist of law Lon Fuller called the 'internal morality of law'.[193] These are the principles implied in the legal system itself such as the requirement of law not to be retroactive, self-contradictory and so forth. Oakeshott mentions these principles as inherently belonging to the system of *lex*.[194] Yet it is clear that they are not those deliberated in the consideration of 'civil desirability' for, according to Oakeshott, those principles are the conditions of any rule if it is to be a proper part of *lex*. Therefore, one can suggest that whatever alterations are advocated in a rule both the current and imagined conditions are supposed to acknowledge the inner morality of law.

But then the difficult question is what is left when considerations of utility, of moral conviction or of inherent qualities of law are excluded. Oakeshott seems to be squaring the circle here and it is not surprising that he prefers to show what this deliberation is not, rather than what it is. Moreover, he argues that there is no abstract answer to this question. The best he can do is to offer some examples of the conditional criteria of the considerations of civil desirability. One such consideration is that a civil prescription is undesirable if it is incapable of enforcement. This may be the unconditional criterion only in respect of the requirement of belief, for beliefs cannot be enforced, but in most cases it is conditioned by specific circumstances. The consideration here is to prevent legislation which would require 'for its enforcement an apparatus of search and inquisition... such as to conflict with the norms of civil conduct... plausi-

---

[191] HC, p. 154. In 'The Rule of Law,' OH, pp. 129-178, he develops this point further, arguing that that the alteration of law may derive from its deliberation in terms of *jus* as distinguished from its authority.
[192] HC, p. 171.
[193] Lon L. Fuller, *The Morality of Law* (New Haven: Yale University Press, 1969).
[194] HC, p. 153n.

bly tolerated by the *respublica*.[195] Another criterion is that the subscription to the civil condition should be required only in respect of the harm inflicted on other agents. Again, this rule is not unconditional, and Mill's mistake was to turn it into an absolute maxim, because no action is exempt in principle from the considerations of civility. Nevertheless, the civil association recognises the 'circumstantial privacy' of the subjects.[196] Finally, any innovation should be such that it can be accommodated into the entire system and the values of continuity and economy should be taken into consideration whilst deliberating any proposed change.

Oakeshott does not offer the general principle of civil desirability yet the above examples are not completely unconnected as they hint at a possible sentiment guiding them. Indeed, all of them are explicitly formulated in such a way as to justify themselves on account of their necessity for the integrity of civil association. However, a more substantive element is implied in at least the first two of these principles which evoke not only the formal concern about the coherence of law but also a more substantive concern about the direction of the legal system. This concern seems to be the preservation of freedom not only as a formal quality but also as the kind of freedom which is familiar to modern people. For these criteria are directed against the increase in the apparatus of the discretionary power of the state and against an excessive interference in the relatively self-regarding actions of individuals.

But civil association tolerates no substantive concerns. Therefore, Oakeshott cannot turn these considerations into unconditional principles. He is careful to emphasise that they are contingent upon historical circumstances and cannot impose *a priori* limits on the content of civil requirements. Although in the purely theoretical world there is no place for this substantive concern, it seems that, for Oakeshott, the ideal character of civil association is circumstantially connected with the kind of freedom that we recognise as belonging to us.

This historical connection between the ideal character of the civil condition and an historical association of human beings is illuminated in Oakeshott's description of the character of a modern European state in the third essay of *On Human Conduct*. Oakeshott claims that this state came to possess a distinct character of its own in the course of contingent gradual modifications of the conditions of medieval life. It replaced a different kind of polity, the medieval realm, and one of its major characteristics was the appearance of a

---
[195] HC, p. 179.
[196] *Ibid*.

sovereign ruler who presided over a more or less diverse collection of subjects and was acknowledged to possess a hitherto unimaginable authority and enjoyed the use of significant power.

This new state was an ambiguous phenomenon and it invited various attempts to understand its character more clearly, either for pragmatic or philosophical reasons. According to Oakeshott, the attempts to understand the modern state, the office of its government, and the character of its subjects can be generally divided into two kinds. The one was understanding the state in terms of *societas*, in which citizens were understood to be joined in the acknowledgement of the rules of the association. The other was understanding the state as *universitas*, in which the terms of the association were not the common rules of conduct, but the common substantive purpose. In other words, these two models of historical artefacts roughly corresponded to the ideal characters of the civil and the enterprise association.[197]

Because of the ambiguity of actually existing states, there was enough material to give some plausibility to both models. Oakeshott offers a significant number of examples for both kinds of understanding, formally trying to maintain the symmetry between them. He seems to suggest that the character of a modern European state is twofold, containing both the potential features of *societas* and *universitas*, and that neither can ultimately prevail at the expense of the other. This because these two characters 'are not friends, but nor are they exactly foes; perhaps... their relationship is that of "sweet enemies".'[198]

However, the symmetry and even-handedness are deceptive. Firstly, as we have seen, Oakeshott's discussion focuses on the civil condition, and the example of the enterprise association is evoked only to create a contrast in order to elucidate the character of the civil association. There is no doubt that Oakeshott regards 'civility' to be the suitable terms of such a comprehensive association as the modern state. Secondly, at least in one respect, the balance between the description of *societas* and *universitas* is not maintained. The number of famous political thinkers associated with *societas* is greater than the number of those associated with *universitas*. Among the latter Oakeshott includes Bacon, cameralists, early socialists (St. Simon, Owen) and Marx. But most authors present in the mainstream of the curriculum of European political philosophy (including Machiavelli, Bodin, Hobbes, Spinoza, Kant, Fichte, Hegel, Locke, Constant,

---

[197] HC, pp. 199-206.
[198] HC, p. 326.

Mill, Ranke, Burke, Montesquieu, Madison and others) are mentioned among those who either implicitly accepted or explicitly theorised the postulates of *societas*.[199] It can be argued that Oakeshott's classification is very questionable and that he adapts the views of these thinkers to fit his conceptual framework. It is doubtful whether thinkers such as Spinoza, Fichte or Hegel would feel themselves comfortably in the company of the theorists of *societas*. Yet, be that as it may, Oakeshott's point is clear: at least on the intellectual level, the superiority of understanding the state as *societas* is unquestionable.

Thirdly, and most importantly, each understanding of the modern state is linked to the different kind of associates who happen to be its citizens. We have already seen that Oakeshott asserts that modern European states are composed of two opposite characters: the individual and the individual *manqué*. He thinks that historically the two characters are likely to recognise different kinds of state as suiting their dispositions. The individual tends to see the state in terms of *societas* because this leaves him the freedom of making choices for himself. Of course, there is nothing in the character of the individual to prevent him from joining a variety of enterprise associations. But the state itself cannot be an enterprise association, because it is a compulsory comprehensive association, the members of which usually have not chosen to belong to it. In contrast, the individual *manqué* tends to regard the modern state as a *universitas*, so that it will make his choices for him.

But we have already seen that the individual is the dominant and most vibrant character in European history, whereas the individual *manqué* is the passive and derivative one, who recognises the modern postulates of individuality but sees them as a burden. So, since the morality of individuality is the major and exclusive development of modern Western consciousness, the state as *societas* corresponds to the attitude which is the drive of Western civilisation. In contrast, the state as *universitas* belongs to the always present but, in some sense, secondary disposition.

Therefore, despite the apparent balance between two understandings of the character of the modern European state, Oakeshott's description implies a preference in favour of *societas*. A modern state can never become *societas*, in the full sense, but the intimations of *societas* in the existing Western states are in some sense the most authentic expressions of our civilisation. Therefore, the virtues of

---

[199] HC, pp. 244-263, 287-310.

civility deserve to be cherished as an exclusive property of this civilisation.

III

Oakeshott's philosophy of the civil condition provoked various responses, elaborations and attempts at criticism and refinement with regard to its different aspects. However, my concern here is not with any particular aspect of Oakeshott's civil philosophy, but with its place within his thought in general. So, the two questions to explore are how his analysis of the civil condition complements the rest of his philosophy of society and how his philosophy of society is related to his philosophy as a whole. And I will concentrate on the analysis of details of his argument only in so far as this is essential for answering these questions.

So, what did *On Human Conduct* contribute to the development of Oakeshott's philosophy of society? At first glance, one can say that there is an obvious link between *On Human Conduct* and Oakeshott's earlier ethical and political writings. The civil condition is the ideal mode of relationship which is complementary to the modern morality of individuality first discussed by Oakeshott in his writings of the fifties.[200] The individual wants to live in a society in which his freedom to pursue choices of his own is not compromised. And the civil condition is presented as the relationship of human beings in which their freedom is not only unrestricted but even inherently belongs to the character of the association.

Furthermore, the articulation of the centrality and mutual dependence of freedom, individuality and the rule of law is reminiscent of the concerns of European liberalism. More specifically, Oakeshott follows the trend of 'Romantic liberalism' which became more salient in his later essays. The civil condition is the relationship of free individuals only in respect of the acknowledged rules, and not in terms of the holistic understanding of a society as the diversity unified in laws and customs, nor of a state as the ultimate completion of various social institutions. The emphasis, here, is on the unified system of impersonal rules promoting the civil freedom of individuals.

However, Oakeshott moves farther than other Romantic liberals, and farther than Oakeshott himself in his earlier essays, would be prepared to go. A liberal is usually content with a more moderate claim that the restriction of freedom by laws is the most economical

---

[200] 'The Masses in Representative Democracy'; MPME.

device of ruling and is conducive to the preservation of the greatest amount of liberty of all citizens.[201] Indeed, this seems to be Oakeshott's own claim in 'On Being Conservative'. However, in *On Human Conduct* Oakeshott claims that freedom is inherent in the civil association and even that it is not compromised by the existence of laws at all. In other words, he postulates not the alliance of freedom and the rule of law but their fundamental identity. In his philosophical exploration of liberal society, Oakeshott goes towards the most extreme point and the novelty of his position lies in this radicalisation and transformation of liberal postulates.

This provokes the question of whether what we identified at first glance as a liberal theory retains its liberal character after such a transformation. There are commentators who doubt the connection between the theory of civil association and liberalism or liberal individualism. According to some of them, Oakeshott's views contradict liberalism[202] whilst others recognise in his views a certain strain of liberalism but claim that it is based on principles different from those of other liberals.[203] I want to focus on two specific arguments supporting those positions. The first claim is that civil association is in some sense an embodiment of morality, being similar to Hegel's *Sittlichkeit*.[204] The second is that Oakeshott spurns the idea of 'negative' freedom understood as the absence of constraint, and that his understanding of civil freedom is qualitatively different.[205] To what extent are these claims correct?

For Oakeshott, civil association is a moral association, being categorially different from both an association in terms of the pursuit of a common purpose and an association in which individuals

---

[201] As, for example, in the following passage: 'Yet while a great deal of silly and harmful legislation would still be possible under the Rule of Law, it is at least not likely that oppressive legislation would be passed under it. The requirement that the laws must be equally applicable to all, that nobody must have the power of dispensing from them, makes this highly improbable. I will admit that some religious fanatics might wish to enforce general rules which others would feel as very severe restrictions of their liberty. But there are at least few rational grounds on which men could wish to impose upon all such restrictions — and where it might be attempted, as in the case of the prohibition of alcoholic drinks and the like, such restrictions are not likely to remain long effective if a substantial number of people regard them as oppressive.' F.A. Hayek, *The Political Ideal of the Rule of Law* (Cairo: National Bank of Egypt, 1955), p. 47.

[202] For example, Robert Devigne, *Recasting Conservatism: Oakeshott, Strauss, and the Response to Postmodernism* (New Haven: Yale University Press, 1994), pp. 119-121.

[203] For example, Franco, *The Political Philosophy of Michael Oakeshott*, pp. 230-236.

[204] *Ibid.*, pp. 172, 182.

[205] Devigne, *Recasting Conservatism*, p. 121.

bargain with each other, pursuing their individual goals. Such a characterisation may provoke the conclusion that Oakeshott sees in the state a kind of moral partnership. Thus, according to Paul Franco, civil association is reminiscent of Hegelian *Sittlichkeit* being 'a living tradition, a way of life', and not simply 'something fixed, finished, or essentially dead'.[206]

There is no doubt that Oakeshott admired Hegel's philosophy and attempted to reinterpret it in line with his own notion of civil association. Thus, according to Oakeshott, Hegel's idea of Right presupposes laws which never demand substantive performances but only prescribe conditions of conduct. Moreover, although Oakeshott recognises that Hegel rejected the authenticity of action as the sole criterion of its moral quality, he nevertheless argues that Hegel attributed the highest importance to the principle of authenticity which is central to preserving the integrity of subjects. For Oakeshott, Hegel remains the philosopher who, far from transcending modern individuality in the holistic framework of the state, based his idea of the state on the full development of the self-awareness of an individual.[207]

This is not how Hegel's philosophy is usually understood. Oakeshott seems to downplay its holistic and teleological aspects, in which the idea of Right reaches its dialectical completion in the system of customs, laws and beliefs of a particular society. *Sittlichkeit* is the moral life as a whole and it is the highest expression of the moral life.[208] And therefore, it is important to discuss whether civil association is similar to *Sittlichkeit* in this respect. Thus, Andrew Sullivan seems to suggest that civil association is the ultimate embodiment of morality, and he equates it with 'practice of all practices', which is Oakeshott's name for the moral practice.[209]

Yet it seems to me that this equation of civil association with the moral life entails a confusion for three reasons. The first is that Oakeshott's specific meaning of morality is not always carefully distinguished from a wider meaning; the second is that civil association is too readily confused with the ultimate moral association; the third is that the contrast between association in terms of practice and association in terms of contract is perceived as an opposition. Let me elaborate these three points.

---

[206] Franco, *The Political Philosophy of Michael Oakeshott*, p. 182.
[207] HC, pp. 256-263.
[208] Not to confuse with *Moralität*, by which Hegel understood the realm of so called 'subjective' morality.
[209] Sullivan, *Intimations Pursued*, p. 312.

Firstly, the peculiar sense of morality in Oakeshott's later philosophy prevents morality from being understood as the fundament capable of cementing a society and turning it into a living whole. This is so because morality is an abstraction relating to only one aspect of human conduct. Morality refers to the aspect of conditionality concerned with a subscription to the variety of practices in which it is the ultimate arbiter. Thus, its jurisdiction falls only on the conditions of conduct and not on its substantive aims and actions. Therefore, even if civil association were the comprehensive moral association, this would not turn it into an association aiming at the good life of its members.

But, secondly, civil association is not comprehensive moral association. It is 'moral' only in the sense that it is not 'instrumental'. This, however, does not mean that civil practice is 'the practice of all practices'. On the contrary, civil association is a relatively limited kind of moral association. For Oakeshott, practices are similar to languages in their flexibility, adaptability to change and relative lack of reflectivity. Usually, explicit rules are secondary to a practice. But this is not the case with civil practice because its distinguishing characteristic is that it is a relationship in terms of identifiable and deliberately enacted rules. Thus, the grammar of this language receives too much importance, making it a relatively poor language. Civil practice refers only to the limited activity of behaving in a 'just' way, leaving aside the more general question of 'good' conduct. It is connected with the general morality but it can only be an imperfect reflection of this morality. It appears as not particularly exciting, being described as the relationship of strangers which does not recognise the languages of love, affection or rivalry.[210] It is the relationship of the equal, but unlike in Aristotle, friendship is not an element of this equality; moreover, civil practice excludes the relationship of friendship almost by definition. Civil intercourse is, therefore, an important part of the social life but it is not the one which leads to some moral or spiritual perfection. As we have seen, Oakeshott is at pains to separate the considerations of 'civil' and 'moral' desirability in the deliberation of changes of *lex*. Law, and not virtue, is the central element of this association.

Thirdly, Oakeshott, of course, clearly rejects the idea of civil association as some sort of 'contract' and distinguishes between the state understood as an agreement between agents pursuing their own interests, and the state understood as a legal framework indifferent to interests of any sort. However, this does not mean that he is a foe

---

[210] HC, p. 123.

of those liberal theories which are often associated with contractualism. At first glance, Oakeshott's distinction may look similar to the one made by Hegel between civil society as a sphere of the competition between individuals and the state as the embodiment of the ultimate resolution of the contradictions within the ethical sphere. Yet a more plausible source of Oakeshott's view seems to be the thought of the neo-Kantian thinker H. Krabbe, who distinguished between the state understood as 'a legal community' and the one understood as 'a community of interests'.[211] The difference of their approach from that of Hegel is that, for Krabbe and Oakeshott, the state as a legal community is not an alternative or an additional social arrangement to the 'community of interests' but is just a better definition for what is often confusedly perceived as a community of interests.

It is true that, on the theoretical level, Oakeshott contrasts the civil condition with both an enterprise association concerned with the pursuit of the agreed common purpose and with a transactional association in terms of rules instrumental to facilitating the bargaining between agents pursuing satisfactions of their own. However, the place of the transactional association, as an 'intermittent' association, is different from that of the enterprise association which is a 'durable' one, being, thereby, the main opponent of the civil association. Moreover, when Oakeshott discusses historical exemplifications of different understandings of the state, transactional association disappears altogether and we are presented with the alternatives of *societas* and *universitas*. At first glance, this absence looks strange since transactional association, best resembling various 'contractualist' theories, should be considered as perhaps one of the central notions of the state in the history of European political thought. Yet Oakeshott simply ignores it. What are the reasons for this?

Oakeshott's interpretation of some political thinkers may provide an explanation. Thus, Oakeshott regarded Hobbes as one of the greatest of all political philosophers and was significantly influenced by him, yet their approaches may look different, even contradictory. Thus, at the centre of Oakeshott's idea of civility there is a concept of the non-purposive association. In contrast, Hobbes argued that everything has its own purpose, otherwise it is vain, and that the purpose of civil commonwealth is peace. Indeed, one of the main criticisms of Oakeshott's theory of civil association was that he

---

[211] H. Krabbe, *The Modern Idea of the State*, trans. G.H. Sabine & W.J. Shepard (New York: D. Appleton and Company, 1922), pp. 226-232.

ignored the fact that peace or stability themselves constituted a purpose.[212] Oakeshott certainly knew that Hobbes envisaged his commonwealth as a purposive association, the explicit goal of which was maintaining peace and security. In one of his lectures, he described Hobbes' understanding of the modern state as 'an "artificial" association of human beings united in an agreed pursuit of "peace" among themselves';[213] nor does his famous introduction to *Leviathan* (1946) suggest otherwise. However, in the revised text of the introduction (1975) Oakeshott seriously changes his assessment of Hobbes' position, making it fit into the general framework of his own thought. Thus, he adjusts Hobbes' terminology to his own vocabulary, changing words such as 'civil society' and 'political' to 'civil association' and 'civil'. Yet the changes of substance are even more important. Thus, in the new edition, Hobbes' philosophy is presented in terms of the distinction between two aspects of human conduct, one being the pursuit of satisfactions of substantive wants and the other being the conditions qualifying this pursuit. In the previous version, Oakeshott described men in the natural condition living in 'their common competitive pursuit of felicity',[214] and this interpretation was faithful to the letter of *Leviathan*, but, in the later version, Oakeshott speaks about a man finding himself in the 'competitive endeavour to satisfy... wants'.[215] Whereas earlier the character of the attempt to pursue felicity was called 'competitive', in the second version the endeavour is 'unconditionally competitive'. Here articles of Peace are understood to be required in order to turn the unconditional competition into a conditional one. Therefore, the requirement of peace cannot be regarded as a substantive purpose but as a condition for pursuing various substantive satisfactions. This interpretation indeed corresponds to Oakeshott's own claim that 'the "security" or the *tranquillitas* of the associates, or their "peace" or moral virtue' are 'not substantive purposes and they do not specify enterprise association.'[216]

Thus, Oakeshott interprets Hobbes' commonwealth as intimating his own idea of civil association, notwithstanding the explicitly 'purposive' vocabulary.[217] This interpretation is not a misunderstanding, but is an attempt to show what Hobbes' philosophy may look

---

[212] D.D. Raphael, Review of *On Human Conduct*, in *Political uarterly* 46(4), 1975, pp. 450-454.
[213] SPP, p. 446.
[214] 'Introduction,' in T. Hobbes, *Leviathan* (Oxford: Basil Blackwell, 1946), p. xxxvi.
[215] HCA, p. 39.
[216] HC, p. 119.
[217] There is, however, one exceptional circumstance in which peace itself *can* become a purpose, but it is only when the civil condition itself becomes a

like when seen through the lenses of Oakeshott's own thought. Therefore, Oakeshott does not claim that the civil association is an alternative to an association based on the agreement to pursue peace. Rather, he implies that the civil condition offers a better articulation of what is often perceived as a contractual association.

Yet one may argue that Hobbes is not a real contractualist because his idea of contract is not typical, for it does not allow the termination of the contract once it has been made. The obligation becomes obsolete only if the sovereign is unable to protect his subjects and not because of some violation of the terms of the contract. Indeed, Hobbes' sovereign cannot violate it, because he is not a party to the contract and therefore has no duties to fulfil. Thus, one may say that both Hobbes and Oakeshott are adversaries of transactional association.

The answer to this is that, while theoretically Oakeshott does regard transactional association as similar to enterprise association in its concern with substantive wants, he avoids attributing this character to various historical expressions of that idea. According to him, most Western political thinkers understood the modern state in terms of *societas*. Even when he admits that a certain thinker did promote the idea of the state in terms of the pursuit of peace as instrumental to the satisfaction of individual wants, he regards this as a confused idea of *societas*. Thus, Oakeshott points out that Marsilius of Padua is 'reputed to have made substantial use of the analogy of corporate association'. Marsilius certainly 'writes of a realm as a *universitas*', however 'his argument does nothing to sustain it in that character'.[218] For him, a human being is an intelligent agent seeking the satisfaction of his wants in transactions with others and it is difficult to sustain this condition without the preservation of what is called human well-being, peace or tranquillity. Therefore, there is a common need for arrangements which would make the satisfaction of wants possible. In order to achieve this, agents unite into a corporation and as its members they acquire the right to make laws and authorise rulers to enforce them. This is an association 'of persons seeking the satisfaction of their different wants in an irreducible plurality of self-chosen actions and responses to actions'.[219] Therefore, 'in spite of this parade of the language of corporate association', a

---

substantive purpose and this may happen when, for example, 'a civil association is threatened with dissolution or destruction.' (HC, p. 146.) Yet this situation is itself 'a suspension of the civil condition.' (p. 147.)

[218] HC, p. 216.
[219] HC, p. 217.

realm does not have 'the essential characteristics of *universitas*'.[220] Now, here a reader might suspect that, while not a *universitas*, this corporation is the clearest example of polity as 'transactional association' in which the rules of peace are designed to facilitate the pursuit of all purposes. However, according to Oakeshott's interpretation, Marsilius' idea of the realm is that of 'a "multitude of men" formally associated in terms of laws...'[221] In other words, Marsilius is just another confused theorist of civil association.

Another example is Oakeshott's account of the thought of the classical economists. They understood modern European states to be composed 'of private persons (or families) seeking the satisfaction of their wants',[222] who constitute an association for the mutual satisfaction of those individual wants. However, this condition was understood not to be self-sustaining. The association required 'defence against external enemies and against internal corruptions' and 'the office of civil authority' was to provide this defence.[223] Also, according to Oakeshott, in this respect, the economists did not advocate a state as *universitas*, a common enterprise in the production and distribution of benefits. Yet he does not even consider the possibility that they might see the state as a transactional association in the pursuit of individual wants. Instead, Oakeshott says that, in their theories, 'a modern European state is to be understood as a *societas cupiditatis* qualified by considerations imposed in civil law, considerations which are not themselves instrumental to the satisfaction of wants.'[224]

Thus, Oakeshott transforms almost any writer who does not clearly adhere to the state as a common enterprise, into an advocate of the civil association, however ambiguous and confused. He does not leave any space for some kind of transactional association. This is so because the civil association for him is not a rival to both the enterprise and transactional association but a substitute for the confused theories of transactional association in order to serve as a better alternative to the enterprise association. In other words, Oakeshott's civil association is a reformulation, but not rejection, of what is recognised in the history of political thought as various kinds of contractual theories. This reformulation represents the radicalisation of what is often perceived as 'liberalism'. Theoretically, the difference between liberals and anti-liberals can be perceived as

---
[220] *Ibid*
[221] HC, pp. 217-218.
[222] HC, p. 293.
[223] HC, p. 294.
[224] *Ibid*.

one of degree. Anti-liberals suggest that the state imposes a certain common allegiance (like a common religion, worldview etc.), whereas liberals prefer to limit the state to a loose purpose of 'peace', 'happiness' or 'progress'. The problem is that the liberal position is a shaky compromise. For, if the purpose of 'peace' is acceptable in the civil condition, there is no definite reason why goals such as 'welfare' or 'prosperity' should be rejected, and so on. Liberalism, however, is guarded against such reduction if this difference of degree is transformed into the difference of kind, and this is what Oakeshott does. His civil philosophy is, therefore, not a rejection of the mainstream liberal intellectual heritage but rather a self-proclaimed attempt to purge this heritage of what he sees as its incoherencies.

IV

Civil association is, therefore, a reformulation of various liberal theories of the modern state in an attempt to elucidate inner postulates of these theories. It is based on the analytical distinction between the substantive and the formal aspect of human conduct so that everything related to the formal conditions of conduct is understood to be incapable of constituting a substantive purpose.

But why is such radical reformulation necessary? My answer is that it enables Oakeshott to reconcile the radical enjoyment of freedom by the modern individual with the existence of social order. Oakeshott's theory of civil association makes it possible to argue that social order does not limit the freedom of subjects at all. This cannot be said with regard to comprehensive and compulsory social arrangements if they derive from the pursuit of substantive wants. Why is this so?

To answer this question it is necessary to consider the character of Oakeshott's theory of civil freedom. It has already been mentioned that some commentators claim that Oakeshott rejects the idea of 'negative' freedom. Roughly speaking, negative liberty can be defined as the absence of constraint from other human beings whereas positive liberty is associated with the ideas of autonomy, self-direction and self-fulfilment.[225] Positive liberty is often linked with the notions of 'real' or 'rational' will as distinguished from a transient whim. Social arrangements are perceived as having the positive function of directing a personality towards the achievement of this real freedom. Now, there is a temptation to say that Oakeshott's idea of civil freedom is not a 'negative' one because of

[225] Isaiah Berlin, 'Two Concepts of Liberty,' in *Four Essays on Liberty* (Oxford: Oxford University Press, 1969), pp. 118-172.

the apparent identity between civil freedom and the rule of law. Of course, even unequivocal theorists of negative liberty such as Paley or Bentham were advocates of some form of the rule of law yet they thought that, being a form of constraint, law constituted a limitation on freedom and that it was important to limit the scope of law as much as possible.[226] For Oakeshott, however, civil freedom is not dependent on the silence of law.[227] One remains free by being a member of the compulsory association in terms of the acknowledgement of the rules of law. This suggestion seems to be unacceptable to many liberal thinkers and incompatible with the idea of negative liberty.

Yet Oakeshott's brief discussion of civil freedom does not support this interpretation. As it has already been said, the members of a civil association are considered free for two reasons. Firstly, they do not regard themselves as being participants in the project of which they do not approve. A state is a comprehensive and compulsory association but, when it is understood as civil association, it does not impose participation in a common undertaking and, therefore, there is nothing here 'to threaten the link between belief and conduct which constitutes "free" agency'.[228] In other words, nothing leads an agent to perceive his performances as actions directed to a purpose not of his own choice. Secondly, the rules of civil association are not commands and they do not demand performance of specific actions. Agents always act in the pursuit of their own purposes, choosing to do *this* rather than *that*. They merely have to subscribe to the general conditions of conduct specified in civil rules. Oakeshott calls this feature of rules 'adverbiality' while pointing out that

> the appearance procedures and rules may have of excluding (forbidding), or more rarely of enjoying, substantive choices and actions is illusive... A criminal law, which may be thought to come nearest to forbidding actions, does not forbid killing or lighting a fire, it forbids killing 'murderously' or lighting a fire 'arsonically'.[229]

In other words, *cives* in civil association are free because they are not compelled or forbidden to perform specific actions.

---

[226] William Paley, 'Of Civil Liberty,' from *Moral and Political Philosophy*, in *Works* (London: Bohn, 1847), pp. 134-136; Jeremy Bentham, *Of Laws in General* (London: The Athlone Press, 1970), pp. 253-254.
[227] See W. John Coats Jr., 'Some Correspondence Between Oakeshott's "Civil Condition" and the Republican Tradition,' *Political Science Reviewer* 21, 1992, pp. 99-115.
[228] HC, p. 158.
[229] HC, p. 58n.

These arguments, especially the latter one, have been severely criticised, often too hastily.[230] The main claim has been that conditions do restrict actions and that some conditions can be very repressive indeed, even if formulated in a general way. Yet the commentators often fail to take into account the Idealistic standpoint of Oakeshott's philosophy. Oakeshott speaks about civil freedom not as a material quality but as a perception of human beings and he attempts to disclose the conditions in which human agents perceive themselves as free.[231] These conditions are that agents do not understand themselves either as being compelled to take part in a project of which they disapprove, or as being compelled to perform specific actions. If subjects perceive their association and its laws as fulfilling those conditions then they will not regard themselves as being constrained by others at all.

Whether this approach is plausible is a matter of philosophical dispute.[232] Be that as it may, the question here is not about the plausibility of Oakeshott's conclusions but about the logic of his argument, for it is the character of argument which determines the place of a notion of freedom within the conceptual distinction between negative and positive freedom. That is, in order to grasp what Oakeshott's idea of civil freedom means, it is more important to understand why he advocates some kind of identity between freedom and law. And even a brief look at the argument reveals that its logic is based on the principle of the absence of constraint. For, Oakeshott does not say that laws are perceived as not limiting civil freedom because they allegedly contribute to self-fulfilment, or allow the freedom of *rational* or *ethical* actions, restricting only irrational or unworthy instincts. Nor does he say that real freedom is life in a society, and that laws make men free by enabling them to exist in a society. Nor, again, is his claim that freedom is preserved when law is understood as a self-enacted rule. Oakeshott's argument is merely that subjects are not compelled or constrained by other human agents to perform actions or to be participants in any common

---

[230] See, for example, John Gray, *Liberalisms: Essays in Political Philosophy* (London: Routledge, 1989), p. 211; Liddington, 'Oakeshott: Freedom in a Modern European State,' p. 313.

[231] 'Since the human relationships are an expression of the self-understanding of the agents so related, to grasp the character of an association must necessarily entail understanding the beliefs of the associates.' Jeremy Rayner, 'The Legend of Oakeshott's Conservatism: Sceptical Philosophy and Limited Politics,' *Canadian Journal of Political Science* 18(2), 1985, p. 331.

[232] See my analysis of Oakeshott's idea of freedom in Efraim Podoksik, 'Oakeshott's Theory of Freedom as Recognized Contingency,' *European Journal of Political Theory* 2(1), 2003, pp. 57-77.

undertaking. This is regardless of whether agents behave wisely or stupidly, ethically or not so ethically. In so far as the association is a pure civil association, freedom from constraint in it is absolute. This is why there is identity between the *lex* of an association and civil freedom.

V

Civil association is, therefore, an association in terms of the acknowledged system of non-purposive law and, by virtue of being such an association, it provides the conditions for the existence of uncompromised civil freedom. Members of such an association recognise themselves as not being constrained by other human beings, their action dependent only on what is perceived as a formal law. This association is, of course, an ideal type, and it is nowhere to be found in reality but the imperfect reflection of this type may be found in a modern European state. Moreover, such an understanding of the state is suitable specifically for a modern Western state because this understanding assumes the existence of individuals who recognise themselves as free agents looking for a way to make the comprehensive organisation of their social life compatible with their enjoyment of freedom.

Oakeshott, therefore, inherits the principles of freedom and the rule of law frequently advocated by European liberals but he radicalises those ideas by transforming their postulates. Law is commonly recognised as a restriction on freedom yet it is acknowledged as a device to maintain the moderate character of government and to provide a defence from arbitrary interference, thus increasing the scope of free action. Oakeshott's claim is, of course, more radical as he postulates absolute freedom in the civil condition.[233] This radical interpretation requires an elaborate conceptual framework, which would be different from the utilitarian one and is offered by Oakeshott in his distinction between the formal and substantive aspect of human conduct.

The theory of the civil condition completes Oakeshott's philosophy of society, the other element of which is the idea of radical individual freedom. But why does Oakeshott need to maintain this radical assertion and come out with seemingly paradoxical claims where he could adopt a more common-sense position? Is it only a

---

[233] Partly ironically, Oakeshott evokes the anarchist theory of Proudhon as specifying the character of the civil condition: 'Trouver un état de l'égalité sociale qui soit ni communauté, ni despotisme, ni morcellement, ni anarchie, mais liberté dans l'ordre et indépendance dans l'unité.' HC, p. 319n.

fancy, a literary adventure of an author ostensibly hostile to whatever is reminiscent of the empirical and utilitarian tradition of English political philosophy? I suggest that that would be a rash judgement. Oakeshott's civil philosophy is indeed radical and reflects the intellectual temperament of the author. However, I suggest a more profound reason which is that Oakeshott attempts to make his entire thought more coherent. Through the theory of the civil condition, his general philosophical approach can become reflected on the level of his philosophy of society, similar to the way in which it is reflected on the level of his philosophy of experience. For, although Oakeshott does not claim that philosophy of society must, or even can be, necessarily deduced from his philosophy of experience, the main aspects of both are analogous.

We have already seen that Oakeshott's philosophy of society and philosophy of experience are theoretical explorations of two levels — the level of understanding and the level of conduct. The level of understanding can be seen as composed of modes of understanding. Each mode represents a homogeneous non-purposive identity. The counterpart of a mode on the level of conduct is an individual, who is understood as a homogeneous ('self') non-purposive ('the end in himself') identity. Oakeshott's civil philosophy is supposed to give an answer to the question of how these identities coexist.

On the level of understanding (experience) the modes (voices, languages, orders of inquiry etc.) coexist in conversation which means that from the standpoint of their inner characters they are completely irrelevant to each other. As they are mutually irrelevant, they allegedly cannot clash while possessing the absolute sovereignty of their own way of imagining. However, this radical plurality cannot maintain unity and, therefore, it is impossible to ensure that some mode does not trespass the limits of its own identity. Therefore, Oakeshott urges restraint for each mode but does not provide the philosophical basis on which such restraint can be defended.

Now, this is analogous to the relationship between individuals in the civil condition. What distinguishes this relationship from one based on the anticipated substantive benefits of action, is that here agents are not directly related to each other for it is the 'relationship between a subject and *lex* which constitutes civil association.'[234] The members are related to a certain kind of practice which is the system of impersonal law. Practices are never direct actions of some individuals on others compelling or persuading them to do *this* rather than *that*. They are considerations which can be taken into account

---
[234] HC, p. 171.

only when they have been learned and understood individually, for there is no collective understanding.[235] Thus, subscription is possible only when a practice is acknowledged by an agent individually. Practice is, therefore, external, in the sense that it is not subjective, and that it is not of an agent's making, who is thrown into it. But it is internal in the sense that it is *his* practice and it can be subscribed to only when it has been individually learned and it is by no means a constraint by other agents. Rules emanate from *lex*, not from the wills of others, and *lex* is a practice which should be internalised. As Oakeshott asserts, in this relation subjects 'are all concerned with the same skill and are specified in the same terms; the relation of flute-players, not of flute-players to audiences'.[236] What is characteristic though, of the relation of flute-players is that, unlike the relation of flute-players to their audiences, the former does not entail a direct interaction. Flute-players do not necessarily interact with each other. Each of them may be an independent player who does not meet others of his kind. He is related to them only in the sense of possessing the same practice of flute-playing.

Therefore, members of the civil association can be free precisely because they are not related to each other but related to *lex*. Similarly, modes of experience cannot clash because they are irrelevant to each other, thus being absolutely free from mutual considerations. *Cives* are also *irrelevant* to each other in this sense. If this is so, it becomes clear why Oakeshott rejects any analogy with the transactional association based on the bargain between different interests, or with any other kind of 'contractualist' approach, with regard to the civil condition. This is because the bargain between individuals about the satisfaction of their individual wants presupposes a clash of interests, an argument, and the mutual limitation of freedom. The civil condition, on the contrary, is based on irrelevance, conversation and uncompromised freedom. If it is claimed that this metaphor of irrelevance is somewhat unattractive, as it excludes the warmth and affection of human contact, one can reply that the civil condition is supposed to be a relatively unattractive condition and that it is not the highest expression of human relationships. It is a relationship between strangers based on justice, but it is necessary in order to enable freely chosen substantive relationships to flourish.

Oakeshott suggests that this understanding of the modern state is deeply embedded in the consciousness of modern Western civilisa-

---

[235] See HC, p. 87.
[236] HC, p. 121.

tion, and is perhaps exclusive to this civilisation. Similarly, the awareness of the fragmentation of various modes is exclusive to modern experience. Yet, in his account of modes of experience, Oakeshott seems to recognise that there is no philosophical system which would provide the necessary unity to buttress such understanding. Is there any such grounding in his philosophy of society? In some senses one can find here a shadow of unity which is the idea of *lex* itself constituting a certain system. Yet this is only a shadow which removes most of the elements of unity present in earlier Oakeshott writings. It took much longer for him to arrive at radical plurality in respect of his philosophy of society than in respect of his philosophy of experience. He started with a neo-Hegelian attempt to advocate unity in diversity on both levels.[237] However, it soon became clear that there was a profound tension between unity and his kind of radical diversity and that it was the aspect of diversity which was pre-eminent and mostly original in his philosophy of experience. With regard to society, however, the general holistic framework remained much longer in the background of his thought, being supported by the congruence of the principle of unity in diversity with the tradition of Whig liberalism. This difference is not surprising for it is much easier to postulate an ordered anarchy within mind (for it does not necessarily require the assent of others), than a similar condition within society. Yet in the end Oakeshott pushes his assertion of plurality as far as possible.

Lex is certainly a system, but it is a very strange system. It cannot itself account for society as a whole, being unconcerned with substantive relationships of human agents. Even in its proper realm, though, it is dependent on the acknowledgement of its authority and this acknowledgement is always made by individuals who are not directly related to each other. Is there any foundation on which the adherence to *lex* can be defended?

We have already seen that there is no unconditional criterion for the consideration of particular provisions of *lex* in terms of their desirability. Laws are alterable but the criteria of change are contingent and cannot be deduced. But can this system of law be supported as a whole? Oakeshott does not deal with this question in *On Human Conduct*. However, this is the concern of the essay 'The Moral Life in the Writings of Thomas Hobbes' (1960).[238] Although it had been written before Oakeshott's synthesis of philosophy of society in *On*

---

[237] 'The Authority of the State,' (1929), RPML, pp. 74-87; EM.
[238] RIP, pp. 295-350.

Human Conduct was completed, it was included in *Hobbes on Civil Association*[239] and was likely to reflect some of his later ideas.

In this essay, Oakeshott identifies Hobbes as one of the philosophers of the morality of individuality, but the question he is dealing with is whether Hobbes may be said to have a moral theory at all. In other words, the question is whether Hobbes' theory not only shows why men behave towards each other in a certain manner but also offers a justification for their conduct. Oakeshott discerns three different contemporary readings of Hobbes, each trying to elucidate his moral theory. The first is provided by Leo Strauss who claims that an obligation to be 'just' originates in the natural necessity, and therefore natural right, of every man to preserve his own nature. Yet a man has no right to do more than this. To endeavour to preserve one's own nature means to endeavour peace and therefore an obligation to be 'just' means merely pursuing peace. To behave otherwise would contradict the man's nature and therefore be irrational. Oakeshott is completely unsatisfied with this answer and he does not even discuss it at length. This reading presupposes that 'reason' has prescriptive force, and this is what Oakeshott wants to deny. For him, this interpretation would lead to the Rationalist fallacy of deriving an ethical doctrine from 'reason' and he certainly does not follow Strauss in this direction.

Two other readings seem more plausible. The difference between them lies in the question of the meaning of Natural Law. That is, whether Hobbes believed Natural Law to be a law in the proper sense, creating obligations of some sort, or whether he regarded it merely as 'rational theorems' about human conduct whilst proper law can exist only when there is an authorised law-giver whose prescriptions can be ascertained and who is present only in the condition of civility.

Oakeshott thinks that the latter interpretation is more coherent, yet he recognises that sometimes Hobbes seems to be expressing the former view. There is a certain inconsistency in Hobbes' writings because he frequently makes contradictory statements on this subject.[240] Oakeshott suggests that the contradiction is intentional, for Hobbes has a twofold purpose. One is to display a theory of obligation absolutely consistent with his general philosophy while the second is to frame it into the familiar idioms of current discourse strongly connected with the theories of Natural Law. The first is

---
[239] HCA, pp. 80-140.
[240] HCA, pp. 122-124.

directed to the 'initiated' and the second is to the ordinary reader to whom 'novelties... must be made to appear commonplaces'.[241]

Thus, Oakeshott holds the view that moral obligation in Hobbes' theory is grounded in the civil condition, that it is self-sufficient and cannot require external moral justification. He denies the possibility of justification of obligation by some metaphysical moral principles, and this implies the existence of a gap between the civil condition and habits of behaviour as such. There is no way to derive 'rational' grounds for obligation from these habits.[242]

Therefore, there is no gradual way to civility. The civil condition should be accepted as a whole without any attempt to find justification for it. This acceptance is not grounded on rational conviction but on a sentiment which presupposes a certain character. This character is the 'individual' who is understood as one making choices for himself. But he belongs to that rare variety in whom individuality is not founded on fear and prudence, which is the dominant passion for most men. He is driven by a special type of pride which comes not from a Satanic self-love of one's own omnipotence, but from self-knowledge and self-respect. This type of pride forms a man 'who (in Montaigne's phrase) "knows how to belong to himself".'[243]

What distinguishes such a character is courage and thus a radical acceptance of himself and his condition. The existence of this character is enormously important, since, according to Oakeshott

> it seems almost to have been Hobbes' view that men of this character are a necessary cause of the *civitas*; and certainly it is only they who, having an adequate motive for doing so, may be depended upon to defend it when dissension deprives the sovereign of his power. And he saw in Sidney Godolphin the emblem of this character.[244]

Now, if we extrapolate this analysis of Hobbes' moral theory to the discussion of the foundations of Oakeshott's own idea of the civil condition then we can conclude that no philosophical system can maintain civility. Civil freedom postulates radical plurality which is irreducible to unity. Therefore, what maintains civil association is the disposition to cherish this condition of radical plurality for its own sake and the quality of courage required to defend it. Similarly

---

[241] HCA, p. 126. This emphasis on the esoteric character of Hobbes' philosophy is probably influenced by Leo Strauss (see L. Strauss, *Persecution and the Art of Writing* [Glencoe, Ill: The Free Press, 1952], pp. 22-37.) Yet, even if Oakeshott adopts here Strauss' method, he rejects Strauss' conclusions in this case.

[242] On Oakeshott's denial of the possibility of an independent justification of the authority of law see also Richard B. Friedman, 'Oakeshott on the Authority of Law,' *Ratio Juris* 2(1), 1989, pp. 27-40.

[243] HCA, p. 128.

[244] HCA, p. 132.

to the fragmentation of experience, the fragmentation of society can be cherished and defended but cannot be philosophically justified.

VI

This is, then, the basic feature of Oakeshott's civil philosophy. He attempts to theorise a certain condition of social arrangements which is suitable to independent individuals cherishing their own freedom of choice. While he does not think that this is the only disposition existing in the modern Western consciousness, he suggests that it is the driving force of Western civilisation whilst its counterpart is derivative of it. Oakeshott's civil philosophy is the disclosure of the postulates of this liberal civilisation, the imperfect copy of which has been contingently intimated in the life of all Western societies. These intimations are valuable in themselves and were cherished by the most admirable characters in European history. Their underlying principle is that of civility.

Oakeshott's civil philosophy is perhaps the most original part of his philosophy of society and of his philosophy in general. It is related to the ideas commonly ascribed to liberalism but it transforms and radicalises them. Thus, a common notion of the association which has a non-specific common purpose, such as 'peace', is transformed into an association with no purpose at all. Or the idea of the affinity between the rule of law and freedom is pushed towards postulating their identity. Through this radicalisation, Oakeshott makes liberalism compatible with his own philosophical approach based on the idea of radical plurality.

CONCLUSION
I

Oakeshott's philosophy of society is an achievement which follows a series of attempts to offer a coherent statement corresponding to his philosophy in general. Two main modifications of Oakeshott's initial view are particularly important in understanding the character of this achievement. One is concerned with the practical life. Whereas in his early writings, practice is a homogeneous mode of experience alongside other modes, in his mature philosophy it is removed outside the level of modes of experience altogether to create a completely different level, the level of conduct. The other modification is a new understanding of human conduct based on the distinction between its substantive and formal aspects.

Let us summarise the main features of this mature philosophy of society. His exploration of modern society implies two parallel dichotomies: that of the characters of the 'individual' and the 'individual *manqué*', and that of understanding a state as either a civil or an enterprise association. These distinctions do not necessarily refer to 'objective' or 'materialist' properties. They are mental constructions through which the character of modern society can be understood.

The alternatives in both of these dichotomies are symmetrical, but not equally balanced. Oakeshott does not conceal his sympathies for the ideas of individuality, freedom and a state understood as civil association. But this is not only a matter of sentiment. For, according to Oakeshott, these ideas reflect our deep understanding of the character of human agency and are, therefore, primary in modern sensibility, whereas the ideas of anti-individuality and a state as an enterprise association are at odds with this modern self-awareness, being merely its negation. Although the negation of freedom and individuality will always be present in modern society, the idea of individuality is capable of maintaining its own superiority because individuality possesses more intellectual and practical resources. Only where the modern perception of individuality has not been fully established, where there are still relics of the morality of communal ties, does anti-individuality have a good chance of asserting itself. Thus, civil association is a central idea of modernity, entailing the understanding of the modern state as a free association composed of independent individuals.

This description of freedom in civil association is the radical elaboration of the assumptions of modern liberalism, at the heart of which there is an ideal of a society of free individuals within the framework of the rule of law. Yet, being more of a political ideology than a pure philosophy, liberalism always qualifies its own assumptions, attempting to find the balance between the freedom of action and the restrictions imposed by law. As a pragmatic belief it is always a compromised ideology. Oakeshott in his philosophical treatise radicalises its assumptions making this balance obsolete. Civil association postulates the full scope of civil freedom within the framework of the general conditions of civil conduct, incapable of limiting freedom by their very nature.

II

Oakeshott's philosophy of society is a part of his thought in general and thus related to his philosophy of experience. This relation is not direct, for philosophy of society and philosophy of experience deal with two different levels, the level of conduct and the level of understanding, which do not constitute a system between themselves. Nevertheless, the expositions of these two levels are analogous to each other. Oakeshott's philosophy of experience postulates the existence of several well-established forms of experience which are homogeneous within themselves, have no external purpose and stand in the relation of complete irrelevance to each other. They are not supported by any comprehensive philosophical framework, yet they are the corner-stone of our civilisation and should be maintained so long as we want this civilisation to exist.

Now, the same reasoning applies to Oakeshott's philosophy of society. Modern society, similar to modern experience, is not and cannot be a whole. It is perceived as consisting of plurality of independent agents. These agents are abstract and they possess qualities similar to those of the modes of experience. They are more or less homogeneous in themselves, because they have a distinct self. They are non-purposive, being ends in themselves. And finally, they stand to each other in the relation of irrelevance, coexisting, so to say, in brilliant isolation. The ideal character of relationships here is that of civil, polite indifference. Similarly, there is no philosophical foundation for the conditions of civility and its maintenance requires not philosophical rigour but civil courage.

Thus, I argue that the same logic and the same vision drive both Oakeshott's philosophy of experience and his philosophy of society. How tenable is this view? It has already been shown that this interpretation can very successfully explain much of what looks strange in Oakeshott's philosophy, such as his rejection of the contractualist approach. Moreover, although the parallel is never explicitly drawn by Oakeshott, some hints can be found in his writings. He was aware of a long tradition of European philosophy from Plato in which the social life is analysed in an analogy to the human soul or mind and he once described this analogy as a parallel between a 'macrocosm' and a 'microcosm'.[245] And in his introduction to Hobbes' *Leviathan* Oakeshott characterised the essence of political philosophy as being 'the relation of political life... to the entire conception of the world that belongs to a civilisation'.[246]

Moreover, sometimes Oakeshott uses the language of his civil philosophy in his philosophy of experience and vice versa. Thus, in 'A Place of Learning' (1975) he describes the relationship between dif-

---
[245] SPP, p. 138.
[246] HCA, p. 4.

ferent languages of understanding in the following way: 'Their relationship is not hierarchical. Nor is it either a co-operative or a transactional relationship. They are not partners in a common undertaking, each with a role to perform, nor are they suppliers of one another's wants.'[247] This is precisely how the relationship between agents in civil association is described. Or, we are already familiar with Oakeshott's characterisation of the relationship of different voices as a relationship of conversation, as distinct from an argument. And in 'Political Education' (1951) Oakeshott refers to politics in the same way, saying that it is 'a conversation, not an argument'.[248] Oakeshott was very aware of the parallel between the idea of the conversation of voices and the idea of the civil intercourse of human agents.

This parallel has been noticed by some commentators, most explicitly by Terry Nardin in his recently published book.[249] I am myself indebted to the insight of Robert Grant who drew the parallel between *Experience and Its Modes* and the Hobbesian notion of sovereignty,[250] although I arrive at a different conclusion with regard to its character.

However, as far as I know, there has been no attempt to articulate the precise character of this parallel, partly in deference to Oakeshott's own insistence that he did not construct a system. Yet, as Oakeshott himself recognised, it was a virtue to be systematic without constructing a system,[251] and this study have tried to show that his thought is certainly systematic, more than it is usually perceived to be. There are indeed nuances, modifications and incoherencies in details of his thought. But their meaningful analysis and criticism are impossible without first understanding the general composition of this philosophy.

Before we can finish this study, however, something else must be explored. We have seen that modernity, being based on the postulates promulgating radical plurality, cannot be philosophically justified. The preservation of modern civilisation requires a sentiment, not an argument. But how does this sentiment appear? In order to see this, we should turn our attention to Oakeshott's writings on education.

---

[247] VLL, p. 38.
[248] RIP, p. 58.
[249] Terry Nardin, *The Philosophy of Michael Oakeshott* (University Park: The Pennsylvania State University Press, 2001), p. 234.
[250] Robert Grant, *Oakeshott* (London, The Claridge Press, 1990), p. 40.
[251] JL, p. 72.

Chapter 4
Education

> The invitation to disentangle oneself, for a time, from the urgencies of the here and now and to listen to the conversation in which human beings forever seek to understand themselves.   *A Place of Learning*, 1975

I

We have now reached the question of Oakeshott's view of education that was omitted from the preceding discussion. His writings on this subject are not themselves a part of his philosophy *per se*. They do not add anything substantially new to what we already know about the main postulates of his thought, nor do they contain as carefully edited and detailed a philosophical exposition as that found in *Experience and Its Modes* or *On Human Conduct*. Yet they are important for our understanding of the vision of modernity which drives his philosophy and for illuminating his answer to the question of how this vision can be upheld even in the face of the impossibility of offering a comprehensive philosophical justification of radical plurality.

Oakeshott was, first and foremost, an educator who spent most of his life as a teacher in leading British universities, and the discussion about his essays on education is important given that his ideas on this subject have not received much attention from commentators.[1]

---

[1] There is a small number of articles dealing with this subject. See Geoffrey Hinchliffe, 'Education or Pedagogy?' *Journal of Philosophy of Education* 35(1), 2001, pp. 31-45; Chris Lawn, 'Adventures of Self-Understanding: Gadamer, Oakeshott and the Question of Education,' *Journal of the British Society for Phenomenology* 27(3), 1996, pp. 267-277; David McCabe, 'Michael Oakeshott and the Idea of Liberal Education,' *Social Theory and Practice* 26(3), 2000, pp. 443-464; R.S. Peters, 'Michael Oakeshott's Philosophy of Education,' in P. King & B.C. Parekh (eds.), *Politics and Experience* (Cambridge: University Press, 1968), pp. 43-63; Michael Smith, 'After Managerialism: Towards a Conception of the School as an Educational Community,' *Journal of Philosophy of Education* 33(3), 1999, pp. 317-336; Kevin Williams, 'The Gift of an Interval: Michael Oakeshott's

Moreover, although Oakeshott's writings on education are not an inherent part of his philosophy, they are intimately connected with it because their concern is with what sort of education is compatible with the view of modern civilisation presented in his thought. We have seen that Oakeshott's vision of modernity can be divided into two aspects. Modern civilisation can find its mirror image in the philosophy of modern experience. This experience is understood as being composed of several established, homogeneous worldviews which are irrelevant to each other. Or, our civilisation can be reflected in the philosophy of modern society. The comprehensive organisation of this society is seen as a relationship of completely free individuals in a non-purposive association.

Oakeshott's writings on education relate to both spheres. In his middle period he was mostly concerned with university education which is discussed in 'The Universities' (1949), 'The Idea of a University' (1950), 'The Study of "Politics" in a University' (1961) and also in 'The Definition of a University' (1967).[2] These essays focus primarily on the question of the initiation into a plurality of voices in human civilisation and so they relate to the philosophy of experience. Other writings, such as 'Learning and Teaching' (1965), 'The Education: The Engagement and Its Frustration' (1972) and 'A Place of Learning' (1975) belong to the later period. They deal mainly with general concepts of education and their concern is the development of autonomous personality. Thus they correspond to his philosophy of society. Of course, the distinction between these two groups of essays is not absolute as they share much in common. However, it is useful for focusing our attention on their most distinctive moments.

Furthermore, this discussion is important not only because it affirms what we have already learned. There are two moments in which it can still contribute something new to our study of Oakeshott's thought. Firstly, as we have found, Oakeshott insists on radical plurality as the main characteristic of modern civilisation but he eliminates any prospect of finding a unifying philosophical ground in which to cement both parts of his philosophy. This account, if accepted, might mean that modernity is logically unsustainable. The existence of modern civilisation is, then, precarious, for modernity might find itself facing the attacks of its enemies without

---

Idea of a University Education,' *British Journal of Educational Studies* 37(4), 1989, pp. 384-397.

[2] Most passages of 'The Definition of a University' are taken from 'The Study of "Politics" in a University,' (1961) but others are borrowed from 'Learning and Teaching' (1967).

knowing how to sustain the loyalty of those who belong to it. Oakeshott's writings on education are an answer to the question of how to implant loyalty to modernity even when it has no philosophical foundations. It will be shown that his remedy is, paradoxically, what looks like a more traditionalist position, in comparison to his other writings. He is often labelled as an advocate of the conservative approach, hostile to modern education.[3] However, this apparently conservative attitude is more modern than is perceived, for it is the only kind of education that may save modern civilisation in the long run.

Secondly, Oakeshott's writings on education reveal a different pattern in his relation to the intellectual debates of his time. In the previous chapters we have seen that, far from being an esoteric philosophy, his thought absorbed many important contemporary influences, yet remained itself relatively unnoticed. In contrast, his views on education are not only an expression of his deep familiarity with the intellectual achievements of his period; here Oakeshott appears as one who has himself influenced and shaped the intellectual life of his society. For, as we shall see, he exercised significant influence on British philosophy of education and on the agenda of its debates.

II

Oakeshott is known as an advocate of 'liberal education'. 'Liberal' education is perceived as an ideal inherited from Classical culture. Oakeshott himself related the origin of 'liberal education' to the Greek and Roman epochs.[4] Yet the concept of 'liberal education' was often evoked in order to deal with circumstances of modern times, offering a view of education which would provide an answer to the modern condition. There is no single view about the precise character of such education; big differences emerge between various advocates of liberal education as well as between them and its rivals. However, one can generally identify several trends, two of which had a particularly strong impact on Oakeshott's thought. These are the nineteenth-century English idea of liberal education with its emphasis on the cultivation of mind for its own sake and the German neo-humanistic and Idealistic philosophies with their emphasis on self-realisation as the true aim of education. Both found their inspiration in ancient culture, yet both were concerned with developing a

---

[3] George F. Kellner, *Movements of Thought in Modern Education* (New York: John Wiley & Sons, 1984), pp. 219-226.
[4] WP.

specifically modern view of education which would break up earlier systems.

Respect for 'liberal education' was established in the English public consciousness well before the nineteenth century. As Sheldon Rothblatt argues, an early eighteenth-century Georgian ideal of 'liberal education' was concerned with the moral education of the higher classes, in which initiation into practices of civility was the most important element. However, towards the middle of the nineteenth century the English concept of 'liberal education' itself underwent an important change. Its previous socio-ethical ideal was transformed into the advocacy of the pursuit of knowledge for its own sake.[5] Rothblatt relates this transformation to the growing role of the universities of Cambridge and Oxford, and to the process of specialisation among dons. The integrity of everyone's field of study, rather than the common civil and ethical education, became the central concern.

This novel approach to education can be found in the thought of John H. Newman and Matthew Arnold. In *The Idea of a University* (1852-1858), Newman advocated the idea of knowledge for its own sake, and claimed for a university the role of the primary guardian of disinterested study. For him, the goal of a university was to teach universal knowledge, which he felt is also liberal knowledge because it is knowledge for its own sake.[6] Quoting Aristotle he sharply distinguished between useful knowledge and liberal knowledge.[7] Only the latter has its place in a university education. This also means that the university is not concerned with forming a socio-religious worldview. Newman maintained that knowledge was a disinterested search for the objective truth and he was sympathetic to the trend of specialisation of different branches as leading to deeper knowledge. However, he was not entirely happy about this fragmentation, arguing that there is a connection and balance between all branches of knowledge and that the aim of liberal education is to provide universal knowledge, the ability to view a whole.[8]

Matthew Arnold was perhaps a less consistent defender of the idea of education as an end in itself. In his views on education he attempted to make a synthesis between two polar ideals of knowl-

---

[5] Sheldon Rothblatt, *Tradition and Change in English Liberal Education* (London: Faber and Faber, 1976).
[6] John Henry Newman, *The Idea of a University* (Oxford: Clarendon Press, 1976), pp. 94-112.
[7] *Ibid.*, p. 102.
[8] *Ibid.*, pp. 94-96, 122-123.

edge as virtue, and knowledge as power.[9] However, the idea of knowledge for its own sake is strongly emphasised in Arnold's definition of 'culture', described by him as 'the best which has been thought and said in the world'.[10] 'Culture' teaches man disinterestedness and the desire to see things as they are. It strives towards a harmonious perfection of man, in which he will recognise 'all the voices of human experience',[11] such as art, science, poetry, philosophy, history and religion.

This ideal of knowledge as virtue is inherited by Oakeshott from these English theorists of liberal education. The title of one of his essays — 'The Idea of a University' — is indeed an allusion to Newman's lectures and also, perhaps, to a more recent book by Karl Jaspers.[12] However, he abandons the view that such knowledge should be 'universal' or lead to 'a harmonious perfection'. There is, according to him, a 'hiatus between the formulated conception of a university — as expounded by Newman or Whewell or Paulsen or Matthew Arnold — and the sort of education a university actually provided at different times'.[13] Being educated in Cambridge Oakeshott inherited not only the theory of liberal learning, but also the actual tradition in which this education was undertaken with its emphasis on specialisation of recognised branches of learning. In his writings, Oakeshott combined the ideal of the pursuit of disinterested knowledge with his philosophy of the radical plurality of experience.

Like other theorists of 'liberal education' Oakeshott postulates the value of disinterested knowledge as a virtue, and sees in a university the main agent for pursuing such knowledge. According to him 'a university is not a machine for achieving a particular purpose or producing a particular result; it is a manner of human activity.'[14] It would be wrong to assign to a university a specific social function. It is a good in itself, and as such it is one of the features of a civilised society. The activity of learning is 'one of the properties, indeed one of the virtues, of a civilised way of living'.[15] Oakeshott, however, sometimes assigns a purpose to this pursuit of learning. This purpose can be described as 'attending' to the inheritance of a civilisa-

---

[9] Ralph White, 'The Anatomy of a Victorian Debate: An Essay in the History of Liberal Education,' *British Journal of Educational Studies* 34(1), 1986, pp. 38-65.
[10] Matthew Arnold, *Culture and Anarchy* (Cambridge: University Press, 1935), p. 6.
[11] *Ibid.*, p. 47.
[12] Karl Jaspers, *The Idea of the University*, trans. H.A.T. Reiche & H.F. Vanderschmidt (London: Peter Owen, 1960).
[13] 'The Universities,' VLL, pp. 119-120.
[14] VLL, p. 96.
[15] *Ibid.*

tion, so that this inheritance is kept intact, and also 'continuously recovering what has been lost, restoring what has been neglected... reshaping and reorganising these advantages of human understanding'.[16] This is, however, not an extraneous purpose, but rather something which is inherent in the tradition of a university activity.

The pursuit of learning is, therefore, an end in itself, a 'luxury'. It belongs to the world of human wants, not needs. It necessarily involves the idea of leisure and it can be regarded as 'waste'. But this luxury must be defended. Oakeshott may be called a Rousseauean anti-Rousseauist. Like Rousseau he is suspicious of the domination of the concept of 'labour' in the system of modern values. Unlike him, Oakeshott thinks that freedom from the burden of work is only possible in a civilised society, one which allows luxury, and which is concerned more with culture than with the maintenance of basic economic needs. The truth for Oakeshott is 'that there is nothing great in the world that does not involve waste'.[17]

Oakeshott attempts to distinguish between universities and other forms of education such as school education or 'vocational' education. Thus, school-education for him is 'learning to speak before one has anything significant to say'.[18] What is learnt in school is miscellaneous information from a variety of disciplines which appears more 'like a stock of ideas, beliefs... than a capital'.[19] Most of it will never be of use. It neither is related to what is immediate, nor initiates a pupil into different ways of human understanding. Rather, it provides some general knowledge and habits of learning. Oakeshott argues against early specialisation in school, considering such specialisation worthless at best.

School education is followed by a higher education which may be either a 'vocational' or a 'university' education.[20] 'Vocational' education is basically professional, utilitarian training in which useful skills are acquired. What worries Oakeshott most is that 'vocational' education may invade universities and corrupt them. University education should be protected from any intrusion of 'vocational' education, since these are two completely different, even incompatible kinds of learning.

As we have seen, the essence of 'university' education is the pursuit of disinterested knowledge. However, this pursuit does not presuppose any quest for 'integrated' or 'universal' knowledge.

---

[16] DU, p. 139.
[17] Ibid.
[18] 'The Study of "Politics" in a University,' RIP, p. 189.
[19] Ibid.
[20] RIP, pp. 190-199.

Oakeshott sharply diverges from English thinkers like Newman and Arnold, or Germans like Schiller and Jaspers, all of whom advocated the unity implied in such universal education.[21] Oakeshott seems to regard this position as a remnant of the old pre-modern hierarchical worldview. He introduces the notion of radical plurality into his writings on education.

Thus, in 'The Universities' Oakeshott discusses Sir Walter Moberly's *The Crisis in the Universities* (1949), in which the author laments a growing specialisation among dons, seeing a modern university education as 'a miscellaneous collection of fragments'.[22] For Moberly this is one of the central problems of the modern university. Oakeshott agrees that over-specialisation is a sort of problem, perhaps for the reason that such narrow specialisation may be a disguised form of professional training. Nevertheless, he dismisses the call for unity, as contrary to his idea of the nature of a university. According to Oakeshott, a university never presented a unified picture. There was always 'a chaotic university'.[23] What was learned in universities was neither one specific form of knowledge, nor the collection of miscellaneous disciplines, 'it was neither an institute in which only one voice was to be heard, nor was it a polytechnic in which only mannerisms of the voices were taught.'[24] The curriculum consisted of several recognised and well-established branches of scholarship. There were no general criteria by which they had been chosen, besides that all of them had come to be recognised as the ways of self-understanding of our civilisation. Therefore, 'no one of these subjects of study was capable of defence on *a priori* grounds'.[25] For Oakeshott, there can be no logical justification for the inclusion of one or another discipline into the university curriculum. The only criterion for such inclusion may be the recognition that a certain branch of scholarship reflects one of the important activities of our self-understanding.

The task of a university is to initiate a student into these different idioms of human understanding. Unlike 'vocational' education, which teaches a specific 'text', 'university' education teaches 'languages' in which these 'texts' are written — texts of science, or reli-

---

[21] Newman, *The Idea of a University*; Arnold, *Culture and Anarchy*; Friedrich Schiller, 'The Nature and Value of Universal History: An Inaugural Lecture [1789],' *History and Theory* 11(3), 1972, pp. 321-334; Jaspers, *The Idea of the University*.
[22] VLL, p. 118.
[23] VLL, p. 120.
[24] VLL, p. 126.
[25] VLL, p. 125.

gion, or history etc.[26] This education will necessarily involve learning some particular 'text', such as the achievements of a certain science, or studies of a particular historical epoch. But this study will not be its main goal. The aim of such education is rather to teach a student to understand the languages of science or of history, to make him see how the scientist or the historian reaches his conclusions.

Oakeshott ridiculed the attempts to unite different disciplines and fill in 'the interstices between the sciences with a sticky mess called "culture",'[27] almost certainly in reference to Arnold. There is no reason for alarm if such a unified concept is nowhere to be found, because 'no extraneous cement to hold it together' is needed.[28] Already in 1949 Oakeshott introduces the notion of conversation in which different voices in a university are engaged.[29] Later he would use the metaphor of voices in conversation in 'The Voice of Poetry'. But here conversation is not just a metaphor. University is literally the co-operative institution, in which scholars from different disciplines work and converse in mutual respect. These are relationships presupposing not assertion or denial, but 'oblique recognition and accommodation'.[30] A student is a spectator who is present at the conversation of these scholars, thus learning to recognise the distinction between different idioms, and also to absorb the rules of civility calling for respect for all voices.

A university, therefore, represents 'the image of a civilisation as a manifold of different intellectual activities',[31] being an institution which most profoundly reflects the essence of modern civilisation. This civilisation is understood by Oakeshott as one characterised by the plurality of voices through which human beings can learn about the world and themselves. A university is the place in which this plurality finds the clearest expression. Oakeshott defends the idea of the pursuit of knowledge for its own sake and rejects any concession to influential currents which advocate the role of the universities as agents of social progress through education to social involvement and professional training.

At first glance, Oakeshott's concept of a university education and the radicalism of style of his essays make him appear as being at odds with reality. Indeed, he himself was quite pessimistic about the current situation. As late as 1972 he lamented that 'the self-corrup-

---

[26] 'The Study of "Politics" in a University,' RIP, p. 195.
[27] 'The Idea of a University,' VLL, p. 98
[28] Ibid.
[29] 'The Universities,' VLL, p. 126.
[30] RIP, p. 195.
[31] RIP, p. 196.

tion of universities exceeds that of any other of the educational engagement of European peoples.'[32] Yet this perception would be one-sided. It has already been shown that Oakeshott followed the tradition of respectable educational thought as well as of the practice of English universities. He himself qualified his pessimism claiming that the engagement of liberal learning 'has survived'.[33] According to him, 'universities still have some genuine and discerning friends... and there are students, alive to the pursuit of understanding...'[34]

Moreover, his own ideas directly influenced the development of English educational thought. Contrary to the perception which Oakeshott's own rhetoric might have created, his ideas found an attentive audience among the English educational establishment. Oakeshott regarded the democratisation and expansion of higher education as one of the major potential threats to his ideal of a university. Governments expected from universities practical outputs, and a great mass of students were coming with demands of acquiring useful skills and social status, the demands which a proper university was not supposed to fulfil. This development was common to all Western countries, yet they coped with it in different ways. Thus, in America this trend coincided with the rise of philosophical pragmatism, from which Dewey's concept of education originated. The advocates of liberal education found themselves on the defensive, and even when they tried to balance Dewey's views, they had to adopt many of his assumptions.[35]

In Europe, however, many a prominent philosopher and educator continued to advocate the ideal of knowledge for its own end. In Germany, for example, it was promoted by prominent intellectuals such as Karl Jaspers, partly as a reaction to Nazi suppression of the universities.[36] But nowhere was the attempt to preserve the tradition of liberal education through educational philosophy so apparent as in Britain. In the forties and fifties there developed a British philosophy of education, which, as Kaminsky argues, was 'methodologi-

---

[32] 'Education: The Engagement and Its Frustration,' VLL, pp. 89-90.
[33] 'A Place of Learning,' VLL, p. 30.
[34] DU, p. 142.
[35] See, for example, *General Education in a Free Society*. Report of the Harvard Committee (Cambridge, Mass: Harvard University Press, 1946).
[36] Jaspers, *The Idea of the University*. See also Ernst Anrich, *Die Idee der deutschen Universität und die Reform der deutschen Universitäten* (Darmstadt: Wissenschaftliche Buchgesellschaft, 1960).

cally radical and intellectually conservative'.[37] According to him, it retained strong allegiance to general philosophy in the reaction to the post-war social reform and to the attempts of the social sciences to appropriate the language and thereby the study of education to themselves.

The turning point was the establishment of the Chair of Educational Philosophy in the London Institute of Education, given to the philosopher L.A. Reid. His books presented an argument broadly similar to that of *Experience and Its Modes*, by stating that every form of experience involved some element of thought and judgement, and that knowledge consisted of many independent forms, though Reid's argument was less radical and influenced by some insights of pragmatism.[38] Reid was succeeded by R.S. Peters who brought to his job the analytical rigour of Oxford and organisational skills. Together with Paul H. Hirst, who later became a professor at Cambridge, Peters shaped the main framework of the educational debate in Britain.[39] Both Peters and Hirst acknowledged their debt to Oakeshott's philosophy.[40] Two of Oakeshott's educational essays were published in books edited by them.[41]

British educational philosophers were not entirely preoccupied with university education, rather concerning themselves with school, and especially secondary school teaching, and with the sixth form. However, their recommendations for the secondary school curriculum were borrowed from Oakeshott's views on the appropriate character of university education. Thus, the report prepared by the Oxford University Department of Education (1960) advocated far-reaching changes in the school curriculum, which were ostensibly intended to eliminate the division between Arts and Science and further promote general education.[42] Yet, according to the report, the main flaw of the English sixth form had been 'the unac-

---

[37] James S. Kaminsky, *A New History of Educational Philosophy* (Westport, Co: Greenwood Press, 1993), p. xx.
[38] See Louis Arnaud Reid, *Ways of Knowledge and Experience* (London: George Allen, 1961).
[39] See Kaminsky, *A New History of Educational Philosophy*, pp. 156-179.
[40] See Peters, 'Michael Oakeshott's Philosophy of Education,' p. 43; P.H. Hirst, 'Liberal Education and the Nature of Knowledge,' in *Knowledge and Curriculum* (London: Routledge and Kegan Paul, 1974), pp. 52-53.
[41] 'Learning and Teaching,' in R.S. Peters (ed.), *The Concept of Education* (London: Routledge and Kegan Paul, 1967), pp. 156-157. Reprinted in VLL, pp. 43-62; 'Education: The Engagement and Its Frustration,' in R.F. Dearden, P.H. Hirst & R.S. Peters (eds.), *Education and the Development of Reason* (London: Routledge & Kegan Paul, 1972), pp. 19-49. Reprinted in VLL, pp. 63-94.
[42] *Arts and Science Sides in the Sixth Form*. A Report of the Gulbenkian Foundation (Abingdon: The Abbey Press, 1960).

knowledged assumption that education means the acquisition of a body of knowledge rather than the development of the power to think'.[43] General education does not mean general knowledge of facts. It consists 'in the development of the understanding in the main modes of human experience'.[44] Although such education always presupposes teaching specific facts, learning such facts cannot be the end in itself. Rather, learning a particular science aims at acquiring the understanding of 'how scientists reach their conclusions'.[45] In a strikingly Oakeshottean style the report claims that a lack of general education is found if one 'confuses a moral with aesthetic judgment, interprets the actions of Asian political leaders in terms of nineteenth century English parliamentarism or believes that the existence of God has been scientifically approved'.[46]

This report is especially important because it is further developed by Hirst in his very influential article 'Liberal Education and the Nature of Knowledge' (1965). There he claims that liberal education 'is concerned with the comprehensive development of the mind in acquiring knowledge, it is always aimed at achieving an understanding of experience in many different ways'.[47] He refers to Oakeshott's 'The Voice of Poetry' as the main inspiration for his views. In *The Logic of Education* (1970) Peters and Hirst mention the term 'modes of experience'[48] and maintain that 'within the domain of objective experience and knowledge, there are such radical differences of kind that experience and knowledge of one form is neither equitable with, nor reducible to, that of any other form.'[49] They refer to Oakeshott's *Experience and Its Modes* and Reid's *Ways of Knowledge and Experience*.[50]

According to Hirst, there can exist neither hierarchical organisation of forms of knowledge, nor any external justification of them. Indeed, to look for such a justification would be self-defeating, if knowledge is valued for its own sake.[51] A proper education would always be the education into these forms of knowledge themselves, and not to the philosophy of these forms.[52] Following Oakeshott,

---

[43] Ibid., p. 13.
[44] Ibid., p. 14.
[45] Ibid., p. 18.
[46] Ibid., p. 13.
[47] Hirst, 'Liberal Education and the Nature of Knowledge,' p. 105.
[48] P.H. Hirst and R.S. Peters, *The Logic of Education* (London: Routledge, 1970), p. 64.
[49] Ibid., p. 65.
[50] Ibid., p. 136n.
[51] Hirst, 'Liberal Education and the Nature of Knowledge,' pp. 41-43.
[52] Ibid., p. 49.

Hirst also denied that this would lead to chaos and ever greater disintegration of mind. The absence of unity is replaced not by a chaos, but by the existence of different well established forms of thinking.[53]

Oakeshott's concept of education, then, strongly influenced the leading figures in the British educational philosophy of the sixties and seventies. However, Peters and Hirst do not follow Oakeshott in all respects, diverging from him at some important points. Firstly, according to them, there is still interdependence, or network of logical relationships between distinct modes of experience, where one domain of thinking often employs elements of another.[54] Peters and Hirst, then, are not ready to go as far as Oakeshott. But this simply shows that Oakeshott's ideas are just a more radical expression of our intuitions. His position is sometimes perceived as esoteric, not because it contradicts modern experience but rather because it offers a purified version of the idea which most people are capable of accepting only in its moderate form. Secondly, and more importantly, Peters and Hirst advocated rationalistic education. Peters was an analytical philosopher and regarded the strict analytical clarification of education's basic concepts to be at the centre of the project of constructing a philosophy of education. One of Peters' criticisms of Oakeshott is directed against the elusive character of the latter's writing. Further, education itself, not only its philosophy, has a rationalistic form, since liberal education, according to Hirst, is 'concerned directly with the development of the mind in rational knowledge'.[55] Peters and Hirst's publication of three volumes of articles about education, to which Oakeshott contributed one of his essays, is dedicated to the question of education and reason.[56] Much later Hirst moderated his previous passionate rationalism, having been influenced, as he admitted, by the criticism of thinkers such as Anthony O'Hear, Charles Taylor and Alasdair MacIntyre.[57] Pointedly, Oakeshott, whom some commentators include in this group of critics of rationalism, was not mentioned by Hirst at this time. Hirst had admitted a debt to Oakeshott in his earlier 'rationalistic' period.

This may seem a paradox, yet after the previous analysis of Oakeshott's own philosophy we should not be surprised. Notwithstanding the general elusiveness of Oakeshott's thought and occa-

[53] *Ibid.*, p. 52; P.H. Hirst, 'Curriculum Integration,' in *Knowledge and Curriculum*, p. 137.
[54] *Ibid*; Hirst and Peters, *The Logic of Education*, pp. 65-66.
[55] Hirst, 'Liberal Education and the Nature of Knowledge,' p. 43.
[56] Dearden, Hirst and Peters, *Education and the Development of Reason*.
[57] P.H. Hirst, 'Education, Knowledge and Practices,' in R. Barrow & P. White (eds.), *Beyond Liberal Education: Essays in Honour of Paul H. Hirst* (London: Routledge, 1993), p. 199n.

sional essays against Rationalism, his analysis of the branches of knowledge has much more in common with the proponents of the typically modernistic view than with radical critics of modernity.

III

There is, however, a different aspect to Oakeshott's educational thinking. Oakeshott was interested in education not only from the standpoint of the development of mind, but also from the standpoint of the development of man. He dealt not only with the character of thinking, but also with the character of human agents. Indeed, the cultivation of man involves the cultivation of mind, but here emphasis is not on knowledge as its own end, but on knowledge that leads to self-development. Oakeshott was indebted not only to the English tradition of liberal education, but also to the German neo-humanistic and Idealistic concept of *Bildung*. One tradition does not deny the other, and some English writers like Arnold were much influenced by German neo-humanism. Yet the latter is distinct by highlighting the humanistic and individualistic side implied in liberal education.

The German idea of *Bildung* originated in the debate about the role of the modern university during the crisis of the revolutionary events at the end of the eighteenth and the beginning of the nineteenth centuries. This notion was coined by thinkers such as Goethe for whom it meant an aspiration towards the harmonious development of personality and the full realisation of spiritual and aesthetic abilities of an individual.[58] Such view was held in common by neo-humanists such as W. von Humboldt or Schleiermacher and by proponents of the new Idealistic post-Kantian school of philosophy such as Fichte and Hegel.

Although neo-humanists and many Idealists referred to the Greek ideal of harmony as an inspiration for their pursuits, they regarded this debate to be a debate about the character of modern education, which would present an alternative to a utilitarian education. Thinkers such as Schiller, Humboldt and Hegel paid debt to the ancients, but they also recognised the specifically modern character of individuality which required a corresponding system of education. Such education was meant to be mainly concerned with the self-realisation of an individual, and it had to be distinct from learning to perform a social role or to acquire useful skills. In Humboldt's

---

[58] R. Steven Turner, 'Universitäten,' in K.-E. Jeismann & P. Lundgreen (eds.) *Handbuch der deutschen Bildungsgeschichte*, Band III 1800-1870 (München: C.H. Beck, 1987), p. 223.

words, it must not aim at some extraneous purpose.[59] To cultivate oneself as a human being, and to learn the independence of mind was the inherent purpose of education.

Neo-humanism, promoted by Humboldt and others, influenced not only the tradition of university education in nineteenth-century Germany, but also its school system. The emphasis on harmonious self-realisation and independence, combined with the rigorous process of learning were popular educational ideas. German schools were even admired by foreign observers for the way that they 'taught independence rather than mere knowledge' and encouraged conversation between teachers and pupils.[60]

This humanistic ideal is strongly present in Oakeshott's later educational essays. Their central theme is a pupil or a student as a human agent, and some of their ideas are fully developed in *On Human Conduct*. According to Oakeshott, learning is an activity characteristic of human beings and only of human beings, since it is possible only to 'an intelligence capable of choice and self-direction in relation to his own impulses and to the worlds around him'.[61] Education initiates a learner 'into the mysteries of a human condition: the gift of self-knowledge and of a satisfying intellectual and moral identity'.[62] It is learning 'how to be at once an autonomous and a civilised subscriber to a human life'.[63]

In the language of liberal Hegelianism, Oakeshott talks about the inescapable human freedom, where the human being is free 'because he is *in* himself what he is *for* himself'.[64] Nobody is born human, yet 'each is what he learns to become', and our permanent engagement is 'to become by learning'.[65] The world we inhabit is the world of learnt meanings in which we can distinguish between artefacts and intelligent beings like ourselves.[66] Therefore, by learning something about the world we learn to recognise the system of meanings we inhabit. Our world of meanings consists of a variety of languages of understanding, and these languages must be recognised 'not merely as diverse modes of understanding the world but

---

[59] Turner, 'Universitäten,' pp. 223-224.
[60] See Karl-Ernst Jeismann, 'American Observation Concerning the Prussian Educational System in the Nineteenth Century,' in H. Geitz, J. Heideking & J. Herbst (eds.), *German Influences on Education in the United States to 1917* (Washington, DC: German Historical Institute, 1995), pp. 31-32.
[61] 'Learning and Teaching,' VLL, p. 43.
[62] 'Education: The Engagement and Its Frustration,' VLL, p. 70.
[63] VLL, p. 71.
[64] 'A Place of Learning,' VLL, p. 19.
[65] VLL, p. 21.
[66] VLL, p. 23.

as the most substantial expressions we have of human self-understanding'.[67]

Education cannot provide a unified picture of the world, which 'has no meaning as a whole; it cannot be learned or taught in principle, only in detail.'[68] Therefore, what should be taught at school is always something specific. The inheritance of our civilisation is contingent and ambiguous. But because this is the only inheritance we have, a teacher has to have 'the courage of his circumstances',[69] and teach pupils the standards of human achievement from what is available.

In his earlier essays Oakeshott writes about the gift of an interval as the central feature of the universities.[70] A university stands in the middle between student's school and adult years, being 'a break in the tyrannical course of irreparable events'.[71] Here a student has an opportunity to put aside the allegiances of youth without acquiring new loyalties. This is the only period where he can dedicate himself to disinterested study. A university is the liberation from 'here' and 'now'. At the same time, a university may help a student to learn to 'lead a more significant life'.[72]

In later essays Oakeshott also discusses earlier stages of education. Thus, already in school a pupil learns independence of thought and begins to recognise intellectual virtues:

> Learning to think is... learning to recognise and enjoy the intellectual virtues. How does a pupil learn disinterested curiosity, patience, intellectual honesty, exactness, industry, concentration and doubt? How does he acquire a sensibility to small differences and the ability to recognise intellectual elegance? How does he come to inherit the disposition to submit to refutation? How does he not merely learn the love of truth and justice, but learn it in such a way as to escape the reproach of fanaticism?[73]

At the same time, this education is a profoundly social education. It presupposes the belief 'that we live in societies which, because they are associations of human beings, depend upon their members being human, that is, being in some degree educated persons'.[74] This does not have anything in common with so-called 'socialisation' in which education is sacrificed to the process of training for a certain

---

[67] VLL, p. 38.
[68] 'Learning and Teaching,' VLL, p. 49.
[69] Ibid.
[70] 'The Idea of a University,' VLL, p. 101; 'The Universities,' VLL, p. 127.
[71] Ibid.
[72] 'The Idea of a University,' VLL, p. 103.
[73] 'Learning and Teaching,' VLL, pp. 60-61.
[74] 'Education: The Engagement and Its Frustration,' VLL, p. 79.

social role. On the contrary, 'socialisation' is inimical to real education.

For Oakeshott, there is a dialectic in which a student's detachment, rather than the concern with relevance, represents the real introduction to the civilised life. Although Oakeshott refers to Greeks and Romans in his search for the origins of humanistic education, and recommends Classics as a legitimate field of the university curriculum, he by no means calls for a return to an ancient system of education. As it has been mentioned, German neo-humanists recognised the crucial differences between the ancient and the modern world, and therefore sought for a specifically modern answer to utilitarianism. So did Oakeshott, who was very familiar with this debate. For him, humanistic education is worthy only when it becomes a living culture of our civilisation. He argued that it is important to recognise learning as 'an inheritance coming to be possessed in such a manner that it loses its second-hand or antique character'.[75]

Education is, therefore, an emancipation. But this emancipation always involves the effort of study. All these intellectual virtues, resulting in the development of an autonomous personality, require discipline. And the initiation into the inheritance of our civilisation can be performed only by limitation. The emancipation presupposes 'detachment from the immediate' and can only be achieved 'in continuous redirection of attention'.[76]

Discipline in studying is not only compatible with the development of independent character which follows it; it is its basis. However, there can be no explicit education in autonomy. What can be explicitly taught is always some branch of learning, and not moral virtues. And yet learning is intimately connected with the development of personality. According to Oakeshott, in every activity of teaching two elements are involved: 'instructing by communicating information' and 'imparting by communicating judgement'. 'Judgement' is a tacit element of knowledge, an ability to apply the information to a particular circumstance. Judgement is indispensable to any ability, especially to complex abilities such as speaking languages or thinking in a certain idiom of thought.[77] Judgement makes it possible to distinguish the irrelevant, and it provides us with the 'style' implied in any human performance. Unlike information, judgement and style can be transmitted not by instruction, but only,

---

[75] 'Learning and Teaching,' VLL, p. 47.
[76] 'Education: The Engagement and Its Frustration,' VLL, p. 69.
[77] 'Learning and Teaching,' VLL, pp. 51-56.

as Oakeshott says, by 'imparting'.[78] Therefore, the ability to speak in an idiom of modern civilisation can never be explicitly taught, it is always 'imparted' in the process of studying something specific. Intellectual virtues are also taught by imparting, and they 'may be only imparted by a teacher who really cares about them for their own sake and never stoops to the priggishness of mentioning them'.[79]

The development of real human and intellectual virtues is, therefore, implicit in the process of teaching and learning. An explicit learning must always involve a thorough study of a specific subject. Oakeshott adopts the radical individualistic ideal of humanistic education, yet he does not fall into the extreme of romantic or post-modernistic spontaneity.

Again, this ideal in which the development of autonomy involves the discipline of learning and not a freedom from the constraints of study became well established in the British educational philosophy during the sixties and seventies. This is the view that Hirst and Peters presented as a middle way between the 'progressive' and 'authoritarian' approaches. 'Progressives' advocate radical changes in the manner of school education, arguing that maximum freedom is conducive to the development of independent personality. In contrast, 'authoritarians' emphasise the acquisition of a body of knowledge, often through mechanical learning. As an alternative to these two extremes, Hirst and Peters argued that the true aim of education had to be the development of autonomous personality but that this could be done only indirectly. Skills required for such development can be acquired only by means of learning specific subjects.[80] Oakeshott, as we have seen, held a similar view. Unlike the idea of plurality of experience, this approach to autonomy was not specifically Oakeshottean. It was a common and established position shared by many educational theorists. Yet Oakeshott remained one of its most articulate advocates, and what he was saying reflected the sentiments of many of his educationalist colleagues.

IV

Oakeshott's conception of education is, therefore, a specifically modern view, although not the prevalent one. It was influenced by

---

[78] VLL, p. 57.
[79] VLL, p. 62.
[80] Hirst and Peters, *The Logic of Education*, pp. 31-32. R.F. Dearden, 'Autonomy as an Educational Ideal,' in S.C. Brown (ed.), *Philosophers Discuss Education* (London: The Macmillan Press, 1975), pp. 3-18.

the nineteenth-century English and German theories of education which presented themselves as alternatives to utilitarianism. Oakeshott's writings strongly influenced his contemporaries, and thus indirectly shaped the character of the British debate on the nature of education.

According to Oakeshott, the essential characteristics of a proper education must be the initiation into the plurality of languages in our civilisation, and the self-recognition of human agents as independent individuals pursuing choices of their own. These two aspects of education correspond to Oakeshott's philosophy of experience and to his philosophy of society.

Although such radicalism coexists with an apparent traditionalism and conservatism in Oakeshott's educational writings, it is not contradicted by this conservatism. Moreover, Oakeshott's conservative approach is a necessary part of his defence of modernity. Oakeshott's philosophy, as we have seen, is incapable of providing a satisfactory logical ground for the radical plurality which it promulgates. This plurality, though the most distinctive and valuable feature of modern civilisation, has no external justification. Although various branches of knowledge and their presuppositions can be explicitly taught and learnt, the relationships of irrelevance and plurality between those branches cannot be preached. Likewise, while specific rules within civil society can be meaningfully deliberated, it is impossible to get a philosophical justification for civil obligation itself.

Hence the importance of teaching by imparting, or of learning through the recognition of tradition. Although radical plurality cannot be rationally justified, it still can be valued as one of the greatest enjoyments that modernity offers. However, in order to value this plurality one must perceive it as a part of his own inheritance, and therefore of oneself. A child, entering the plurality of sounds and colours, is in no need of justifying it. He is amused by this polyphony because it brings him an immediate joy and because by enjoying this plurality he makes it a part of himself. Likewise, a pupil or a student initiated into the plurality of worldviews is amused by it and thus feels its importance. And he recognises other individuals as ends in themselves because freedom is not his doctrine, but a part of his way of life.

This position entails a paradox. In order to teach what is most valuable in modern society, modern education should be strikingly traditionalist. This paradox is what makes liberal education vulnerable. The recognition that our civilisation is a contingent historical event is so intolerable, that attempts to break out of this tension and to find the final rational justification for modernity will always be made. Rational thinking will be diverted from within the modes of experience towards their justification and the endeavours to build a system. This system will be none other than ideology and will always fall short of the expectations it will provoke. It will always be guilty of the 'crippling error' of irrelevance. Indeed, this attempt to shore up modern civilisation through ideology is the major threat to it. When people cease to value this plurality unreflexively, it will simply vanish.

It is no surprise, then, that Oakeshott's pessimism, or even 'alarmism', becomes most apparent in his educational writings. The main concern of 'Rationalism in Politics', one of his most pessimistic essays, is not politics but rather education, where the influence of Rationalism is much more pernicious.[81] However, this pessimism is never overwhelming. Even when Oakeshott thinks that the situation is grave, he still finds some hope for liberal education. There are still many people who come to a university in search of such an education, and this is what counts in the end. However influential the *theories* of post-modernism or the vulgarity of masses may be, they will not prevail so long as those institutions which are guardians of the inheritance of our civilisation, first and foremost the universities, impart the values of plurality to the intellectual elite. Then, if an historian, or scientist conducts objective research, or if an artist pursues what is aesthetically satisfactory, notwithstanding what they may have learnt at the courses of the philosophy of science, or art or history; if a citizen still recognises the virtue of civility and plurality, notwithstanding what he may have heard from radical political ideologies, it means that liberal education is still alive. It is not philosophical certainty that supports this education but an implicit belief in its value for our civilisation. As Oakeshott once said, 'I speak as a believer, not (in this matter) as a critical sceptic.'[82]

---

[81] RIP, pp. 37-42.
[82] DU, p. 129.

Epilogue

I

This book has been an attempt to elucidate the vision of modernity implied in the general structure of Michael Oakeshott's thought. In order to prevent possible misunderstandings, however, it seems appropriate to conclude with some qualifications with regard to the claims of the study.

Firstly, Oakeshott's thought and his analysis of modernity do not refer to modernity understood as some 'objective' reality, but to his interpretation of what is going on. His purpose, more precisely, is to show us a more or less coherent way of reconciling ourselves to the world in which we find ourselves. Oakeshott does not seem to believe, however, that this can be done by constructing an absolutely perfect philosophical system. His philosophy is not such a system for two reasons. One is the lack of logical unity between the level of experience and the level of society. The other is his rejection of holistic structure, on the ground that these levels consist of radically independent and mutually irrelevant abstractions. As was observed at the outset, however, Oakeshott's rejection of philosophy in the sense of system does not mean that his thought lacks rigour. On the contrary, he maintains a remarkable consistency in the course of exploring the inner logic of each of the abstractions, while an overall coherence is achieved by means of analogy.

Secondly, although Oakeshott's thought is about understanding modern Western civilisation, it is not a mere summary of familiar and explicit features of modern intellectual life. Instead, it offers what can be claimed to be a very coherent critique of the essential postulates of the often confused and ambiguous self-understanding which underlies our civilisation.

Thirdly, his thought does not claim to offer a complete account of modern Western civilisation, but only to identify the postulates of modernity which seem to be exclusive to this civilisation. Oakeshott concentrates, that is, on the postulates which distinguish our life from that of other civilisations. It is, accordingly, with these postulates that the present study has been especially concerned.

Finally, it would be wrong to conclude that Oakeshott's concentration on what is distinctive about the modern period of Western civilization means that he believes other periods offer nothing of value. Certainly, pre-Renaissance European life, with its grand system of ethics comprising other forms of knowledge and with its warm morality of communal ties, had many attractive features. Oakeshott's contention, however, is that any attempt to retrieve it would be futile, since the outcome would only be a purely artificial resemblance to the original organic unity. On the level of experience, this leads to intellectual confusion, and on the level of society, results in a totalitarian type of solidarity. Therefore, the only appropriate response to modernity is radical acceptance. Such an acceptance does not merely mean a compromise, or a temporary retreat. It means, rather, an unconditional admission that the modern, essentially fragmented way of life is the only one open to us. This admission implies in turn a determination to protect modernity against those who dream of replacing it with a more integrated or organic mode of existence.

Oakeshott is relatively optimistic about the prospect of carrying out the defence of modernity successfully, suggesting that fully 'modern' societies are not going to be easily seduced by the dream of restoration because the postulates of modernity are engrained in them. He acknowledges, however, that the dream of restoration is likely to be attractive to those half-modern societies in which the relics of a former unity are still recognisable enough to create the illusion of a possible return. Despite Oakeshott's optimism, there are moments in which he reveals an occasional pessimism. At such times, he sees modernity as bearing the seeds of its own destruction. This is particularly true about his writings on education, in which any attempt to modernise the system of education is regarded as likely to lead to the loss of what is valuable in modernity. In addition, his last essay, 'The Tower of Babel' (1983), is a description of how a hedonistic free society finally succumbs to the dream of restoring unity and achieving immortality.[1] On the whole, however, the dominant sentiment in Oakeshott's writings is an appreciation of present enjoyment even when decay is inevitable, as it is for everything historically contingent.

---

[1] 'The Tower of Babel,' OH, pp. 179-210.

Bibliography

Oakeshott's Works

Books and Articles

'A Place of Learning,' in *The Voice of Liberal Learning*, pp. 17-42. (First published in *Colorado College Studies* 12, January 1975, pp. 6-29.)

'Contemporary British Politics,' *Cambridge Journal* 1(8), 1948, pp. 474-490.

'Dr. Leo Strauss on Hobbes,' in *Hobbes on Civil Association*, pp. 141-158. (First published in *Politica* 2, 1937, pp. 364-379.)

'Education: The Engagement and Its Frustration,' in *The Voice of Liberal Learning*, pp. 63-94. (First published in R.F. Dearden, P.H. Hirst & R.S. Peters (eds.), *Education and the Development of Reason*. London: Routledge & Kegan Paul, 1972, pp. 19-49.)

'Edward Bullough,' *Caian* 43(i), 1934, pp. 1-11.

Experience and Its Modes. Cambridge: University Press, 1933.

Hobbes on Civil Association. Indianapolis: Liberty Fund, 2000. (First published by Basil Blackwell, 1975.)

'Introduction to *Leviathan*,' in *Hobbes on Civil Association*, pp. 1-79. (An earlier version was first published in T. Hobbes, *Leviathan*. Oxford: Basil Blackwell, 1946, pp. vii-lxvi.)

'John Locke,' *Cambridge Review* 54, 1932, pp 72-73.

'Learning and Teaching,' in *The Voice of Liberal Learning*, pp. 43-62. (First published in R.S. Peters (ed.), *The Concept of Education*. London: Routledge and Kegan Paul, 1967, pp. 156-157.)

'Lord Acton,' *Caian* 31(i), 1922, pp. 14-23.

'Mr. Carr's First Volume,' *Cambridge Journal* 4(6), 1951, pp. 543-554.

'On Being Conservative,' in *Rationalism in Politics and Other Essays*, pp. 407-437. (Originally given as a lecture at the University of Swansea in 1956. First published in the original edition of *Rationalism in Politics*, 1962.)

On History and Other Essays. Indianapolis: Liberty Fund, 1999. (First published by Basil Blackwell, 1983.)

On Human Conduct. Oxford: Clarendon Press, 1975.

'Political Education,' in *Rationalism in Politics and Other Essays*, pp. 43-69. (First published by Bowes and Bowes, 1951.)

'Rational Conduct,' in *Rationalism in Politics and Other Essays*, pp. 99-131. (First published in *Cambridge Journal* 4(1), 1950, pp. 3-27.)

'Rationalism in Politics,' in *Rationalism in Politics and Other Essays*, pp. 5-42. (First published in *Cambridge Journal* 1(2-3), 1947, pp. 81-98, 145-157.)

Rationalism in Politics and Other Essays. Indianapolis: Liberty Fund, 1991. (The first edition was published by Methuen and Co., 1962.)

'Religion and the Moral Life,' *Religion, Politics and the Moral Life*, pp. 39-45. (First published in 'The "D" Society Pamphlets' 2, 1927, pp. 13.)

'Science and Society,' *Cambridge Journal* 1(11), 1948, pp. 689-697.

'Scientific Politics,' in *Religion, Politics and the Moral Life*, pp. 97-110. (First published in *Cambridge Journal* 1(6), 1948, pp. 347-358.)

'Shylock the Jew,' *Caian* 30(i), 1921, pp. 61-67.

'The Activity of Being a Historian,' in *Rationalism in Politics and Other Essays*, pp. 151-183. (First appeared in *Historical Studies* 1, T.D. Williams (ed.). London: Bowes and Bowes, 1958, pp. 1-19.)

'The Authority of the State,' (1929), in *Religion, Politics and the Moral Life*, pp. 74-87. (First published in *Modern Churchman* 19(6-8), 1929, pp. 313-327.)

'The B.B.C.' *Cambridge Journal* 4(9), 1951, pp. 543-554.

'The Claims of Politics,' in *Religion, Politics and the Moral Life*, pp. 91-96. (First published in *Scrutiny* 8, 1939, pp. 146-151.)

'The Concept of a Philosophical Jurisprudence,' *Politica* 3, 1938, pp. 203-222, 345-360.

'The Customer is Never Wrong,' in *Religion, Politics and the Moral Life*, pp. 111-118. (First published in *Listener* 54, 1955, pp. 301-302.)

'The Definition of a University,' *Journal of Educational Thought* 1, 1967, pp. 129-142.

'The Idea of a University,' in *The Voice of Liberal Learning*, pp. 95-104. (First published in *Listener* 43, 1950, pp. 424-426.)

'The Masses in Representative Democracy,' in *Rationalism in Politics and Other Essays*, pp. 363-383. (First published as 'Die Massen in der repräsentativen Demokratie,' in A. Hunold (ed.), *Masse und Demokratie*. Erlenbach-Zürich und Stuttgart: Rentsch, 1957, pp. 189-214. Appeared in English in A. Hunold (ed.), *Freedom and*

Serfdom: An Anthology of Western Thought. Dordrecht: Reidel, 1961, pp. 151-170.)

'The Moral Life in the Writings of Thomas Hobbes,' in *Hobbes on Civil Association*, pp. 80-140. (Originally given as a lecture at the University of Nottingham in 1960. First published in the original edition of *Rationalism in Politics*, 1962.)

'The Political Economy of Freedom,' in *Rationalism in Politics and Other Essays*, pp. 384-406. (First published in *Cambridge Journal* 2(4), 1949, pp. 212-229.)

'The Rule of Law,' in *On History and Other Essays*, pp. 129-178.

The Social and Political Doctrines of Contemporary Europe. Cambridge: University Press, 1939.

'The Study of "Politics" in a University,' in *Rationalism in Politics and Other Essays*, pp. 184-218. (First published in the original edition of *Rationalism in Politics*, 1962.)

'The Tower of Babel,' in *Rationalism in Politics and Other Essays*, pp. 465-487. (First published in *Cambridge Journal* 2(1), 1948, pp. 67-83.)

'The Tower of Babel,' in *On History and Other Essays*, pp. 179-210.

'The Universities,' in *The Voice of Liberal Learning*, pp. 105-135. (First published in *Cambridge Journal* 2(9), 1949, pp. 515-542.)

The Voice of Liberal Learning, T. Fuller (ed.). New Haven: Yale University Press, 1989.

'The Voice of Poetry in the Conversation of Mankind,' in *Rationalism in Politics and Other Essays*, pp. 488-541. (First published by Bowes and Bowes, 1959.)

Posthumously Published Works

Morality and Politics in Modern Europe, S. Robin Letwin (ed.). New Haven: Yale University Press, 1993. (Lectures first given at Harvard in April 1958.)

'Political Philosophy,' in *Religion, Politics and the Moral Life*, pp. 138-155.

'Religion and the World,' in *Religion, Politics and the Moral Life*, pp. 27-38.

Religion, Politics and the Moral Life, T. Fuller (ed.). New Haven: Yale University Press, 1993.

'The Concept of a Philosophy of Politics,' in *Religion, Politics and the Moral Life*, pp. 119-137.

The Politics of Faith and the Politics of Skepticism, T. Fuller (ed.). New Haven: Yale University Press, 1996.

'Work and Play,' *First Things* 54, 1995, pp. 29-33.

Book Reviews

Review of H. Butterfield, *The Origins of Modern Science, 1300-1800*, in *Times Literary Supplement*, November 25, 1949, pp. 761-763.

Review of R.G. Collingwood, *The Idea of History*, in *English Historical Review* 62, 1947, pp. 84-86.

Review of R.G. Collingwood, *The Principles of Art*, in *Cambridge Review* 59, 1938, p. 487.

Review of G.C. Field, *Principles and Ideals in Politics*, in *Cambridge Journal* 2(7), 1949, pp. 444-446.

Review of B. de Jouvenel, *Sovereignty*, in *Crossbow* 1, 1957, pp. 43-44.

Review of H. Marcuse, *Reason and Revolution*, in *Spectator* 194, 1955, pp. 404-405.

Review of J. Needham (ed.), *Science, Religion and Reality*, in *Journal of Theological Studies* 27, 1926, pp. 317-319.

Review of M. Polanyi, *Personal Knowledge*, in *Encounter* 11(iii), 1958, pp. 77-80.

Review of J.C. Powys, *The Meaning of Culture*, in *Cambridge Review* 51, 1930, pp. 367-368.

Review of R. Scruton (ed.), *Conservative Thoughts: Essays from The Salisbury Review*, in *Spectator* 261, July 9, 1988, p. 60.

Review of K.C. Wheare, *Government by Committee*, in *Spectator* 194, 1955, p 129.

Unpublished Archive Material

'A Discussion of Some Matters Preliminary to the Study of Political Philosophy.' LSE Archives.

'An Essay on the Relations of Philosophy, Poetry, and Reality.' LSE Archives.

'A Study of Political Thought' (A Series of Lectures of Michael Oakeshott). LSE Archives.

Letter to F.A. Hayek, April 30, 1968. Hoover Institute Archives.

Letter to K. Popper, January 28, 1948. Hoover Institute Archives.

'The Cambridge School of Political Science,' [April 1924]. LSE Archives.

'The Idea of "Character" in the Interpretation of Modern Politics,' [1954]. LSE Archives.

Secondary Sources

Published Sources and Dissertations

Abel, Corey. *Michael Oakeshott's Liberalism: The Epistemology of Experience and the Morality of Individualism*. PhD diss., Chicago University, 1995.

Adorno, Theodor W. and Max Horkheimer. *Dialectic of Enlightenment*, trans. J. Cumming. London: Verso, 1979.

Aliotta, Antonio. *The Idealistic Reaction Against Science*, trans. A. McCaskill. London: Macmillan and Co., 1914.

Anderson, Perry. 'The Intransigent Right at the End of the Century,' *London Review of Books* 14, September 24, 1992, pp. 7-11.

Angermann, Erich. *Robert von Mohl 1799-1875: Leben und Werk eines altliberalen Staatsgelehrten*. Neuwied: Hermann Luchterhand, 1962.

Annan, Noel. *Our Age: Portrait of a Generation*. London: Weidenfeld and Nicolson, 1990.

Anrich, Ernst. *Die Idee der deutschen Universität und die Reform der deutschen Universitäten*. Darmstadt: Wissenschaftliche Buchgesellschaft, 1960.

Arnold, Matthew. *Culture and Anarchy*. Cambridge: University Press, 1935.

Arts and Science Sides in the Sixth Form. A Report of the Gulbenkian Foundation. Abingdon: The Abbey Press, 1960.

Auspitz, Josiah Lee. 'Individuality, Civility and Theory: The Philosophical Imagination of Michael Oakeshott,' *Political Theory* 4(3), 1976, pp. 261-294.

Ayer, Alfred Jules. *Language, Truth and Logic*. London: Victor Gollancz, 1967.

Barber, Benjamin R. 'Conserving Politics: Michael Oakeshott and Political Theory,' *Government and Opposition* 11, 1979, pp. 446-463.

Beardsley, Monroe C. *Aesthetics: Problems in the Philosophy of Criticism*. Indianapolis: Hackett Publishing Company, 1981.

Bell, Clive. *Art*. Oxford: Oxford University Press, 1987.

Bell-Villada, Gene H. *Art for Art's Sake and Literary Life*. Lincoln: University of Nebraska Press, 1996.

Bentham, Jeremy. *Of Laws in General*. London: The Athlone Press, 1970.

Berki, R.N. 'Oakeshott's Concept of Civil Association: Notes for a Critical Analysis,' *Political Studies* 29(4), 1981, pp. 570-585.

Berlin, Isaiah. 'Two Concepts of Liberty,' in *Four Essays on Liberty*. Oxford: Oxford University Press, 1969, pp. 118-172.

Blaas, P.B.M. *Continuity and Anachronism: Parliamentary and Constitutional Development in Whig Historiography and in the Anti-Whig Reaction Between 1890 and 1930*. The Hague: Martinus Nijhoff, 1978.

Blackmore, John T. *Ernst Mach: His Work, Life and Influence*. Berkeley: University of California Press, 1972.

Bloom, Allan. *The Closing of American Mind*. London: Penguin Books, 1988.

Boucher, David. 'The Creation of the Past: British Idealism and Michael Oakeshott's Philosophy of History,' *History and Theory* 23(2), 1984, pp. 193-214.

Boucher, David. 'Human Conduct, History and Social Science in the Works of R.G. Collingwood and Michael Oakeshott,' *New Literary History* 24, 1993, pp. 697-717.

Boucher, David. 'Overlap and Autonomy: The Different Worlds of Collingwood and Oakeshott,' *Storia, Antropologia e Scienze del Linguaggio* 4, 1989, pp. 69-79.

Boucher, David and Andrew Vincent. *British Idealism and Political Theory*. Edinburgh: Edinburgh University Press, 2000.

Bradley, F.H. *Appearance and Reality*. Oxford: Clarendon Press, 1930.

Bradley, F.H. *Ethical Studies*. Oxford: Clarendon Press, 1927.

Bradley, F.H. *The Presuppositions of Critical History*. Don Mills: J.M. Dent & Sons, 1968.

Bradley, J. *Mach's Philosophy of Science*. London: The Athlone Press, 1971.

Browning, Reed. *Political and Constitutional Ideas of the Court Whigs*. Baton Rouge: Louisiana State University Press, 1982.

Bullough, Edward. *Aesthetics: Lectures and Essays*. London: Bowes and Bowes, 1957.

Burckhardt, Jakob. *The Civilization of the Renaissance in Italy*, trans. S.G.C. Middlemore. London: Phaidon, 1995.

Burgh, W.G. de. Review of *Experience and Its Modes*, in *Hibbert Journal* 33, 1934, pp. 144-150.

Burke, Peter. *The French Historical Revolution: The* Annales *School, 1929-1989*. Cambridge: Polity, 1990.

Burrow, J.W. *Whigs and Liberals: Continuity and Change in English Political Thought*. Oxford: Clarendon Press, 1988.

Buruma, Ian. *Voltaire's Coconuts, or Anglomania in Europe*. London: Weidenfeld & Nicolson, 1999.

Butler, L.J. and Anthony Gorst (eds.), *Modern British History: A Guide to Study and Research*. London: I.B. Tauris, 1997.

Butterfield, Herbert. *The Whig Interpretation of History*. London: G. Bell and Sons, 1931.

Caird, Edward. *The Social Philosophy and Religion of Comte*. Bristol: Thoemmes Press, 1999.

Carr, Edward H. *What Is History*. London: Macmillan & Co., 1962.

Casey, John. 'Philosopher of Practice,' in J. Norman (ed.), *The Achievement of Michael Oakeshott*. London: Duckworth, 1993, pp. 58-66.

Cassagne, Albert. *La Théorie de l'Art Pour l'Art: En France chez les Derniers Romantiques et les Premier Réalistes*. Seyssel: Champ Vallon, 1997.

Coats, W. John Jr. 'Michael Oakeshott as Liberal Theorist,' *Canadian Journal of Political Science* 18(4), 1985, pp. 773-787.

Coats, W. John Jr. *Oakeshott and His Contemporaries*. Selinsgrove: Susquehanna University Press, 2000.

Coats, W. John Jr. 'Some Correspondence Between Oakeshott's "Civil Condition" and the Republican Tradition,' *Political Science Reviewer* 21, 1992, pp. 99-115.

Cockroft, Eva. 'Abstract Expressionism, Weapon of the Cold War,' in F. Frascina & J. Harris (eds.), *Art in Modern Culture*. London: The Open University, 1992, pp. 82-90.

Collingwood, R.G. *The Idea of History*. Oxford: Clarendon Press, 1993.

Collingwood, R.G. *Principles of Art*. Oxford: Oxford University Press, 1958.

Collingwood, R.G. Review of *Experience and Its Modes*, in *Cambridge Review* 55, 1934, pp. 249-250.

Collingwood, R.G. *Speculum Mentis or The Map of Knowledge*. Oxford: Clarendon Press, 1924.

Collini, Stefan. *Public Moralists: Political Thought and Intellectual Life in Britain 1850-1930*. Oxford: Clarendon Press, 1991.

Collinson, Diané. 'Aesthetic Experience,' in O. Hanfling (ed.), *Philosophical Aesthetics: An Introduction*. Oxford: Blackwell, 1992, pp. 117-178.

Covell, Charles. *The Redefinition of Conservatism: Politics and Doctrine*. London: Macmillan, 1986.

Cowling, Maurice. *Religion and Public Doctrine in Modern England*. Cambridge: Cambridge University Press, 1980.

Crick, Bernard. 'The World of Michael Oakeshott: or the Lonely Nihilist,' *Encounter* 20(6), 1963, pp. 65-74.

Croce, Benedetto. *History as the Story of Liberty*. Indianapolis: Liberty Fund, 2000.

Croce, Benedetto. *Logic and the Science of the Pure Concept*, trans. D. Ainsle. London: Macmillan, 1917.

Croce, Benedetto. *Theory and History of Historiography*, trans. D. Ainsle. London: George G. Harrap & Co., 1921.

Davis, Howard. 'Poetry and the Voice of Michael Oakeshott,' *British Journal of Aesthetics* 15(1), pp. 59-68.

Dearden, R.F. 'Autonomy as an Educational Ideal,' in S.C. Brown (ed.), *Philosophers Discuss Education*. London: The Macmillan Press, 1975, pp. 3-18.

Dearden, R.F., P.H. Hirst and R.S. Peters (eds.), *Education and the Development of Reason*. London: Routledge & Kegan Paul, 1972.

Deleuze, Gilles and Félix Guattari. *Anti-Oedipus: Capitalism and Schizophrenia*, trans. R. Hurley, M. Seem & H.R. Lane. New York: The Viking Press, 1977.

Devigne, Robert. *Recasting Conservatism: Oakeshott, Strauss, and the Response to Postmodernism*. New Haven: Yale University Press, 1994.

Dickey, Laurence. *Hegel: Religion, Economics and the Politics of Spirit 1770-1807*. Cambridge: Cambridge University Press, 1987.

Dray, William H. 'Michael Oakeshott's Theory of History,' in P. King & B.C. Parekh (eds.), *Politics and Experience*. Cambridge: University Press, 1968, pp. 19-42.

Dunn, John. *Locke*. Oxford: Oxford University Press, 1982.

Dunn, John. *The Political Thought of John Locke*. Cambridge: Cambridge University Press, 1969.

Eddington, Arthur S. *The Nature of the Physical World*. Cambridge: University Press, 1928.

Elster, Jon (ed.). *The Multiple Self*. Cambridge: Cambridge University Press, 1986.

Elton, G.R. *Political History: Principle and Practice*. London: Allen Lane, 1970.

Elton, G.R. *The Practice of History*. London: Methuen and Company, 1967.

Evans, Richard J. 'Afterword,' in G.R. Elton, *The Practice of History*. Oxford: Blackwell, 2002, pp. 165-203.

Falck, Colin. 'Romanticism in Politics,' *New Left Review* 18, 1963, pp. 60-72.

Farr, Anthony. *Sartre's Radicalism and Oakeshott's Conservatism: The Duplicity of Freedom*. London: Macmillan Press, 1998.

Flathman, Richard E. *The Practice of Political Authority*. Chicago: The University of Chicago Press, 1980.

Forster, E.M. 'Art for Art's Sake,' in *Two Cheers for Democracy*. London: Edward Arnold & Co., 1951, pp. 98-104.

Franco, Paul. 'Michael Oakeshott as Liberal Theorist,' *Political Theory* 18(3), 1990, pp. 411-436.

Franco, Paul. 'Oakeshott's Critique of Rationalism Revisited,' *Political Science Reviewer* 21, 1992, pp. 15-43.

Franco, Paul. *The Political Philosophy of Michael Oakeshott*. New Haven: Yale University Press, 1990.

Friedman, Richard B. 'Oakeshott on the Authority of Law,' *Ratio Juris* 2(1), 1989, pp. 27-40.

Frisby, David. *Fragments of Modernity: Theories of Modernity in the Work of Simmel, Kracauer and Benjamin*. Cambridge: Polity Press, 1985.

Frohnen, Bruce P. 'Oakeshott's Hobbesian Myth: Pride, Character and the Limits of Reason,' *Western Political Quarterly* 43(4), 1990, pp. 789-809.

Fuller, Lon L. *The Morality of Law*. New Haven: Yale University Press, 1969.

Fuller, Timothy. 'Foreword,' in M. Oakeshott, *On History and Other Essays*. Indianapolis: Liberty Fund, 1999, pp. ix-xx.

Fuller, Timothy. 'Introduction,' in M. Oakeshott, *Religion, Politics and the Moral Life*. New Haven: Yale University Press. 1993, pp. 1-26.

Furet, François. 'Quantitative History,' in F. Gilbert & R. Graubard (eds.), *Historical Studies Today*. New York: W.W. Norton & Company, 1972, pp. 45-61.

General Education in a Free Society. Report of the Harvard Committee. Cambridge, Mass: Harvard University Press, 1946.

Gerencser, Steven A. *The Skeptic's Oakeshott*. New York: St. Martin's Press, 2000.

Gordon, Scott. *The History and Philosophy of Social Science*. London: Routledge, 1991.

Grant, Robert. *Oakeshott*. London: Claridge Press, 1990.

Gray, John. *Liberalisms: Essays in Political Philosophy*. London: Routledge, 1989.

Gray, John. *Post-liberalism: Studies in Political Thought*. New York: Routledge, 1993.

Greenleaf, W.H. *Oakeshott's Philosophical Politics*. London: Longman's Green, 1966.

Grosby, Steven. 'Pluralism in the Thought of Oakeshott, Shils and Weber,' *Journal of Classical Sociology* 2(1), 2002, pp. 43-58.
Guerlac, Henry E. 'Science and French National Strength,' in E.M. Earle (ed.), *Modern France: Problems of the Third and Fourth Republic*. Princeton: Princeton University Press, 1951, pp. 81-105.
Guyer, Paul. *Kant and the Experience of Freedom*. Cambridge: Cambridge University Press, 1993.
Hare, R.M. *The Language of Morals*. Oxford: Clarendon Press, 1952.
Hartz, Louis. *The Liberal Tradition in America*. New York: Harcourt, Brace & World, 1955.
Haslam, Jonathan. *The Vices of Integrity: E.H. Carr, 1892-1982*. London: Verso, 1999.
Hauser, Arnold. *Sozialgeschichte der Kunst und Literatur*. München: C.H. Beck, 1972.
Hayek, F.A. *The Political Ideal of the Rule of Law*. Cairo: National Bank of Egypt, 1955.
Hayek, F.A. *The Road to Serfdom*. London: George Routledge & Sons, 1944.
Hegel, G.W.F. *Elements of the Philosophy of Right*, trans. H.B. Nisbet. Cambridge: Cambridge University Press, 1991.
Hempel, Carl G. 'The Function of General Laws in History,' in *Aspects of Scientific Explanation*. New York: The Free Press, 1965, pp. 231-243.
Himmelfarb, Gertrude. 'Supposing History Is a Woman – What Then?' *American Scholar* 53(4), 1984, pp. 494-505.
Hinchliffe, Geoffrey. 'Education or Pedagogy?' *Journal of Philosophy of Education* 35(1), 2001, pp. 31-45.
Hirst, P.H. 'Curriculum Integration,' in *Knowledge and Curriculum*. London: Routledge and Kegan Paul, 1974, pp. 132-151.
Hirst, P.H. 'Education, Knowledge and Practices,' in R. Barrow & P. White (eds.), *Beyond Liberal Education: Essays in Honour of Paul H. Hirst*. London: Routledge, 1993, pp. 184-199.
Hirst, P.H. 'Liberal Education and the Nature of Knowledge,' in *Knowledge and Curriculum*. London: Routledge and Kegan Paul, 1974, pp. 30-53.
Hirst, P.H. and R.S. Peters. *The Logic of Education*. London: Routledge, 1970.
Hobbes, Thomas. *On the Citizen*, trans. R. Tuck. Cambridge: Cambridge University Press, 1998.
Holliday, Ian. 'On Michael Oakeshott,' *Government and Opposition* 27(2), 1992, pp. 131-147.

Horton, John. 'The Fetishism of Sociology,' in J.D. Colfax & K.L. Roach (eds.), *Radical Sociology*. New York: Basic Books, 1971, pp. 171-193.

Humboldt, Wilhelm von. *The Limits of State Action*, trans. J.W. Burrow. Indianapolis: Liberty Fund, 1993.

Jaffe, Kineret S. 'The Concept of Genius: Its Changing Role in Eighteenth-Century French Aesthetics,' in P. Kivy (ed.), *Essays on the History of Aesthetics*. Rochester: University of Rochester Press, 1992, pp. 224-244.

Jaki, Stanley L. *Uneasy Genius: The Life and Work of Pierre Duhem*. The Hague: Martinus Nijhoff, 1984.

Jaspers, Karl. *The Idea of the University*, trans. H.A.T. Reiche & H.F. Vanderschmidt. London: Peter Owen, 1960.

Jeismann, Karl-Ernst. 'American Observation Concerning the Prussian Educational System in the Nineteenth Century,' in H. Geitz, J. Heideking & J. Herbst (eds.), *German Influences on Education in the United States to 1917*. Washington, DC: German Historical Institute, 1995, pp. 21-41.

Jenkins, Keith. *On "What is History": From Carr and Elton to Rorty and White*. London: Routledge, 1995.

Johnson, Matthew. *Michael Oakeshott's Critique of Modernity: Science, Ideology and Reason*. PhD diss., Nebraska University, 1999.

Johnson, Nevil. 'Die Politische Philosophie Michael Oakeshotts,' *Zeitschrift für Politik* 32(4), 1985, pp. 347-374.

Jouvenel, Bertrand de. *Sovereignty: An Inquiry into the Political Good*, trans. J.F. Huntington. Indianapolis: Liberty Fund, 1997.

Kaminsky, James S. *A New History of Educational Philosophy*. Westport, Co: Greenwood Press, 1993.

Kant, Immanuel. *The Critique of Judgement*, trans. J.C. Meredith. Oxford: Clarendon Press, 1978.

Kaufman, Paul. 'Heralds of Original Genius,' in *Essays in Memory of Barrett Wendell*. New York: Russell & Russell, 1967, pp. 189-217.

Kellner, George F. *Movements of Thought in Modern Education*. New York: John Wiley & Sons, 1984.

Kelly, George Armstrong. *The Human Comedy: Constant, Tocqueville and French Liberalism*. Cambridge: Cambridge University Press, 1992.

Kenyon, John. *The History Men: The Historical Profession in England since the Renaissance*. London: Weidenfeld and Nicolson, 1993.

King, Preston. 'Michael Oakeshott and Historical Particularism,' *Politics* 16(1), 1981, pp. 85-102.

Kirk, Russell. *The Conservative Mind*. London: Faber and Faber, 1954.

Koselleck, Reinhart. 'Historia Magistra Vitae: The Dissolution of the Topos into the Perspective of a Modernized Historical Process,' in *Futures Past: On the Semantic of Historical Time*, trans. K. Tribe. Cambridge, Mass: The MIT Press, 1985, pp. 21-38.

Krabbe, H. *The Modern Idea of the State*, trans. G.H. Sabine & W.J. Shepard. New York: D. Appleton and Company, 1922.

Knox, T.M. Review of *Experience and Its Modes*, in *Oxford Magazine* 52, 1934, pp. 551-552.

Koerner, Kirk F. *Liberalism and its Critics*. London: Croom Helm, 1985.

Kolakowski, Leszek. *Positivist Philosophy: From Hume to the Vienna Circle*, trans. N. Guterman. Harmondsworth: Penguin Books, 1972.

Kuhn, Thomas. *Structure of Scientific Revolutions*. Chicago: University of Chicago Press, 1970.

LaCapra, Dominic. *History and Criticism*. Ithaca: Cornell University Press, 1985.

Laclau, Ernesto and Chantal Mouffe. *Hegemony and Socialist Strategy: Towards a Radical Democratic Politics*. London: Verso, 1985.

Lamprecht, S.P. Review of *Experience and Its Modes*, in *Journal of Philosophy* 31(6), 1934, pp. 163-164.

Langewiesche, Dieter. *Liberalism in Germany*, trans. Ch. Banerji. London: Macmillan Press, 2000.

Lawn, Chris. 'Adventures of Self-Understanding: Gadamer, Oakeshott and the Question of Education,' *Journal of the British Society for Phenomenology* 27(3), 1996, pp. 267-277.

Lepenies, Wolf. *Between Literature and Science: The Rise of Sociology*, trans. R.J. Hollingdale. Cambridge: Cambridge University Press, 1988.

Liddington, John. 'Hall and Modood on Oakeshott,' *Political Studies* 30(2), 1982, pp. 177-183.

Liddington, John. 'Oakeshott: Freedom in a Modern European State,' in Z. Pelczynski & J. Gray (eds.), *Conceptions of Liberty in Political Philosophy*. London: The Athlone Press, 1984, pp. 289-320.

Losee, John. *A Historical Introduction to the Philosophy of Science*. Oxford: Oxford University Press, 1993.

Lyotard, Jean-François. *The Postmodern Condition: A Report on Knowledge*, trans. G. Bennington & B. Massumi. Manchester: Manchester University Press, 1984.

McCabe, David. 'Michael Oakeshott and the Idea of Liberal Education,' *Social Theory and Practice* 26(3), 2000, pp. 443-464.

Mach, Ernst. *The Analysis of Sensations*, trans. C.M. Williams. London: Routledge, 1914.

Manuel, Frank E. *The New World of Henri Saint-Simon*. Cambridge, Mass: Harvard University Press, 1956.

Mapel, David R. 'Civil Association and the Idea of Contingency,' *Political Theory* 18(3), 1990, pp. 392-410.

Megill, Allan. '"Grand Narrative" and the Discipline of History,' in F. Ankersmith & H. Kellner (eds.), *A New Philosophy of History*. London: Reaktion Books, 1995, pp. 151-173.

Minogue, Kenneth. 'Oakeshott's Idea of Freedom,' *Quadrant*, October 1975, pp. 77-83.

Montesquieu, Charles de Secondat, baron de. *The Spirit of the Laws*, trans. T. Nugent. New York: Hafner, 1949.

Moore, George Edward. *Principia Ethica*. Cambridge: Cambridge University Press, 1971.

Nardin, Terry. *The Philosophy of Michael Oakeshott*. University Park: The Pennsylvania State University Press, 2001.

Newman, John Henry. *The Idea of a University*. Oxford: Clarendon Press, 1976.

Nietzsche, Friedrich. *Untimely Meditations*, trans. R.J. Hollingdale. Cambridge: Cambridge University Press, 1983.

Novick, Peter. *That Noble Dream: The "Objectivity Question" and the American Historical Profession*. Cambridge: Cambridge University Press, 1988.

Olson, Mancur. *The Logic of Collective Action: Public Goods and the Theory of Groups*. Cambridge, Mass: Harvard University Press, 1965.

O'Sullivan, Luke. 'Michael Oakeshott on European Political History,' *History of Political Thought* 21(1), 2000, pp. 132-151.

O'Sullivan, Luke. *Oakeshott on History*. Thorverton: Imprint Academic, 2003.

O'Sullivan, Noël. 'Visions of Freedom: The Response to Totalitarianism,' in J. Hayward, B. Barry & A. Brown (eds.), *The British Study of Politics in the Twentieth Century*. Oxford: Oxford University Press, 1999, pp. 63-88.

Paley, William. 'Of Civil Liberty,' from *Moral and Political Philosophy*, in *Works*. London: Bohn, 1847, pp. 134-136.

Parekh, Bikhu. 'Oakeshott's Theory of Civil Association,' *Ethics* 106, 1995, pp. 158-186.

Parker, Christopher. *The English Idea of History from Coleridge to Collingwood*. Aldershot: Ashgate, 2000.

Pascal, Roy. *Culture and the Division of Labour: Three Essays on Literary Culture in Germany*. Coventry: University of Warwick, 1974.

Passmore, John. *A Hundred Years of Philosophy*. London: Duckworth, 1966.

Pater, Walter. *The Renaissance: Studies in Art and Poetry*. London: Collins, 1967.

Paul, Harry W. 'The Debates Over the Bankruptcy of Science in 1895,' *French Historical Studies* 5(3), 1968, pp. 299-327.

Pearson, Karl. *The Grammar of Science*. London: Adam and Charles Black, 1911.

Peters, R.S. 'Michael Oakeshott's Philosophy of Education,' in P. King & B.C. Parekh (eds.), *Politics and Experience*. Cambridge: University Press, 1968, pp. 43-63.

Pilbeam, Bruce. 'Conservatism and Postmodernism: Consanguineous Relations or "Different" Voices?' *Journal of Political Ideologies* 6(1), 2001, pp. 33-54.

Pinkard, Terry. *Hegel: A Biography*. Cambridge: Cambridge University Press, 2000.

Pitkin, Hanna F. 'The Roots of Conservatism: Michael Oakeshott and the Denial of Politics,' *Dissent* 20, 1973, pp. 496-525.

Pocock, J.G.A. 'Introduction,' in E. Burke, *Reflections on the Revolution in France*. Indianapolis: Hackett, 1987, pp. vii – lvi.

Podoksik, Efraim. 'How Oakeshott Became an Oakeshottean,' *European Journal of Political Theory*, forthcoming.

Podoksik, Efraim. 'Oakeshott's Theory of Freedom as Recognized Contingency,' *European Journal of Political Theory* 2(1), 2003, pp. 57-77.

Poincaré, Henri. *Science and Hypothesis*. London: The Walter Scott Publishing Co., 1905.

Poincaré, Henri. 'Sur la Valeur Objective de la Science,' *Revue de Métaphysique et de Morale* 10, 1902, pp. 263-293.

Poincaré, Henri. *La Valeur de la Science*. Paris: Ernest Flammarion, 1908.

Popper, Karl. *The Logic of Scientific Discovery*. London: Hutchinson, 1959.

Popper, Karl. *The Open Society and Its Enemies*. London: Routledge, 1995.

Postan, M. 'The Revulsion from Thought,' *Cambridge Journal* 1(7), 1948, pp. 395-408.

Pyle, Andrew. 'Introduction,' in H. Poincaré, *Science and Method*, trans. F. Maitland. London: Routledge, 1996, pp. v-xxi.

Quinton, Anthony. *The Politics of Imperfection: The Religious and Secular Traditions of Conservative Thought in England from Hooker to Oakeshott*. London: Faber and Faber, 1978.
Raphael, D.D. Review of *On Human Conduct*, in *Political Quarterly* 46(4), 1975, pp. 450-454.
Rasch, William. *Niklas Luhmann's Modernity: Paradoxes of Differentiation*. Stanford: Stanford University Press, 2000.
Rayner, Jeremy. 'The Legend of Oakeshott's Conservatism: Sceptical Philosophy and Limited Politics,' *Canadian Journal of Political Science* 18(2), 1985, pp. 313-338.
Reid, Louis Arnaud. *Ways of Knowledge and Experience*. London: George Allen, 1961.
Ringer, Fritz K. *The Decline of the German Mandarins: The German Academic Community, 1890-1933*. Cambridge, Mass: Harvard University Press, 1969.
Rorty, Richard. *Objectivity, Relativism, and Truth*. Cambridge: Cambridge University Press, 1997.
Rosenblum, Nancy. *Another Liberalism: Romanticism and the Reconstruction of Liberal Thought*. Cambridge, Mass: Harvard University Press, 1987.
Rotenstreich, Nathan. *Philosophy, History and Politics: Studies in Contemporary English Philosophy of History*. The Hague: Martinus Nijhoff, 1976.
Rothblatt, Sheldon. *Tradition and Change in English Liberal Education*. London: Faber and Faber, 1976.
Ruggiero, Guido de. *The History of European Liberalism*, trans. R.G. Collingwood. London: Oxford University Press, 1927.
Runciman, David. *Pluralism and the Personality of the State*. Cambridge: Cambridge University Press, 1997.
Schiller, Friedrich. *On the Aesthetic Education of Man*, trans. E.M. Wilkinson & L.A. Willoughby. Oxford: Clarendon Press, 1967.
Schiller, Friedrich. 'The Nature and Value of Universal History: An Inaugural Lecture [1789],' *History and Theory* 11(3), 1972, pp. 321-334.
Schmitt, Carl. *The Crisis of Parliamentary Democracy*, trans. E. Kennedy. Cambridge, Mass: The MIT Press, 1985.
Schorske, Carl E. *Fin-de-Siècle Vienna: Politics and Culture*. New York: Alfred A. Knopf, 1980.
Schweitzer, Albert. *Civilization and Ethics: The Philosophy of Civilization Part II*, trans. J. Naish. London: A. & C. Black, 1923.
Scruton, Roger. *Modern Philosophy*. London: Sinclair-Stevenson, 1994.

Segal, Jacob. 'A Storm from Paradise: Liberalism and the Problem of Time,' *Critical Review* 8(1), 1994, pp. 23-48.
Shils, Edward. 'The Antinomies of Liberalism,' in *The Virtue of Civility*. Indianapolis: Liberty Fund, 1997, pp. 123-187.
Siedentop, Larry. 'Two Liberal Traditions,' in A. Ryan (ed.), *The Idea of Freedom: Essays in Honour of Isaiah Berlin*. Oxford: Oxford University Press, 1979, pp. 153-174.
Simmel, Georg. 'Christianity and Art,' in *Essays in Religion*, trans. H.J. Helle. New Haven: Yale University Press, 1997, pp. 65-77.
Simmel, Georg. *Lebensanschauung: vier metaphysische Kapitel*. München: Duncker & Humboldt, 1918.
Simmel, Georg. 'On the Nature of Philosophy,' in K.H. Wolff (ed.), *Georg Simmel, 1858-1918: A Collection of Essays with Translations and a Bibliography*. Columbus: The Ohio State University Press, 1959, pp. 282-309. Originally published in *Hauptprobleme der Philosophie*. Leipzig: Sammlung Goschen, 1910, pp. 8-43.
Simmel, Georg. *The Sociology of Georg Simmel*, trans. K.H. Wolff. Glencoe, Ill: The Free Press, 1950.
Skinner, Quentin. 'Sir Geoffrey Elton and the Practice of History,' *Transactions of the Royal Historical Society* 7, 1997, pp. 301-316.
Smith, Gordon. 'Between Left and Right: The Ambivalence of European Liberalism,' in E.J. Kirchner (ed.), *Liberal Parties in Western Europe*. Cambridge: Cambridge University Press, 1988, pp. 16-28.
Smith, Michael. 'After Managerialism: Towards a Conception of the School as an Educational Community,' *Journal of Philosophy of Education* 33(3), 1999, pp. 317-336.
Smith, Steven B. *Hegel's Critique of Liberalism: Rights in Context*. Chicago: The University of Chicago Press, 1989.
Smith, Thomas W. 'Michael Oakeshott on History, Practice and Political Theory,' *History of Political Thought* 17(4), 1996, pp. 591-614.
Snow, C.P. *The Two Cultures*. Cambridge: Cambridge University Press, 1993.
Southgate, Beverly. *History: What and Why? Ancient, Modern and Postmodern Perspectives*. London: Routledge, 1996.
Stebbing, L. Susan. Review of *Experience and Its Modes*, in *Mind* 43, 1934, pp. 403-405.
Stevenson, John. 'Social History,' in L.J. Butler & A. Gorst (eds.), *Modern British History: A Guide to Study and Research*. London: I.B. Tauris, 1997, pp. 207-217.

Stone, Lawrence. *The Past and the Present Revisited*. London: Routledge & Kegan Paul, 1987.
Strauss, Leo. *Natural Right and History*. Chicago: The University of Chicago Press, 1953.
Strauss, Leo. *Persecution and the Art of Writing*. Glencoe, Ill: The Free Press, 1952.
Stump, David. 'Henri Poincaré's Philosophy of Science,' *Study in History and Philosophy of Science* 20(3), 1989, pp. 335-363.
Sullivan, Andrew. *Intimations Pursued: The Voice of Practice in the Conversation of Michael Oakeshott*. PhD diss., Harvard University, 1990.
Sullivan, Andrew. 'Taken Unseriously,' *The New Republic*, May 6, 1991, p. 42.
Taylor, Peter J. *Modernities: A Geohistorical Interpretation*. Minneapolis: University of Minneapolis Pres, 1999.
Tocqueville, Alexis de. *Democracy in America*, trans. G. Lawrence. London: Fontana, 1994.
Tönnies, Ferdinand. *Community and Civil Society*, trans. J. Harris & M. Hollis. Cambridge: Cambridge University Press, 2001.
Townsend, Dabnew. 'From Shaftesbury to Kant: The Development of the Concept of Aesthetic Experience,' in P. Kivy (ed.), *Essays on the History of Aesthetics*. Rochester: University of Rochester Press, 1992, pp. 205-223.
Tregenza, Ian. 'The Life of Hobbes in the Writings of Michael Oakeshott,' *History of Political Thought* 18(3), 1997, pp. 531-557.
Trilling, Lionel. *The Liberal Imagination*. New York: Doubleday, 1953.
Tseng, Roy. *The Sceptical Idealist: Michael Oakeshott as a Critic of the Enlightenment*. Thorverton: Imprint Academic, 2003.
Tully, James. *An Approach to Political Philosophy: Locke in Context*. Cambridge: Cambridge University Press, 1993.
Turner, R. Steven. 'Universitäten,' in K.-E. Jeismann & P. Lundgreen (eds.) *Handbuch der deutschen Bildungsgeschichte*, Band III 1800-1870. München: C.H. Beck, 1987, pp. 221-249.
Vandenberghe, Frédéric. *Comparing Neo-Kantians: Ernst Cassirer and Georg Simmel*. Manchester: University of Manchester, 1996.
Voegelin, Eric. *The New Science of Politics: An Introduction*. Chicago: The University of Chicago Press, 1987.
Walsh, W.H. 'The Practical and Historical Past,' in P. King & B.C. Parekh (eds.), *Politics and Experience*. Cambridge: University Press, 1968, pp. 5-18.
Weber, Alfred. 'Die Bedeutung der geistigen Führer in Deutschland,' *Die neue Rundschau* 29, 1918, pp. 1249-1268.

Weingartner, Rudolph H. *Experience and Culture: The Philosophy of Georg Simmel*. Middletown, Co.: Wesleyan University Press, 1962.

White, Hayden. *Metahistory: The Historical Imagination in Nineteenth-Century Europe*. Baltimore: John Hopkins University Press, 1973.

White, Ralph. 'The Anatomy of a Victorian Debate: An Essay in the History of Liberal Education,' *British Journal of Educational Studies* 34(1), 1986, pp. 38-65.

Williams, Kevin. 'The Gift of an Interval: Michael Oakeshott's Idea of a University Education,' *British Journal of Educational Studies* 37(4), 1989, pp. 384-397.

Williams, Michael 'Liberalism and Two Conceptions of the State,' in D. MacLean & C. Mills (eds.), *Liberalism Reconsidered*. Totowa, NJ: Rowman & Allanheld, 1983, pp. 117-129.

Winch, Peter. *The Idea of Social Sciences and Its Relation to Philosophy*. London: Routledge & Kegan Paul, 1958.

Wolin, Sheldon S. 'The Politics of Self-Disclosure,' *Political Theory* 4(3), 1976, pp. 321-334.

Wood, G.O. Review of *Experience and Its Modes*, in *Times Literary Supplement*, April 26, 1934, p. 294.

Worthington, Glenn. 'Michael Oakeshott and the City of God,' *Political Theory* 28(3), 2000, pp. 377-398.

Worthington, Glenn. 'Michael Oakeshott on Life: Waiting with Godot,' *History of Political Thought* 16(1), 1995, pp. 105-119.

Worthington, Glenn. 'Oakeshott's Claims of Politics,' *Political Studies* 45, 1997, pp. 727-738.

Wuthenow, Ralph-Reiner. *Muse, Maske, Meduse: Europäischer Ästhetizismus*. Frankfurt am Main: Suhrkamp, 1978.

Archive Material

Gonville and Caius College's archive, Cambridge. The register of the borrowed books.

LSE Archive, Oakeshott collection. Caius Papers.

Index

A

Absolute Idealism, see *Idealism*
'Activity of Being an Historian, The', 44, 50, 52, 93, 125
Acton, Lord, 48, 106n, 142, 165
Adorno, Theodor, 26, 177
aesthetic education, see *education*
aestheticism, 55, 62, 104-106, 115, 120
aesthetics, 7, 22, 99, 103-104, 110, 119, 131, see also *art, poetry*
Aliotta, Antonio, 59
Annan, Noel, 56
anthropology, 71, 76
anti-individual, 149, 156, 178, 208, see also *individual, individual manqué*
Aristotle, 29, 47, 53, 149, 193, 214
Arnold, Matthew, 107, 142, 214, 217-218, 223
art, 6, 11-12, 18, 23-25, 41, 43, 50, 55, 61, 104, 106-111, 113-116, 120, 131, 133, 215, 229, see also *aesthetics, poetry*
association,
    civil, 53, 183-188, 191-199, 201-203, 206, 208, 210
    cultural, 170
    enterprise, 183, 185, 188-189, 194-197, 208
    moral, 170, 183, 185-186, 191-193
    transactional, 183, 194, 196-197, 203
'Authority of the State, The', 170
Ayer, A.J., 138

B

Bacon, Francis, 175, 177, 188
Bagehot, Walter, 179
Beardsley, Monroe, 106, 114
Bell, Clive, 105-107
Bell-Villada, Gene, 115
Bentham, Jeremy, 151, 199
Bergson, Henri, 46, 61, 105, 133
Berlin, Isaiah, 165
Bildung, 223
Blake, William, 78
Bloom, Alan, 27
Bodin, Jean, 188
Bosanquet, Bernard, 15, 47
Boucher, David, 78, 80n
Bradley, F.H., 38, 40-42, 57, 79-80, 86, 135, 142
British Idealism, see *Idealism*
Broch, Hermann, 17, 24

Bullough, Edward, 110, 113-114, 116, 122
Burckhardt, Jakob, 25, 153, 165
Burgh, W.G. de, 43
Burke, Edmund, 151, 174, 189
Buruma, Ian, 179-180
Bury, J.B., 89, 99
Butterfield, Herbert, 73, 81

C

Carr, E.H., 95, 97, 122
Casey, John, 35
character, 107, 142, 149, 153
Chateaubriand, F.-R. de, 171
civil association, see *association*
'Claims of Politics, The', 109
Clifford, W.K., 62
Coats, W.J., 37, 45
Collingwood, R.G., 10-19, 22, 27, 40-41, 52, 57-58, 71-72, 78-80, 82-84, 86-87, 89, 91-92, 95, 101-103, 108-109, 122
Collini, Stefan, 142
Comte, Auguste, 23
'Concept of a Philosophical Jurisprudence, The', 43-44
conditional understanding, see *understanding*
conservatism (conservative), 1, 10, 20, 24, 27, 31-32, 131, 141, 144, 158-160, 163, 167, 174-177, 179, 213, 220, 228
Constant, Benjamin, 163n, 166, 188
contingency (contingent), 89, 99-100, 152, 184, 204, 207, 225, 228, 232
contract, 192-194, 196-197, 203, 209

conversation, 39, 44, 52, 93, 110, 117, 123-124, 167, 202-203, 210, 218
Croce, Benedetto, 16, 31, 40, 57-58, 79-80, 82-84, 86-87, 89-90, 92, 103, 122
cultural association, see *association*
culture, 18, 20, 22, 25, 27, 107-108, 169, 214, 218

D

Danto, Arthur, 79
'Definition of a University, The', 212
Deleuze, Gilles, 24, 28
Descartes, René, 175
Dewey, John, 219
Dilthey, Wilhelm, 56n, 79
'Discussion of Some Matters Preliminary to the Study of Political Philosophy, A', 47-49, 149, 169
doing, see *level of doing*
Droysen, J.G., 79
Duhem, Pierre, 73
Duns Scotus, 11

E

economics, 70-71
Eddington, Arthur, 63-64, 66-67, 122
education, 7-8, 33, 54, 56, 125, 179, 210-229, 232
    aesthetic, 106, 116, 120
    liberal, 8, 213-214, 219, 222-223, 229
    scientific, 56
'Education: The Engagement and Its Frustration', 212
Eliot, T.S., 107

Elton, G.R., 98, 100, 101n, 103
empiricism, 16, 18, 62, 80-82, 84, 102
Enlightenment, 26, 166, 174
    Scottish, 25
enterprise association, see *association*
Epicurean, 107, 161, 167
Epicurus, 107
'Essay on the Relations of Philosophy, Poetry and Reality, An', 47
Eucken, Rudolf, 133
Evans, Richard, 98
existentialism, 103
Experience and Its Modes, 6, 9-10, 13-15, 18-19, 30, 35-39, 43-45, 48-52, 54-58, 63, 73, 75, 78-79, 84, 92-93, 95, 99-101, 108, 110-111, 117, 119, 121, 123, 128, 131-132, 134, 137-138, 140, 143, 147-150, 170, 210-211, 220-221

F

fabricating, 119
Fichte, J.G., 17, 188-189, 223
Flaubert, Gustave, 81, 105
Forster, E.M., 115
fragmentation, 9-11, 14, 16-18, 20, 22-28, 32-33, 133, 204, 214, 232, see also *self, fragmented*
fragmented self, see *self*
Franco, Paul, 192
freedom (liberty), 14-15, 107, 116, 135, 149, 155-156, 159, 161-165, 168-169, 177, 179-180, 182, 185, 187, 189-191, 198-201, 203, 206-208, 224, 228
    negative, 198-200

positive, 198, 200
friendship, 52, 117, 119, 143, 167, 169, 193
Fry, Roger, 105
Furet, François, 82n

G

Gallie, W.B., 79
George, Stefan, 23
Gerencser, Steven, 35
Gibbon, Edward, 92
Godolphin, Sidney, 206
Goethe, J.W. von, 78, 223
Grant, Robert, 54, 93, 210
Gray, John, 21
Green, T.H., 15
Greenleaf, W.H., 56n, 103, 118
Guizot, François, 163n
Guyer, Paul, 116

H

Hare, R.M., 185n
Hartz, Louis, 162n
'Harvard lectures', 151
Hayek, F.A., 129, 165, 176-177
Hegel, G.W.F., 16-17, 22, 25, 38, 47, 103, 149, 151, 163, 188-189, 192, 194, 223
Heidegger, Martin, 46, 50, 137
Helmholtz, Hermann von, 57
Hempel, Carl, 80
Herder, J.G., 166
Herzen, Alexander, 179-180
Himmelfarb, Gertrude, 93
Hirst, Paul H., 220-222, 227
historical positivism, see *positivism*
history, 5-7, 12-13, 23, 25, 29, 41, 43-44, 48-50, 52, 55-58, 71, 78-104, 106, 114-115, 120-125,

127, 131-134, 136-139, 215, 218, 229
Hobbes, Thomas, 7, 29-30, 53, 138, 151, 173, 181, 188, 194-196, 204-206, 209-210
Hobbes on Civil Association, 182, 205
Hooker, Richard, 174
Horkheimer, Max, 26, 177
human conduct, 44, 76, 99-100, 118-119, 131, 139-141, 147-149, 151-153, 155-157, 182-183, 193, 195, 198, 201, 203, 205, 207
human sciences, see *social sciences*
Humboldt, Wilhelm von, 166, 167n, 168, 223-224
Husserl, Edmund, 46

I

'Idea of a University, The', 212, 215
Idealism (Idealist), 37, 55, 58, 71-72, 77, 103, 117, 169, 200, 213, 223, see also *neo-Hegelianism, neo-Kantianism*
  Absolute, 16, 19, 38, 40, 42-43, 48-49, 57, 92
  British, 15-16, 78, 170-171
individual, 119, 149-151, 154-157, 174, 178, 182, 189-190, 202, 206-208, 228, see also *anti-individual*
individual manqué, 155-156, 174, 178, 189, 208, , see also *anti-individual*

individualism, 14-15, 25, 27, 107, 116, 149, 160-161, 176, 191, 223, 227
  methodological, 149, 153
individuality, 14-15, 25, 28, 31-32, 132, 149-157, 166, 168-169, 173-174, 179, 182, 190, 192, 206, 208, 223
irrelevance, 1, 18-19, 33, 42, 44, 51, 53-54, 72-73, 88, 96-97, 106, 110, 112, 116-117, 132-134, 136, 139, 157, 184, 202-203, 209, 212, 226, 228-229, 231

J

Jacobinism, 163
Jaspers, Karl, 215, 217, 219
Jouvenel, Bertrand de, 129

K

Kaminsky, James, 219
Kant, Immanuel, 17, 47n, 63, 112, 116-117, 143, 150-151, 188
Kirchnoff, G.R., 60
Kolakowski, Leszek, 62
Knox, T.M., 42
Krabbe, H., 194
Kuhn, Thomas, 62, 64-65, 83, 122

L

Lamprecht, S., 43
Langlois, Charles, 80
law, 43, 130, 146, 166, 169, 174, 183-187, 190-191, 193, 197, 199-205, 206n
  rule of, 163-164, 168-169, 179, 190-191, 199, 202, 207-208

Lawrence, D.H., 150
'Learning and Teaching', 212
Leibniz, G.W. von, 17, 54
Le Roy, Edouard, 61
level of doing (conduct), 6, 121, 139-140, 149, 157, 202, 209
level of understanding, 6, 121, 139-140, 149, 157, 202, 209
liberal education, see *education*
liberalism (liberal), 1, 7, 21, 25, 28, 31, 97, 115, 131, 155, 158-180, 190-191, 194, 197-198, 201, 207-208, 224
    Romantic, 159, 161, 166, 168-169, 174, 179, 190
    Whig, 159, 161-166, 168-169, 171, 174, 179, 204
libertarian, 164n, 175
liberty, see *freedom*
Lichtenberg, G.C., 78
Locke, John, 4, 151, 161, 188
logical positivism, see *positivism*
Lotze, R.H., 59n
love, 52, 117, 119, 143, 151, 193
Lyotard, J.-F., 24, 26

M

Mach, Ernst, 59-60, 62-63, 66, 68, 70
Machiavelli, Niccolò, 176, 188
MacIntyre, Alasdair, 24, 222
McTaggart, J.M.E., 46, 57
Madison, James, 165, 189
Maitland, F.W., 81, 87, 142
Mallarmé, Stéphane, 105
Marsilius of Padua, 196
Marx, Karl, 176, 188
'Masses in Representative Democracy, The', 154, 178
Megill, Allan, 83

methodological individualism, see *individualism*
Mill, J.S., 62, 77, 80, 142, 151, 168, 179, 187, 189
Moberly, Walter, 217
modernity, 7, 10, 14-17, 20-22, 24-33, 53, 55, 78, 94, 102, 114-115, 120, 124, 144, 174, 181, 203-204, 208, 211-213, 223, 226-229, 231-232
Mohl, Robert von, 162
Montaigne, Michel de, 105, 107
Montesquieu, Ch.-S. baron de, 162-163, 172, 189
Moore, G.E., 143
moral association, see *association*
'Moral Life in the Writings of Thomas Hobbes, The', 204
morality, 82, 106, 114, 116, 130-132, 135, 138-149, 154-157, 163, 180, 182, 185-186, 191-193, 206
    of communal ties, 30, 154-155, 178, 208
    of custom, 109, 118, 144-148
    of ideals, 145-148, 179
    of individuality, 29, 149, 151, 153-154, 173, 178, 190, 205
    of rules, 145, 147-148
    reflective, 118, 144-146, 148
Morgenthau, Hans, 76, 177

N

Nardin, Terry, 93, 210
negative freedom, see *freedom*
neo-Hegelianism (neo-Hegelian), 13, 15, 18-19, 39n, 41, 49, 59, 143, 149, 204, see also *Idealism*

neo-Kantianism (neo-Kantian), 16-19, 27, 38, 44, 57, 82, 91, 194, see also *Idealism*
New Criticism, 115
Newman, John H., 214, 217
Nietzsche, Friedrich, 17, 20, 24-25, 38, 53, 109, 143, 145
nihilism, 27-28, 114, 143, 145-146, 155
non-purposive, see *purposeless*
Novick, Peter, 82, 94

O

objectivity (objective), 25-27, 31, 55, 61, 72, 77, 83, 85, 87, 93, 97-99, 101, 103, 122, 208
O'Hear, Anthony, 222
'On Being Conservative', 52, 167, 174-175, 191
On History, 19, 37-38, 44, 52, 54, 98-100, 119, 182
On Human Conduct, 6, 15, 30, 36-37, 44, 50, 54n, 74, 98-100, 118-119, 121, 128-129, 131-132, 139, 141, 147, 149, 151, 154, 156-159, 167n, 173-174, 179-180, 182, 187, 190-191, 204-205, 211, 224
O'Sullivan, Luke, 79, 93
Owen, Robert, 188

P

Paley, William, 199
Pascal, Blaise, 78
Pater, Walter, 23, 105
Paulsen, Friedrich, 215
Pavlov, Ivan, 73
Pearson, Karl, 59, 62, 68
Peters, R.S., 220-222, 227
Pilbeam, Bruce, 31
'Place of Learning, A', 209, 212
Plato, 47, 113, 209
plurality, 7, 9, 18-20, 27-28, 32-33, 36, 49, 53-54, 124-125, 170, 174n, 196, 202, 204, 206-207, 209-212, 215, 217-218, 228-229
poetry, 5, 29, 39, 44, 47, 49-50, 52, 55, 98, 103-121, 124, 127, 132-133, 138, see also *aesthetics, art*
Poincaré, Henri, 31, 48, 59-63, 66-67, 83, 122
Polanyi, Michael, 73
'Political Economy of Freedom, The', 164
'Political Education', 171, 210
political philosophy, 5-6, 35, 42-44, 46, 127-131, 157, 173, 180, 188, 209
political thought, 78, 98, 128, 157-159, 179-181, 194, 197
politics, 5-6, 36, 56, 76-77, 103, 109, 130, 158, 167, 170-173, 175-179, 185, 210
Politics of Faith and The Politics of Scepticism, The, 36
Popper, Karl, 64, 80, 165, 177
positive freedom, see *freedom*
positivism, 55, 65
  historical, 24, 79-80, 82, 84
  logical, 15-16, 59, 67, 122, 138
  scientific, 24, 26-27, 55, 57-60, 62, 64-65, 67-69, 71-72, 75-77, 106, 121, 129
post-modern, 8, 10-11, 20-21, 24-26, 28, 30-32, 55, 80, 83, 98, 122, 227, 229
practical experience (voice, imagining), 43-44, 50, 52, 108, 110-115, 124, 132-136, 138-141, 150-151, 157

practice, 5, 35, 49-50, 61, 72, 75, 94, 96, 98, 103, 116-117, 121, 131-141, 146-148, 180, 182-183, 192-193, 202-203, 207
practices, 139-140, 147, 149, 182-183, 192-193, 202
pragmatism, 58, 122, 133, 219-220
pre-modern, 20-21, 24-28, 32, 168, 176, 217
progress, 20, 116, 160-161, 171-172, 198, 218
Proudhon, P.-J., 201n
Proust, Marcel, 105
pseudo-modes, 42-44
psychology, 70-71, 75-76
purposeless (non-purposive), 51-54, 73, 102, 140, 157, 183, 194, 201-202, 207, 209, 212

R

Ranke, Leopold von, 81, 189
'Rational Conduct', 109
rationalism, 31, 35, 76, 129, 175-179, 205, 222-223
'Rationalism in Politics', 76, 118, 131, 144, 175, 177-178, 229
Rationalism in Politics and Other Essays, 36, 38, 44, 109n, 110, 118, 158-159
realism, 15, 79, 83-86, 102
reflective morality, see *morality*
Reid, L.A., 220-221
relativism, 8, 24, 27-28, 62, 64, 83, 85-86, 93, 97, 102-103, 122-123, 129
religion, 11-12, 18, 22-24, 41, 43, 46n, 71-73, 108, 119, 135, 137, 140, 143, 147, 163, 169, 198, 214-215, 217-218

Renaissance, 14, 103, 105, 154, 175-177, 232
Rickert, Heinrich, 56n, 91
Riehl, Alois, 57
Romantic liberalism, see *liberalism*
romanticism, 103, 105, 142, 173, 227
Rorty, Richard, 21, 24, 26n
Rosenblum, Nancy, 166
Rothblatt, Sheldon, 214
Rousseau, J.-J., 216
Ruggiero, Guido de, 162n
rule of law, see *law*
'Rule of Law, The', 182
Ruskin, John, 105
Russell, Bertrand, 56n, 62

S

Saint-Simon, Henri, 23, 188
Sartre, J.-P., 26n
scepticism, 5, 28, 32, 35-36, 47, 64, 83, 85-87, 92-93, 102, 121, 123
Schiller, Friedrich, 17, 116-117, 217, 223
Schleiermacher, Friedrich, 223
Schmitt, Carl, 175
Schopenhauer, Arthur, 113
Schweitzer, Albert, 133-134
science, 6-7, 11-12, 18, 22-23, 25-26, 29, 41, 43, 48-50, 52, 55-78, 80-83, 88-92, 94, 96, 102, 104, 106, 114-115, 120-125, 127, 129, 131-134, 136-137, 139, 215, 217-218, 220-221, 229
'Science and Society', 77
scientific education, see *education*
'Scientific Politics', 177

scientific positivism, see *positivism*
Scottish Enlightenment, see *Enlightenment*
Scruton, Roger, 26, 179-180
Seignobos, Charles, 80
self, 28, 32, 107, 111, 132, 135, 138, 140, 149-153, 157, 202, 209
  fragmented, 151-152, see also *fragmentation*
Shakespeare, William, 104
Shelley, P.B., 113
Shils, Edward, 162n
Sidney, Philip, 113
Simmel, Georg, 18-20, 25
Simons, H.C., 164
Sittlichkeit, 192
Skinner, Quentin, 98
Smith, Adam, 151
Snow, C.P., 77
social sciences (human sciences), 56, 68-71, 73, 75-76, 97, 130, 220, see also *sociology*
societas, 188-189, 194, 196
sociology, 25, 69, 76, 130, 171-172, see also *social sciences*
Speculum Mentis, 10-15
Spencer, Herbert, 62
Spinoza, Benedict, 47, 188-189
Staël, Madame de, 163n
Stebbing, L. Susan, 42, 56
Strauss, Leo, 24, 26, 29, 205, 206n
Stubbs, William, 81
'Study of "Politics" in a University, The', 212
Sullivan, Andrew, 50, 103, 134, 137, 192
systematic thinking, 3-4, 6, 132, 210, 231

T

Taylor, Charles, 222
Tocqueville, Alexis de, 163, 165, 171-172
Tolstoy, Lev, 112
Tönnies, Ferdinand, 25
totalitarian, 155, 178, 232
'Tower of Babel, The' (1948), 109, 118, 131, 144, 146-147, 149, 175
'Tower of Babel, The' (1983), 232
tradition, 33, 35, 146, 162n, 170, 172-173, 175-176, 192, 228
traditionalism (traditionalist), 141, 144-145, 162n, 165, 175-176, 179, 213, 228
transactional association, see *association*
Trilling, Lionel, 115

U

unconditional understanding, see *understanding*
understanding
  conditional, 38, 44, 51
  level of, see *level of understanding*
  unconditional, 38, 44, 51
universitas, 188-189, 194, 196-197
'Universities, The', 212, 217
utilitarian, 16, 36, 138, 143, 160, 167, 201-202, 216, 223, 226, 228

V

Voegelin, Eric, 24, 27
'Voice of Poetry in the Conversation of Mankind, The', 19, 35-36, 38-39, 50, 52,

54, 74, 110-111, 115, 119, 121, 123, 132, 137-138, 218, 221

W

Watson, J.B., 70
Weber, Alfred, 16
Weber, Max, 17, 20, 26, 53
Whewell, William, 215
Whig liberalism, see *liberalism*
White, Hayden, 97
Whitehead, Alfred, 59n, 62-63
Wilde, Oscar, 105
William the Conqueror, 96
Winch, Peter, 118
Windelband, Wilhelm, 56n, 82, 91
Wittgenstein, Ludwig, 38
Wood, G.O., 43
Woolf, Virginia, 105
Wordsworth, William, 113
'Work and Play', 50, 138-139